WHEN THE END BEGINS

REFUTING A RAPTURE IN MATTHEW 24-25

DOUGLAS D. STAUFFER
ANDREW B. RAY
FOREWORD BY RANDY KING

When the End Begins—Rapture Commentary Series volume 2
Copyright © 2017
McCowen Mills Publishers & LTB Publications
All rights reserved
Printed in the United States of America
Text Design: Rick Quatro (Carmen Publishing Inc., Hilton, NY)
Jacket Design: Chris Taylor (SeraphimChris, Pahrump, NV)

ISBN 978-1-9424521-2-6

No part of this book may be reproduced or transmitted in any form or by any means—electronic or mechanical, including photocopying, recording, or by any information storage and retrieval system—without permission in writing from the publisher. However, it is the desire of the authors to disseminate this information so permission is granted to copy a page for study so long as the copy includes credit.

Scripture quotations from the King James Bible need no permission to quote, print, preach, or teach. For clarity, all scripture is in italics with reference and any emphasis in bold print. Any deviation from the King James Bible is not intentional.

For more information, contact:

McCowen Mills Publishers

Dr. Douglas D. Stauffer, President
5709 North Broadway Street
Knoxville, TN 37918
(866) 344-1611 (toll free)
Website: *www.BibleDoug.com*
Email: *Doug@BibleDoug.com*

LTB Publications

Dr. Andrew B. Ray, Pastor
5709 North Broadway Street
Knoxville, TN 37918
(865) 688-0780 (Antioch Baptist Church)
Website: *www.LearntheBible.org*
Email: *pastorray@LearntheBible.org*

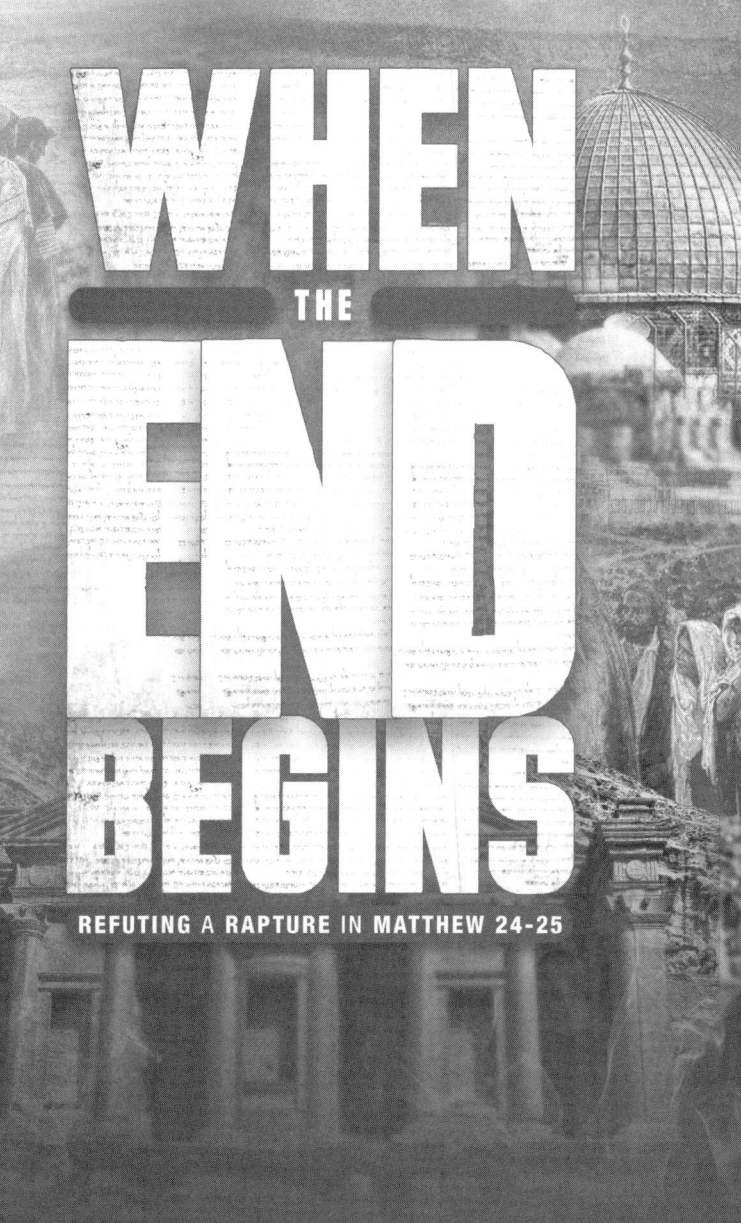

Works by the Authors

Co-authored books by Stauffer/Ray:

- ***When the End Begins***—*Refuting a Rapture in Matthew chapter 24* **(2016, 224 pages, ISBN: 978-1-942452-12-6)**
- ***Reviving the Blessed Hope of Thessalonians***—*The Rapture Commentary Series Volume 1* **(2016, 176 pages, ISBN: 978-1-942452-02-7)**
- ***Josiah: The Boy Who Would Be King***—*A Children's Bible Story and Coloring Book* **(2016, 64 pages, ISBN: 978-1-942452-07-2)**
- ***Daily Strength 1***—*Devotions for Bible Believing Study* **(2014, 455 pages, ISBN: 978-1-942452-17-1)**
- ***Daily Strength 2***—*Devotions for Bible Believing Study* **(2015, 439 pages, ISBN: 978-1-942452-27-0)**
- ***Daily Strength 3***—*Devotions for Bible Believing Study* **(2016, 455 pages, ISBN: 978-1-942452-37-9)**
- ***Daily Strength 4***—*Devotions for Bible Believing Study* **(2017, 418 pages, ISBN: 978-1-942452-47-8)**
- ***That Blessed Hope***—*Teaching and Defending the Doctrine of the Rapture of the Church* (Co-authored with James Knox and others) **(2017, 286 pages)**

By Andrew B. Ray:

- *The Fingerprint of God* (2011, 153 pages, ISBN: 978-1-602082717)

By Douglas D. Stauffer:

- ***One Book One Authority***—*2,000 Years of Church and Bible History* **(2012, 888 pages, ISBN: 978-0-967701-60-8)**
- ***One Book Stands Alone***—*The Key to Believing the Bible* **(2001, 434 pages, ISBN: 978-0-9677016-7-7)**
- ***One Book Rightly Divided***—*The Key to Understanding the Bible* **(2006, 276 pages, ISBN: 978-0-967701-61-5)**
- ***Freedom's Ring***—*Life, Liberty and the Pursuit of Salvation* **(2008, 400 pages, ISBN: 978-0-967701-69-1)**
- ***The DaVinci CON***—*The Great Deception* **(2006, 128 pages)**
- ***The Chronicles of Narnia***—*Wholesome Entertainment or Gateway to Paganism?* **(2006, 236 pages)**

- *One Book Stands Alone*—Roman Catholicism—volume 2, **(2001)**, volume 1 OUT OF PRINT)

Other books, DVDs and CDs on eschatology:

- *Will the Church Go Through the Tribulation?* (2013, 144 pages)
- *After the Rapture:* Be Not Ignorant Brethren **(11 CD set, 12+ hours, UPC: 6-89076-67751-6)**
- *Changed by the Book*—Learn to Study the Bible God's Way **(7 DVD set, 7+ hours, UPC: 6-89076-44624-2)**
- *In the Last Days* **(4 DVD set, 434 minutes, UPC: 6-89076-677615)**
- *God's Wrath versus the Pre-tribulation Rapture* **(3 DVD set, 384 minutes, UPC: 6-89076-67741-7)**

Dedication

This volume is affectionately dedicated to our faithful wives (Judy and Lula) and children (Justin and Heather; Noah, Hannah, Sara, Charity, and Isaac). Thank you for your encouragement and understanding as God tasked us to write yet another book together. No man will ever complete the work of God so the sacrifice continues. Our prayer is that you will be richly rewarded in this life and eternally rewarded in the life to come. We could never do the work without the faithful support of each and every one of you!

> *"…but as his part is that goeth down to the battle, so shall his part be that tarrieth by the stuff: they shall part alike"* **(1 Samuel 30:24b).**

We would also like to expand this dedication to those who truly want to know the truth of scripture. Without lovers of truth, there would be no need to write any Bible-based books. A special thank you toward those who have charged, and encouraged, and strengthened us though your prayers, input, and support. God knows who you are and so do we!

> *"But the hour cometh, and now is, when the true worshippers shall worship the Father in spirit and in truth: for the Father seeketh such to worship him. God is a Spirit: and they that worship him must worship him in spirit and in truth"* **(John 4:23-24).**

Contents

List of Illustrations . . . . *ix*
Extended Author Biographies . . . . *xi*

Introduction 15
Prologue 29
  1. The Conversation Concerning the Last Days 33
  2. The Temple Distraction 43
  3. The Beginning of Sorrows 55
  4. The Outpouring of Hatred 69
  5. The Gospel of the Kingdom 87
  6. The Abomination of Desolation 103
  7. The Time of Great Tribulation 115
  8. The Sign of Christ's Coming 129
  9. The Parable of the Fig Tree 149
10. The Days of Noah and Lot 161
11. The Exhortations to Watchfulness 171
12. The Parable of the Ten Virgins 179
13. The Parable of the Talents 191
14. The Judgment of the Nations 203
Appendix: Who Is This Israel in the Land? 213

    Scripture Index 215
    Index 221

Acknowledgements

The authors would like to express their deepest appreciation to the following:

Most preeminently, the precious Lord Jesus Christ for His saving and sustaining grace.

Those who invested the time and effort into our spiritual development, along with the men and women who have been persecuted and sometimes put to death for the faith and their trust in the Saviour and His word.

Our devoted wives for their constant support, encouragement, and understanding through our years of marriage and ministry together. They are truly God's *second* greatest gift to each of us **(Romans 6:23)**.

Mrs. Lois Barnes for her many hours of proofreading and grammatical suggestions.

Dr. Randy King and Mr. John Wright for their input after reading the manuscript.

Mr. Rick Quatro and Mr. Jonathan Judy for their invaluable assistance in formatting the book text.

Mr. Chris Taylor for his creativity reflected in an impressive cover design.

Lastly, the members of Antioch Baptist Church, Knoxville, TN for their faithful support and encouragement during this process of writing another book while faithfully serving with them.

List of Illustrations

Chart	Title	Page
1.10	The Interruption	34
1.20	This Generation Redefined	36
2.10	The Disciples' Questions	48
2.20	These Things	49
2.30	The End of the World	52
3.10	The Days of Deception	58
3.20	The Beginning of Sorrows	65
4.10	Synagogues Vs. Churches	71
4.20	Cancelling a Curse	76
4.30	When Love Grows COLD	78
4.40	Understanding the Confusion	85
5.10	The Everlasting Gospel	90
5.20	The Shifting Message	97
5.30	Inclusiveness After Cross	98
5.40	World Evangelized	99
6.10	The Hinge of Daniel's 70th Week	104
6.20	God's Offer Prior to Wrath	105
6.30	Precursors to the Abomination	106
6.40	Michael the Archangel	108
6.50	The Abomination	109
6.60	The Abomination Prophesied and Fulfilled	112
6.70	Concerns at "the Abomination"	114
7.10	Threats Heightened	115
7.20	The Assyrian	116
7.30	The Times of the Gentiles	118
7.40	Why All the Trouble?	119
7.50	Where Is Christ?	123
7.60	Christ's Coming: the Imagery	126
8.10	The Jews Require a Sign	130

8.20 After Those Days	131
8.30 Old Testament Prophecy	133
8.40 The Sign of the Son of Man	135
8.50 Angels & the Trumpets	137
8.60 Christ with His Armies	138
8.70 The Lord's Vengeance	139
8.80.1 The Day of the Lord Cometh I	140
8.80.2 The Day of the Lord Cometh II	141
8.80.3 Gathering the Scattered	143
8.90.1 The Tribulation?	147
8.90.2 Tribulation Throughout Time	148
9.10 Fig Tree Parable	154
9.20 End of the Church Vs. End of the World	159
10.10 Those Taken Vs. Those Left Behind	163
10.20 Worldwide Wickedness	164
10.30 Those Taken Vs. Left Behind	165
10.40 One Taken, Other Left	168
11.10 The Thief	173
11.20 The Servant: Wise or Evil?	176
11.30 Who Are the Evil Servants?	178
12.10 The Bridegroom Cometh	186
12.20 The Foolish Buy Oil	189
12.30 Who Are the Foolish Virgins?	190
13.10 Christ Received the Kingdom	194
13.20 Christ Returns with Kingdom	195
13.30 The Reckoning	197
13.40 Well Done!	199
13.50 The Wicked and Slothful	200
14.10 Christ Returns in Glory	205
14.20 The Gathering of the Nations	206
14.30 Dividing the Sheep from the Goats	210

Extended Author Biographies

Dr. Douglas D. Stauffer is an internationally recognized authority in the fields of Bible history, apologetics, and prophecy. He is a prolific author, having written seventeen books along with numerous writings published in Christian periodicals. Because of his biblical expertise, *Oxford University Press* commissioned Dr. Stauffer to work as one of two contributing editors for the notes on the *New Pilgrim* King James study Bible.

Immediately, following high school, Doug served a four year tour of duty in the USAF. Upon discharge, he returned to Pennsylvania to attend *The Pennsylvania State University*, graduating with a BS degree in accounting. A few months later he began attending Bible college.

While attending Bible college, Dr. Stauffer passed the CPA exam. He then worked as controller of several organizations. In 1994, he gave up his work as CFO of a multimillion dollar company along with managing his own firm when God began dealing with him about dedicating his time more fully to the ministry. Since that time, he has earned his ThM and then his PhD in Religion from *International Baptist Seminary*.

Along with being a frequent guest speaker on radio and television, he has served ten years in the pastorate and logged thousands of hours teaching in churches and at the college level. Dr. Stauffer currently serves as an evangelist and president of *Partners for Truth Ministries*. Doug and his wife Judy are blessed with two children, Justin and Heather.

Dr. Andrew B. Ray is the pastor of Antioch Baptist Church in Knoxville, Tennessee. He has a heart for the Lord, His word, the church, the family, as well as the next generation. He spends countless hours counseling and obediently declaring *"all the counsel of God."* As a diligent student of the scriptures, he earned his Doctor of Theology degree and faithfully preaches and teaches at the church, as well as the Bible institute.

Before becoming pastor in May 2007, Dr. Ray served as assistant pastor for four years at Antioch Baptist Church under Dr. David F. Reagan. Upon Dr. Reagan's death, Andrew was unanimously voted as pastor of Antioch Baptist Church.

Bro. Ray is the author of *The Fingerprint of God* along with a four year series of devotional books called *Daily Strength: Devotions for Bible-Believing Study*. He has also written several gospel tracts and is currently serving as an editor for a songbook that incorporates scriptural songs, bringing back original lyrics altered or removed by modern hymnals. He is truly what the Bible defines as a man who labours in the word and doctrine *(1 Timothy 5:17)*.

God has blessed Bro. Ray and his wife Lula with five children: Noah, Hannah, Sara, Charity, and Isaac.

Foreword

When the End Begins definitively answers the age-old question: *"Lord, wilt thou at this time …?"* Every sincere, Bible-believing Christian yearns for the day that the Lord will fulfill His divine purpose and His expressed will for this sin-sick world (and for each of us). Nevertheless, Christians today seem more uncertain than ever, wondering if anyone can truly know the prophetic sequence of events with any degree of certainty.

Yet, God gave man prophecy for a purpose! He wants man to know the truth and experience the freedom and peace that results from knowing that truth. With this in mind, Andrew Ray and Doug Stauffer again tackle the most hotly debated prophetic subjects *"head on"* in this thorough, scholarly exploration of Matthew chapters 24 and 25! This work is plainly written and thoughtfully laid out and provides an invaluable resource for both the beginner and the theologian alike.

When the End Begins pierces through the confusion, despair, and heresy entangled within much of today's prophecy teaching. This wonderful treatise offers hope and understanding through proper biblical interpretation without all of the hype and pointless sensationalism. With these spiritual insights, the reader can properly apply the scriptures concerning the Rapture of the Church, God's dealings with Israel in the Last Days, and God's future millennial kingdom. The book's centerpiece points directly to their defense of the Pre-tribulation Rapture as contrasted with God's dealing with Israel during Daniel's Seventieth Week.

This volume is a tremendous follow-up to their book, Reviving the Blessed Hope, a masterful commentary on the prophetic aspects of Paul's epistles to the Thessalonians. I encourage you to get both of these books, read them for all they are worth, and share them with everyone you know. These materials serve as faithful guideposts to God's true agenda and will greatly benefit every believer searching for the whole truth and nothing but the truth.

My sincere prayer is that God will use these works to renew our faith in the Blessed Hope as an *"anchor to our souls."* May God grant that every Christian be *"approved unto God"* and one day soon stand before Him unashamed **(2 Timothy 2:15)**.

Pastor Randy King
Oshkosh, Wisconsin

Recommendations

When the End Begins is the best book that I have ever read on Matthew chapters 24 and 25. It is evident that the men who wrote this book are not only students of the Bible but also lovers of the God of the Bible. The truths of End Time events are explained in great detail coupled with brilliant simplicity.

You will notice almost immediately that the Bible, as opposed to the ideas of men, is used to bring to light the truth concerning End Time events. ***When the End Begins*** contains numerous charts and graphs that are well thought out and prepared to provide ease of clarity. To the sincere Bible student much can be learned from this great work. Simply put, the content of this book is phenomenal.

Pastor Tim Crotts
Cana, Virginia

When the End Begins is the clearest, simplest, and best faithful-to-God's-word explanation of Matthew chapters 24 and 25 that I have ever read. It contains no sensationalism or extra non-biblical theories—just scripture-with-scripture truths that clear away the confusion caused by those who simply seek to gain a following.

Far too many Bible students, after reading Matthew chapters 24 and 25 (whether one time, ten times, or fifty, or more), have unanswered questions and doubts about their meaning and application. ***When the End Begins*** answers many of the most perplexing questions that have plagued God's people for far too long. Fortunately, this careful analysis encourages readers to write notes in their Bible margins next to those difficult passages so they never again wonder to whom God directed these particular teachings.

John Wright
Knoxville, Tennessee

Introduction

Groundwork for the Gospels

The New Testament begins with a section of scripture collectively identified as *the Gospels*. This portion of the Bible is made up of four distinct books containing a total of eighty-nine chapters with a narrative spanning just over thirty-three years. Although these books reference truths as far back as eternity past *(John 1:1-3)*, the actual story line chronologically commences with the conception of John the Baptist—the forerunner and cousin of Jesus, called *Messias* **(Luke 1:5-25)**. The attention in the Gospels quickly shifts to Christ's supernatural conception.

These books then cover the entirety of Christ's life which includes His earthly ministry, His death, crucifixion, and resurrection. This section chronologically concludes with Christ's ascension to the Father in Heaven **(Luke 24:49-53)**. This scene (the ascension) aligns with the first major event recorded in the book following the four Gospels—the book of Acts **(Acts 1:9)**.

In order to comprehend the various divisions found within scripture, one must recognize how God's word distinguishes between each of the Bible's messengers and their particular messages. For instance, the apostle Paul specifically identified and delineated his gospel as the death, burial, and resurrection **(1 Corinthians 15:1-4)**, yet everything covered in the first four books of the New Testament is collectively known as, or at least classifiable as, "the gospel." Mark, for example, describes his writings as:

*Mark 1:1 **The beginning of the gospel** of Jesus Christ, the Son of God;*

This truth is also clearly expressed in the titles of the first four books (i.e., ***The Gospel*** *According to Matthew, etc.*). Why is all of this so important? A more thorough examination and study reveals that the Bible defines *gospel* simply as *good tidings* (compare **Isaiah 61:1** with **Luke 4:18**, and **Isaiah 52:7** and **Nahum 1:15** with **Romans 10:15**).

Isaiah 61:1 *The Spirit of the Lord GOD is upon me; because the LORD hath anointed me to* **preach good tidings** *unto the meek; he hath sent me to bind up the brokenhearted, to proclaim liberty to the captives, and the opening of the prison to them that are bound;*

Luke 4:18 *The Spirit of the Lord is upon me, because he hath anointed me to* **preach the gospel** *to the poor; he hath sent me to heal the brokenhearted, to preach deliverance to the captives, and recovering of sight to the blind, to set at liberty them that are bruised,*

Certainly everything about the birth, life, ministry, death, resurrection, and ascension of Christ was *good tidings* for a world void of hope and, according to Luke, sitting *"in darkness and in the shadow of death."* Luke described the world's condition as such:

Luke 1:79 *To give light to them that sit in darkness and in the shadow of death,* *to guide our feet into the way of peace.*

As the story unfolds in the earliest New Testament books, the reader finds the Jewish nation in complete disarray. This was the scene upon which John the Baptist and the Lord Jesus Christ began each of their respective ministries. God's people (the Jews) were living under Roman domination and rule *(John 11:48)*. The spiritual condition of the religious leaders—those sitting in Moses' seat—was absolutely deplorable. Jesus made it a point to tell His followers not to follow their hypocritical example.

Matthew 23:2 *Saying, The* **scribes and the Pharisees** *sit in Moses' seat: 3 All therefore whatsoever they bid you observe, that observe and do; but* **do not ye after their works: for they say, and do not.**

In fulfillment of prophecy, the God they claimed to worship appeared in the flesh. Yet, the religious leaders failed to (or refused to) recognize Jesus Christ as the fulfillment of scripture. Their problem was simply a *heart* condition which demonstrated a complete lack of spiritual discernment. They "worshipped" God by giving Him lip service, yet denied Him with their lives and actions, revealing the wicked condition of their hearts.

*Matthew 15:8 This people draweth nigh unto me with their mouth, and honoureth me with their lips; but **their heart is far from me.***

Because of God's love for His creation, God the Son took upon Himself the form of man and lived a life completely free of sin. While robed in a body of flesh, He never ceased being God. One would think that those most familiar with scripture (the Pharisees) would have humbly yielded to Christ's obvious authority **(Luke 4:36)**. Yet, these religious leaders repeatedly sought to entrap the Lord in His gracious words. The religious leaders knew that the identity of the Lord Jesus and His presence upon the earth exposed their religious hypocrisy. This is why they desired to cast doubt upon the identity of Jesus' Father to which Jesus replied that had they *known* His Father, they would have certainly known and recognized the Son of God also.

*John 8:19 Then said they unto him, Where is thy Father? Jesus answered, Ye neither know me, nor my Father: **if ye had known me, ye should have known my Father also**.*

Although the nation as a whole rejected the Messiah, there were individuals within the nation who believed Christ's message and accepted Him for who He was. A few of the religious leaders also accepted Christ's message, but the vast majority of His followers consisted of the common people. From the larger number of those who believed in Him, the Lord chose twelve men to be His key disciples. They are called the twelve apostles.

Why Four Gospels?

Stating that these chosen twelve turned the world completely upside down is a gross understatement. They began as the Lord's *disciples* (or students) and became His *apostles* (sent ones or messengers). Only a few of the twelve apostles penned inspired epistles or Gospels. In fact, only two of the apostles (Matthew and John) were moved by the Holy Ghost *(2 Peter 1:21)* to chronicle the life and ministry of the Lord Jesus Christ.

Two other men, outside the ranks of the twelve (Mark and Luke), were chosen to write gospel accounts which make up the four Gospels. Why would God give man four Gospel books? The answer is quite simple. A wise and omniscient God chose to abide by His own rules of establishing a credible witness by selecting multiple witnesses to record His Son's earthly ministry. Here is the principle found in the Old Testament.

> ***Deuteronomy 19:15*** *One witness shall not rise up against a man for any iniquity, or for any sin, in any sin that he sinneth:* **at the mouth of two witnesses, or** *at the mouth of* **three** *witnesses,* **shall the matter be established.**

Regardless of the precise reasoning of the omniscient God,[1] choosing four witnesses validated the witness of Christ's earthly ministry. We are told that Christ's earthly ministry *"was not done in a corner"* **(Acts 26:26)** but chronicled by *"eyewitnesses of his majesty."* As such, the Gospels record firsthand accounts and not simply hearsay potentially corrupted by man's opinion or bias.

> ***2 Peter 1:16*** *For* **we have not followed cunningly devised fables, when** *we made known unto you the power and coming of our Lord Jesus Christ, but* **were eyewitnesses of his majesty.**

Absolute Unity with Distinct Perspectives

As would be the case with any four eyewitnesses, the writers of the Gospels observed the same person, message, and lifetime, but saw and recorded different aspects of these events. Interestingly, the Lord moved them to present Christ's earthly ministry from four distinct perspectives:

1) Matthew's Gospel emphasized Christ as **the King of the Jews.**

2) Mark's Gospel emphasized Christ as **the Servant.**

3) Luke's Gospel emphasized Christ as **the Son of man.**

4) John's Gospel plainly declared Christ as **the Son of God.**

Yet, with so many distinctive details, the four Gospels NEVER contradict one another. Each distinction serves an important and unique purpose. Yet the most important distinction is the difference between

---

[1] The choice of four witnesses most likely revealed that number's association with earthly things. The Bible speaks of *"the* ***four*** *corners of the earth"* **(Isaiah 11:12),** *"****fourfooted*** *beasts of the earth"* **(Acts 10:12),** *"****four*** *angels standing on the* ***four*** *corners of the earth, holding the* **four** *winds of the earth"* **(Revelation 7:1),** *and the "****four*** *quarters of the earth"* **(Revelation 20:8).** Perhaps the connection was to present the Lord Jesus Christ from four perspectives matching the four heavenly beasts. These *"****four*** *living creatures"* **(Ezekiel 1:5)** were described as follows:

> ***Ezekiel 1:10*** *As for the likeness of their faces,* ***they four*** *had the face of a man, and the face of a lion, on the right side: and* they four *had the face of an ox on the left side;* ***they four*** *also had the face of an eagle.*

John's Gospel and the other three Gospels (commonly known as the Synoptic Gospels). John's Gospel is quite unique from the other three. Matthew, Mark, and Luke parallel each other but offer varying details. In fact, Luke pointed out that he took *"in hand to set forth in order a declaration of those things which are most surely believed among us, Even as they delivered them unto us, which from the beginning were eyewitnesses, and ministers of the word"* **(Luke 1:1-2)**. He further states, *"It seemed good to me also ... to write unto thee in order"* **(Luke 1:3)**.

As much as possible, Matthew, Mark, and Luke reported events as eyewitnesses. Although their viewpoints and their points of emphases differed, they recorded many of the same events. They did so in an orderly and thorough fashion. In fact, the only way to grasp the complete details of any single recorded event is by considering each of the accounts given in the Gospels which cover any particular event.

Although John included many similar statements, he testified that his record was specifically written *"that ye might believe that Jesus is the Christ, the Son of God; and that believing ye might have life through his name"* **(John 20:31)**.[2]

Jews, Disciples, Apostles, and the Church

Some Bible teachers today debate the intended audience for the various written Gospel records; however, no dispute exists concerning the audience present as the events unfolded in the Gospels. For instance, the apostle John testified that the Lord Jesus *"came unto his own"* **(John 1:11)**. Much of the Lord's earthly ministry was specifically (and only) intended for the Jews. In fact, when sending out disciples for the purpose of propagating His teaching, the Lord instructed the men to go specifically *"to the lost sheep of the house of Israel"* **(Matthew 10:6)**. Their message and intended audience was national Israel. The exceptions to this (where at times they ministered to the Gentiles) simply testify to the veracity of the rule.

As discussed earlier, the Lord Jesus chose men to be His disciples. The overall number of disciples was a much higher number. At one

---

[2] This emphasis reveals why so many tract publishers choose to distribute smaller booklets containing the books of John and Romans. Their hope is that these two books portray a sufficient witness for any lost person to understand salvation leading him to come to a saving knowledge of Christ.

point, *"the Lord appointed other seventy also, and sent them two and two"* ***(Luke 10:1)***, but out of that number the Lord chose twelve to eventually serve as His most prominent witnesses. A *disciple* is simply a student of a certain discipline or a *scholar **(1 Chronicles 25:8; Malachi 2:12)**.* This position can best be understood when contrasted to the *master* or *teacher **(Matthew 10:24)**.*

As the twelve took on additional responsibilities of preaching, they became known as *apostles*—the sent ones or messengers. The fact is that **all of the recorded events took place prior to what we now know and refer to as the New Testament Church.** Those who have chosen to ignore or dismiss this particular truth have fallen into some of the most egregious of errors.

The question as to when the New Testament Church was *founded* has been debated for nearly as long as its existence. This debate takes upon itself even greater significance when considering the audience of the Gospels. If the New Testament Church merely continues the Old Testament *"church"* ***(Acts 7:38)***, then the rules of the Old Testament, along with those directions found within the Gospels, equally and completely apply to the New Testament Church today. However, the New Testament Church is not a continuation of any Old Testament group but a distinct entity.

This confusion concerning application explains why some groups have chosen to follow practices matching the Old Testament priesthood including the propagation of the unscriptural and unsavory marriage between church and state. Furthermore, Bible-believing Christianity resoundingly rejects the doctrinal position that the New Testament Church's origin was prior to Christ's sacrificial death on the cross. The Church was certainly *in view* or in the mind of God before the cross, but it is wrong to claim that it could have been *in existence* prior to that time.[3] Granted, many of the truths taught by Christ universally transcend time and dispensations, but the prophecies specifically aimed at Israel cannot and should not be usurped by the Church even by those with the best of intentions.

---

[3] In fact, it is important to note that the **New** Testament does not begin until after the death of the testator (Jesus Christ). Read **Hebrews 9:16-17** for an understanding concerning the NEW Testament and the necessity for Christ to die before the New Testament is in force.

Many Christians propose that the New Testament Church began during the earthly ministry of Christ. After all, the principle of the church was established *(Matthew 16:18; Matthew 18:20)*; Jesus Christ could have served as its head *(Matthew 23:8)* and pastor *(John 10:11, 14)*; the group had rules for discipline *(Matthew 18:15-17)*, and practiced baptism *(Matthew 28:16-20)* and the Lord's Supper *(Matthew 26:26-29)*. Those who subscribe to this doctrinal position tend to believe that the teachings presented in the Gospels are almost without exception directly applicable to the New Testament Church. This would also apply to the End-Times prophetic events mentioned by the Lord during His earthly ministry.

These same teachers typically suggest that Noah and Lot are pictures of the supernatural protection of the New Testament Church and that Matthew chapter 24 provides doctrinal insights into the details of the Church's Rapture. Regardless of the increasing prevalence of this position, it contains serious irreconcilable flaws which will be examined in greater detail later within this work.

Here is one simple point to ponder before moving forward. During Christ's earthly ministry, He spoke of the Church's protection and the failure of the gates of hell to prevail—both of which He spoke of using a future tense. For example, Christ promised, *"I **will build** [future] my church" (Matthew 16:18)*. The Lord's allusion to building something yet unconstructed most definitely provides the context as to the Church's origin being yet future.

In the Old Testament, Christ was prophesied as a stone refused by the builders (the nation of Israel).[4] These Old Testament references show that the Rock was manifest to Israel in the context of the Davidic kingdom with veiled prophetic references to Daniel's Seventieth Week *(Daniel 2:34-35)*. These references most assuredly look forward to the

---

[4] ***Psalm 118:22*** *The **stone** which the builders refused is **become the head stone of the corner**.*

*Isaiah 8:14 And he shall be for a sanctuary; but for **a stone of stumbling and for a rock** of offence to both the houses of Israel, for a gin and for a snare to the inhabitants of Jerusalem.*

*Isaiah 28:16 Therefore thus saith the Lord GOD, Behold, **I lay in Zion for a foundation a stone, a tried stone, a precious corner stone, a sure foundation:** he that believeth shall not make haste.*

rejected stone and are fulfilled in the New Testament and are directly associated to Christ's rejection and crucifixion *(Mark 12:10; Luke 20:17-18; Acts 4:11)*. The rejected Christ became the precious corner stone (the head of the corner).

> **Matthew 21:42** *Jesus saith unto them, Did ye never read in the scriptures,* **The stone which the builders rejected, the same is become the head of the corner**: *this is the Lord's doing, and it is marvellous in our eyes?*

Paul later declared Christ as the *foundation (**1 Corinthians 3:11**)* and *chief corner stone* of the one body consisting of Jews and Gentiles *(**Ephesians 2:20**)*. These truths all point to Christ's crucifixion as the time of initial construction—a crucifixion announced in the context of the initial proclamation of the Church *(**Matthew 16:21-23**)*. Concerning the Church and its construction, Christ simply prophesied of events that were yet future, not something presently being fulfilled.

The New Testament Church

In the same context after the Christ's crucifixion, the Lord identified the Church as *"my church"*—a purchase certainly *not* consummated prior to His crucifixion. In fact, the first reference to the *"church of God"* (a phrase denoting possession or ownership of the Church) suggests that the Church became His Church through a blood purchase that He made upon the cross of Calvary.

> **Acts 20:28** *Take heed therefore unto yourselves, and to all the flock, over the which the Holy Ghost hath made you overseers, to feed* **the church of God, which he hath purchased with his own blood.**

The concept of this blood purchase matches other New Testament teachings like that found in Ephesians and Colossians. The believers' redemption or purchase resulted from the blood shed upon Calvary—it was through HIS blood.

> **Ephesians 1:7** *In whom we have* **redemption through his blood**, *the forgiveness of sins, according to the riches of his grace;*

> **Colossians 1:14** *In whom we have* **redemption through his blood**, *even the forgiveness of sins:*

The purchase was made through the shedding of blood, but the transaction was only completed once Christ, the Great High Priest, placed His blood upon the mercy seat in Heaven *(Hebrews 9:12-14)*. Furthermore, the Bible identifies the Holy Ghost, given to believers, as the *earnest* (a sum given denoting a promise of future completed payment) of this purchase *(Ephesians 1:14)*. This payment in earnest involved an acquisition that will be finalized when the **bodies** of the saved are fully redeemed *(Romans 8:23)*.

In support of these truths, God's word emphasizes that the New Testament was not in effect until after the death of the testator, Jesus Christ. After the death of the testator, the testament was in force with the **new testament** as its instrument.

> ***Hebrews 9:16** For where a testament is, there must also of necessity be the death of the testator. 17 For a testament is of force after men are dead: otherwise **it is of no strength at all while the testator liveth.***

Most of those who have recognized the combination of all of these elements believe that the **New Testament** Church was at least birthed from the womb on the Day of Pentecost but not before. After all, it is at this point that the Bible says that *"the Lord added **to the church** ... such as should be saved" **(Acts 2:47)***. However, this truth alone does not account for all of the necessary pieces of the puzzle.

Perhaps the most accurate, safe, and scriptural teaching proclaims that there was also a church (called out assembly) present during the earthly ministry of Christ. The following two passages seem to indicate this truth.

> ***Matthew 18:17** And if he shall neglect to hear them, **tell it unto the church**: but if he neglect to hear the church, let him be unto thee as an heathen man and a publican.*

> ***Hebrews 2:12** Saying, I will declare thy name unto my brethren, **in the midst of the church** will I sing praise unto thee.*

Most assuredly, there was a called out assembly (a church) present when Jesus walked the earth and before.[5] However, it is important to note that the church to which Jesus referred could not be the **New Testa-**

---

[5] The book of Acts references *"the **church** in the wilderness" **(Acts 7:38)***. It is important to note that *church* can simply refer to a called out assembly or a congregation. Comparing scripture with scripture offers the following: **Hebrew 2:12** *"church"* quotes **Psalm 22:22** which used *"congregation."*

ment Church as the New Testament was not in effect until the death of Christ upon the cross—the death of the testator of the New Testament.[6]

The Ascensions

The Church could not be rightfully called *"my church"* by Christ until purchased with His blood *(Acts 20:28)* at Calvary. Obviously, until Christ hung and died upon the cross, this blood was not shed. However, the completion of the transaction did not take place until Christ sprinkled His blood upon the mercy seat in Heaven. That sprinkling took place between the events recorded in the next two passages (the two ascensions).

> **Before 1st Ascension:** *John 20:17 Jesus saith unto her,* **Touch me not; for I am not yet ascended to my Father**: *but go to my brethren, and say unto them, I ascend unto my Father, and your Father; and to my God, and your God.*

Christ's statement in John clearly shows that He had *not* yet initially ascended to the Father. Yet, the latter narrative recorded in Matthew chapter 28 below shows that by this time He had both ascended to the Father and returned back to earth again. This truth is reflected in the fact that He could now be touched.

> **After 1st Ascension but Before Final Ascension:** *Matthew 28:9 And as they went to tell his disciples, behold, Jesus met them, saying, All hail.* **And they came and held him by the feet**, *and worshipped him.*

These combined truths reveal some things that we know for sure: the New Testament Church did not begin before Christ placed His blood upon the mercy seat in Heaven. However, it must have begun by the day of Pentecost recorded in Acts chapter 2 because something cannot

---

[6] The sequence of events and their close proximity in scripture sometimes offers some of the greatest insights into some of the most important truths. Mark chapter 15 tells us that Christ gave up the ghost (signifying that He died) in verse 37. The next verse continues the account by stating that the temple veil was rent in two from the top to the bottom. This severing of the temple veil opened the way into the most holy place and allowed all to see that God's glory was no longer there but had departed.

Mark 15:37 And Jesus cried with a loud voice, and **gave up the ghost.** *38 And the* **veil** *of the temple was* **rent** *in twain from the top to the bottom.*

be added to that which had not yet commenced. The Bible says that the Lord *"added"* to the Church *(Acts 2:47)* so it certainly had to be in existence, even if at that time it only consisted of a Jewish membership *(Romans 11:17; Ephesians 3:6)*. Thus, these truths would narrow the beginning of the New Testament Church to sometime between the events of *John 20:17* and *Acts 2:47*.

Regardless of the timing of the actual onset of the New Testament Church, we can be assured that there was NO **New Testament** Church present when the Lord prophesied to His Jewish disciples in the Olivet Discourse *(Matthew 24:3)*. This Discourse covered events that would take place in the last days (Daniel's Seventieth Week) pertinent to the Jews and their Seventieth Week' compatriots. Fortunately, every true Bible student agrees that the Olivet Discourse detailed in Matthew chapters 24 and 25 took place prior to Christ's death and His ascension(s) into Heaven.

John's Gospel Record

It is time to build upon the foundation now laid. In order to do so, we must consider some details relative to the Gospel of John. John recorded the actual crucifixion in *John 19:30* followed by the resurrection account *(John 20:1)* which took place upon the first day of the week when Mary and the others visited the now empty tomb. John chapter 20 also records three appearances of Jesus: first to Mary Magdalene at the sepulcher—*John 20:14*; then the apostles without Thomas—*John 20:19*; and then eight days later to all the apostles including Thomas—*John 20:26*.

It is important to note that John plainly declared that the disciples did not yet understand the resurrection prior to Christ's meeting with them. The next verse eliminates any claim to ambiguity concerning this point. Read it carefully and with a believing heart.

*John 20:9 For as yet **they knew not** the scripture, **that he must rise again from the dead**.*

It is inconceivable that any Christian could underestimate the significance of Christ's death, burial, and resurrection since they are the most pivotal events in all of human history. Yet, the disciples themselves were not completely aware of the ramifications resulting from the resurrection until sometime **after** Christ's resurrection. Additionally, the Bible points out that Christ's first appearance to the disciples took place upon the same day as the resurrection by twice stating it in the same verse –

*"Then the **same day** at evening, being the **first day of the week**…" (John 20:19)*. There are no vain words in the Bible and this double witness is not given by accident.

What happened during this meeting is likely the *pivotal* event concerning the Church. Upon **the first day of the week**, Jesus came and breathed upon the disciples and they received the Holy Ghost. All of the necessary elements for a **New Testament** Church were now in place: (1) Jesus died on the cross, (2) Jesus journeyed to the mercy seat in Heaven and placed His blood upon it, and (3) now He breathed upon His disciples for them to RECEIVE the Holy Ghost.

> ***John 20:22** And when he had said this, he breathed on them, and saith unto them, **Receive ye the Holy Ghost:***

Following this event, Peter and the apostles were different, yet still imperfect. Jesus likely referred to this event as Peter's *conversion* even though Peter already knew and followed the Lord.[7]

> ***Luke 22:32** But I have prayed for thee [**Peter**], that thy faith fail not: and **when thou art converted**, strengthen thy brethren.*

---

[7] When the Bible speaks of *"conversion,"* it generally focuses squarely upon the nation of Israel and not the new birth that occurs when one is born again.

> **Matthew 13:15** *For this people's heart is waxed gross, and their ears are dull of hearing, and their eyes they have closed; lest at any time they should see with their eyes, and hear with their ears, and should understand with their heart, **and should be converted**, and I should heal them.*

> **Matthew 18:3** *And said, Verily I say unto you, **Except ye be converted**, and become as little children, ye shall not enter into the kingdom of heaven.*

> **Mark 4:12** *That seeing they may see, and not perceive; and hearing they may hear, and not understand; lest at any time they should **be converted**, and their sins should be forgiven them.*

> **John 12:40** *He hath blinded their eyes, and hardened their heart; that they should not see with their eyes, nor understand with their heart, and **be converted**, and I should heal them.*

> **Acts 3:19** *Repent ye therefore, and **be converted**, that your sins may be blotted out, when the times of refreshing shall come from the presence of the Lord;*

> **Acts 28:27** *For the heart of **this people** is waxed gross, and their ears are dull of hearing, and their eyes have they closed; lest they should see with their eyes, and hear with their ears, and understand with their heart, and **should be converted**, and I should heal them.*

Those teachers who have failed or refused to recognize the distinctions between Israel and the New Testament Church have caused irreparable harm. Those who continue to espouse the error of the Church replacing Israel (i.e., "spiritually" receiving the promises and blessing given to Israel) will stand accountable for this false teaching. The focus of this work delves into the application of the prophecy of Matthew chapters 24 and 25. Simply put, the New Testament Church was not in existence during the pronouncements of the Olivet Discourse prophecy nor will it be present during the fulfillment of said prophecy.

With this foundational material firmly established, we can now consider what is commonly referred to as the Olivet Discourse. Always keep in mind to whom Jesus directed His remarks, and the correct interpretation and application will reveal itself. Prior to the New Testament Church, there was a distinction between the Jew and the Greek (the Gentile), not so during the Church Age where Paul wrote:

> **Galatians 3:28** *There is **neither Jew nor Greek**, there is neither bond nor free, there is neither male nor female: for ye are all one in Christ Jesus.*

Within the body of Christ in the Church Age, God spiritually eliminates some of the long-held distinctions. This same truth cannot be said concerning Daniel's first sixty-nine weeks of years nor the yet unfulfilled Seventieth Week (commonly referred to as the seven-year Tribulation period). After all, the scripture plainly declares that the seventy weeks are upon one certain people identified in one certain locale.

> **Daniel 9:24 *Seventy weeks are determined upon thy people and upon thy holy city**, to finish the transgression, and to make an end of sins, and to make reconciliation for iniquity, and to bring in everlasting righteousness, and to seal up the vision and prophecy, and to anoint the most Holy.*

These three pertinent points need to be emphasized in order to grasp the context of Daniel's prophecy and the future application of his prophecy.

- *"Seventy weeks"*—the entire 490 years!
- *"Thy people"*—Israel!
- *"Thy holy city"*—Jerusalem!

The Olivet Discourse delineates the fulfillment of Daniel's Seventieth Week. As such, the Olivet Discourse—Matthew chapters 24 and 25—applies to the same group and the same locale as the original prophecy found in Daniel and throughout the Old Testament. No doubt, confusion abounds, yet God does not leave the diligent Bible student groping in the dark. The best way to understand the pronouncements surrounding the Olivet Discourse is by first discovering the context of the verses leading up to the Discourse. This context is clearly recorded in Matthew chapter 23.

Prologue

Purpose of this Book

Matthew chapters 24 and 25 record what is commonly referred to as the Olivet Discourse. Sadly, this portion of scripture is one of the most misapplied sections of scripture. In this work, we purpose to address many of the most puzzling issues. Our method will be to simply believe what the Book says and apply these expressed truths within God's intended CONTEXT.

In this Discourse, the Lord purposefully directed the *prophecy* toward a certain group—the nation of Israel. Likewise, the fulfillment of the prophecy also directly applies to Israel. In fact, it is important to recognize that the New Testament Church was not in existence during the Olivet Discourse, nor will it be on earth during its future prophetic fulfillment. The only hope for doctrinally sound Bible study comes from understanding these truths. It is therefore important for every Bible student to distinguish between NATIONAL Israel and the New Testament Church.

The first volume in this Rapture Commentary Series was entitled **Reviving the Blessed Hope**. It examined the prophetic portions of First and Second Thessalonians. Of course, the study's perspective primarily focused upon the Church to whom the Blessed Hope of the Rapture was directed. This particular book focuses upon the Olivet Discourse and considers the people group (the Jews) addressed by the Lord during His earthly ministry. After all, the Jews are the focus of the Olivet Discourse and subsequently of Daniel's Seventieth Week (commonly referred to as the seven-year Tribulation Period).[1]

---

[1] This work tries to consistently refer to the period following the Rapture of the Church as *"Daniel's Seventieth Week"* in lieu of the more well-known *"Tribulation Period"* since tribulation happens to all and is not limited to this seven-year period.

Introductory Remarks

No doubt we are living today in a tumultuous period identified in the Bible as *"perilous times" (2 Timothy 3:1)*. Fear and apprehension are escalating. These two emotions motivate people in different ways, but rarely in any consistently positive fashion. This applies especially to discussions revolving around the Bible's End-Times teachings. Rather than diligently searching for the truth, Bible teachers seem more interested in playing things safe, sensationalizing doom-and-gloom "prophecies," and date-setting.

Additionally, some Christians have chosen to prepare for their supposed entry into Daniel's Seventieth Week. They believe that such preparations are like hedging one's bet or *"covering all the bases."* This mentality is comparable to the man who chooses to believe that he can lose his salvation, reasoning that if he is wrong, he at least erred on the safe side. People fail to realize that playing things safe by accepting false doctrines has a crippling effect upon themselves and upon those whom they influence.

Increasingly, God's children are shying away from acceptance of truth because of the prevailing false perception that the truth cannot be known with any high degree of certainty. Unfortunately, this condition applies directly to the Pre-tribulation Rapture. People are increasingly disinterested, shortsighted, or completely disconnected from the teaching of the imminent return of Christ. This mentality damages the Church in many ways.

Believers must please the Lord which only comes from being firmly anchored in faith rather than being tossed around by every fearful teaching that comes along. Be sure to keep the next point in mind as you study prophecy. Everyone needs to live in the present and yet prepare for the future (and the Lord's return). Jeremiah serves as a great example when the king of Judah imprisoned him for preaching. It may help the Christian to realize these three things:

- Difficult times are here to stay only worsening in the days to come;
- Jesus is coming for the Church prior to any part of Daniel's Seventieth Week; and

- These two realities must not preclude Christians from their God-given responsibilities to **watch** for the Saviour, **wait** for the Saviour, and **work** for the Saviour.

Furthermore, the Bible teaches that many forms of tribulation and persecution have and will come **upon the Church.** Unfortunately, scripturally anemic Christians are paralyzed by the seeming conflict attached to the message of the Pre-tribulation Rapture.

- Why work if Jesus is coming?
- Why get married?
- Why save or invest for the future?
- Why get life insurance?
- Why stay in good health?
- Why raise a family?
- Why join a church?
- Why start a long-term ministry?
- Why prepare to go to the mission field?

After all, if Jesus is soon coming, why plan for a future that may never take place? Interestingly, the Old Testament offers many of these types of perplexing conundrums and offers insights into God's expectations during these times. Jeremiah provides a great example! The Lord instructed him to embark upon some rather "questionable" actions—actions that seemed to contradict the God-given message and the certain inevitability of future events.

Jeremiah preached that the nation was headed into Babylonian captivity. This was not a message that would provoke a man to start a family, build a house, start a new job, or further his education. However, despite God's call and message for Jeremiah, the LORD instructed him to follow a most perplexing course of action—make a land purchase!

> *Jeremiah 32:7 Behold, Hanameel the son of Shallum thine uncle shall come unto thee, saying, **Buy thee my field** that is in Anathoth: for the right of redemption is thine to buy it. 8 So Hanameel mine uncle's son came to me in the court of the prison according to the word of the LORD, and said unto me, Buy my field, I pray thee, that is in Anathoth, which is in the country of Benjamin: for the right of inheritance is thine, and the redemption is thine; buy it for thyself. Then I knew that **this was the word of the LORD**.*

Think about it! What did Jeremiah do as he waited in prison for the inevitable removal from the land? He bought a field! Why would he do something seemingly so imprudent? He simply obeyed what God had told him to do! Likewise, Christians, fully expecting Jesus could return at any moment, should wholly follow the Lord even when the call or direction seems useless should the Lord return soon. Again, every Christian should **watch** for the Saviour, **wait** for the Saviour, AND **work** for the Saviour until He comes for the Church!

Unfortunately, confusion and uncertainty have had a debilitating effect upon far too many believers. We offer this book as a guide and a source of hope and direction. God's people simply cannot allow themselves to be lulled into a false sense of *"whatever will be, will be"* because they have concluded that no one can know the truth with any high degree of certainty. Keep these three promises in mind as you read this work:

*__John 8:32__ And **ye shall know the truth**, and the truth shall make you free.*

*__John 16:13__ Howbeit when he, **the Spirit of truth**, is come, he **will guide you into all truth**.*

__John 17:17__ Sanctify them through thy truth: thy word is truth.

The Bible points out:

- You can know the truth!
- God provides the means for you to know the truth!
- Every Christian has access to the source of truth through God's word!

Our prayer is for this book to help believers remove the man-made blinders causing the loss of focus so prevalent today. The solution is quite simple! During times of distress, especially when things seem so hopeless, the Bible always admonishes God's people to direct their focus upward. This is how the people of God experience true victory—they choose to look above for their redemption and hope. We too should continually repeat, *"our eyes are upon thee"* **(2 Chronicles 20:12)**. Believers would be wise to consistently embark upon this same course of action. We pray that this book assists every reader to focus and stay focused upon the Lord.

1

The Conversation Concerning the Last Days

The Synoptic Gospels of Matthew, Mark, and Luke each cover **the Olivet Discourse**[1] from their own distinct perspective. This is one reason why it is crucial to compare scripture with scripture *(1 Corinthians 2:13)* in hopes of gaining the most comprehensive understanding of any particular Bible passage.

The only complete and comprehensive grasp of the Olivet Discourse comes to those who consider Mark chapter 13 and Luke chapter 21 together with Matthew chapters 24 and 25. Additionally, it is vitally important to recognize that Christ's statements recorded in **Matthew 23:34-39** provide the CONTEXT for the questions asked by the disciples in **Matthew 24:3**. *"Tell us, when shall **these things** be? and what shall be the sign of thy coming, and of the end of the world?"* Any discussion of the Olivet Discourse should start with the chapter preceding that discourse, or at least the last six verses of chapter 23.

Matthew Chapter 23

In order to avoid an incomplete and incorrect understanding, we consider the three Synoptic Gospels together. As mentioned already, to fully understand the Olivet Discourse, the reader must establish the context by looking back to Matthew chapter 23. The first two verses of Matthew chapter 24 serve as an **interruption of thought** in the context of the Olivet Discourse.

---

[1] The Olivet Discourse is simply Christ's teachings while on the Mount of Olives as recorded in Mathew chapters 24 and 25, **Mark 13:1-37**, and **Luke 21:5-36** just prior to His betrayal and crucifixion.

As recorded in Matthew chapter 23, Jesus made some statements about the End-Times prior to ascending the Mount of Olives. These statements became the impetus behind what was asked in private concerning the End-Times. Those teachers who fail to take into account this *interruption* in thought and dialog have caused incalculable damage to End-Times doctrines. It is time to put the whole teaching into its proper perspective.

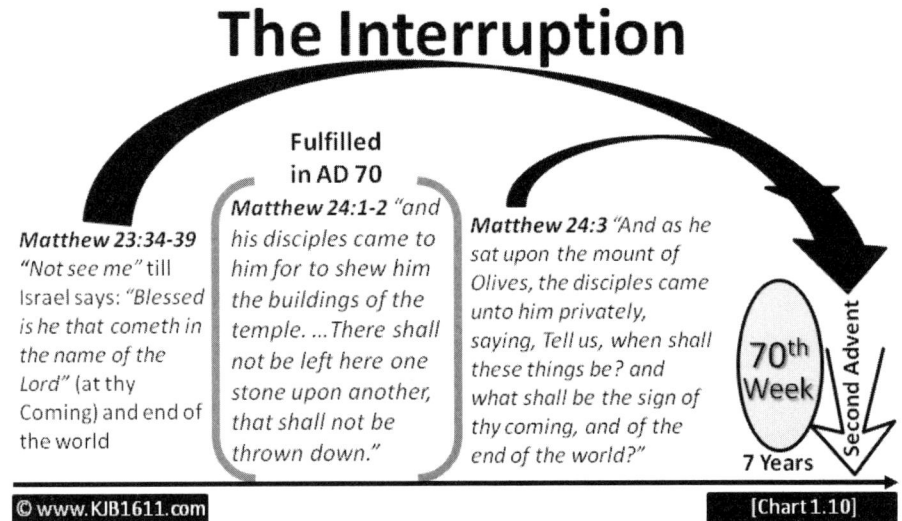

In the first 33 verses of Matthew chapter 23, the Lord harshly rebuked the hypocrisy and inordinate pride of Israel's religious leadership. Their hypocrisy moved the Lord to send prophets, wise men, and scribes to them. The Lord stated:

> **Matthew 23:34 Wherefore, behold, I send unto you** *prophets, and wise men, and scribes: and some of them ye shall kill and crucify; and some of them shall ye scourge in your synagogues, and persecute them from city to city:*

The Lord further prophesied that Israel would kill, crucify, scourge, and persecute these sent ones. In response, God would hold them responsible for all the blood shed throughout the Old Testament's recorded history starting with Abel and ending with Zechariah (recorded in the first book [Genesis] and last book of the Hebrew scriptures [Second Chronicles]).[2]

> *Matthew 23:35* That **upon you may come all the righteous blood shed upon the earth, from the blood of righteous Abel unto the blood of Zacharias** *son of Barachias, whom ye slew between the temple and the altar.*

This pronouncement of judgment only makes complete sense when combined with Daniel's End-Times prophecy against Israel. The purposes of Daniel's Seventy Weeks include *finishing the transgression, making an end of sins, and making reconciliation for iniquity* **(Daniel 9:24)**. This prophetic pronouncement indicates why the wicked over the millennia of time are held accountable for all innocent blood. In fact, these judgments in Matthew refer to a particular generation with the same wicked characteristics, not a generation alive during a certain point in time.

> *Matthew 23:36* *Verily I say unto you,* **All these things shall come upon this generation***.*

It is important not to miss how the Lord sandwiched most of the Olivet Discourse and End-Times preaching between the two statements concerning this single generation and the *"these things"* mentioned. One chapter later, we read: *"Verily I say unto you,* **This generation shall not pass, till all these things be fulfilled"** *(Matthew 24:34).*

The remainder of Matthew chapter 23 (prior to the Olivet Discourse) identifies what piqued the interest and the questioning of the apostles concerning the End-Times.

> *Matthew 23:37* *O Jerusalem, Jerusalem, thou that killest the prophets, and stonest them which are sent unto thee, how often would I have gathered thy children together, even as a hen gathereth her chickens under her wings, and ye would not! 38 Behold, your house is left unto you desolate. 39 For I say unto you,* **Ye shall not see me henceforth, till ye shall say, Blessed is he that cometh in the name of the Lord.**

---

[2] Unlike the English, the Tanakh (the Hebrew Bible) starts in Genesis and ends with Second Chronicles (rather than Malachi) so this pronouncement covered all the innocent blood shed from cover to cover in the Hebrew Old Testament. In the Hebrew Bible, Able was the first innocent blood shed **(Genesis 4:8)** while Zechariah was the <u>last</u> as recorded in **2 Chronicles 24:20-21**.

According to the Lord, the nation of Israel would not see Him again until they accepted Him on a national scale. The worldwide persecution in the End-Times will surely bring this proud and haughty nation to their knees. This humiliation of the nation of Israel will precede Christ's return to deliver them and will, no doubt, prepare them for that return.

Redefining the "Terminal" Generation

Most prophecy teachers claim varying dates for the beginning of this so-called *final* or *terminal generation*. In fact, the biblical length and meaning of this *terminal generation* serves as one of the most sought after and perplexing figures for these teachers. Yet, God never intended for this confusion to exist *(1 Corinthians 14:33)*. In order to grasp the truth, the student and teacher need to first clear their minds of the preconceived theological clutter on this matter. In other words, forget what you have been taught to believe about this so-called final generation because it is most likely wrong!

Two controversial verses of the Olivet Discourse involve what has come to be identified as the *final generation*. However, in order to conclude that Jesus was referring to the people of a certain time period, one generally makes assumptions like the following: (1) the fig tree referenced in the Olivet Discourse *(Matthew 24:32)* is 1948 Israel, and (2) the phrase *"this generation" (Matthew 23:36; Matthew 24:34)* refers to people covering a restricted period of time. Both of these assumptions are false. Consider two negative points with the two associated key phrases from the two key verses:

- THESE THINGS are coming upon THIS GENERATION: *"Verily I say unto you, All **these things shall come upon** this generation" **(Matthew 23:36).***
- THESE THINGS will all be fulfilled before THIS GENERATION dies off: *"Verily I say unto you, This generation **shall not pass**, till all these things be fulfilled" **(Matthew 24:34).***

It helps to explore the negatives associated with *"this generation"* in order to define the context. For instance, the word *"pass"* in **Matthew 24:34** is clearly interpreted and defined in verse 35 as to **pass** away, cease to exist, or die off. Additionally, the pronounced judgments found in the Olivet Discourse will come *"upon this generation"* and the judgments only end when *"this generation"* is completely wiped out at Christ's Second Coming **(Revelation 19:15)**. These truths certainly offer a different perspective.

Commonly held viewpoints fail to examine the full context of what is meant by *"this generation."* Two of the most common misconceptions are that: (1) *"this generation"* involved those living during the Lord's earthly ministry with the fulfillment occurring when Titus conquered Jerusalem in AD 70, or (2) *"this generation"* involved those alive in 1948 when Israel became a nation with the fulfillment to occur at some future time after 1948 depending upon one's quantitative definition of a generation (40, 60, 70, 100 years, etc.).[3]

Both of these interpretations only further muddy the waters. First, the prophesied troubles were not fulfilled in AD 70 when Titus ransacked Jerusalem. Secondly, the fig tree specifically spoke of those *alive* in Daniel's Seventieth Week, not those specifically alive in 1948 and prior to the commencement of Daniel's Seventieth Week. While these truths may seem to minimize the problem encountered in **Matthew 24:34**, they do not yet address the problems associated to **Matthew 23:36**.

For a moment, clear your mind of preconceived notions of what constitutes a generation in the Bible. There is no need to quantify or

---

[3] Interestingly, seventy years from 1948 falls in the year 2017 with yet another prophetic pronouncement concerning a "supernatural event" that will supposedly culminate on September 23, 2017.

identify a biblical generation by placing it into a first or twenty-first century generational time period. It is true that the word *generation* can be descendants at the same stage in a line of any descent. Yet, both historically and scripturally, the word *generation* frequently refers to a specific life (see **Matthew 1:1**) or people who SHARE SPECIFIC TRAITS (like the *"untoward generation"* in **Acts 2:40**). Keep this last definition in mind as we further explore what the Lord intended.

Furthermore, it is important to keep in mind that the phrase *"all these things"* in both **Matthew 23:36** and **Matthew 24:34** encompasses the judgments to be fulfilled upon the wicked who are alive at the Second Coming of Christ. In fact, *"This generation shall not pass, till **all these things** be fulfilled."* What things? The things (judgments) mentioned in the context.

The Bible frequently references *"this generation"* so it is important to consider each instance with their corresponding contexts. For example, the Lord referred to *"this generation"* as alive at the First Advent of Christ *(**Mark 8:12**)*; yet, *"this generation"* was also in the wilderness *(**Deuteronomy 1:35; Psalm 95:10**)*. The Bible refers to *"this generation"* as those who sought to do harm to God's word *(**Psalm 12:7**)* throughout various periods of time. In fact, *"this generation"* will be judged by the men of Nineveh and the queen of the south *(**Matthew 12:41-42**)*. Why does *"this generation"* refer to so many people over so many different generational periods? The answer is quite simple.

The word *generation*, as used in scripture, frequently includes those who span various periods of time, sharing either a lineage or common behavioral traits. The Lord confirmed this truth when He stated, *"That the blood of all the prophets, which was shed from the foundation of the world, may be required of **this generation**" (**Luke 11:50**)*. He further stated that He spoke of blood shed from beginning to end of the Old Testament from *"the blood of Abel unto the blood of Zacharias"* *(**Luke 11:51**)*. The Lord was *not* suggesting that some generational group alive at a certain point in time would be accountable for Abel's shed blood. After all, it was Cain who shed Abel's blood. Instead, the Lord referred to a certain people with similar traits. That generation (a group existing throughout history) was responsible for all the innocent blood shed.

Maybe considering another viewpoint will bring further clarity. What generation will God insure finally ceases to exist *(**Matthew 24:34**)*? Upon what generation does God want *"all these things"* [the judgments] to be fulfilled? In the context, it refers *not* to a group of people with a common span of life, but to those with a degraded moral likeness—the sons or children of Belial **(Deuteronomy 13:13; 1 Samuel 2:12)**; those whose father is the devil **(John 8:44)**; the children of disobedience **(Ephesians 2:2; Ephesians 5:6; Colossians 3:6)**.

Consider the context of generation in the Gospel of Matthew from the various depictions constantly and consistently referred to by Jesus:

- the *"generation of vipers"* **(Matthew 3:7; Matthew 12:34; Matthew 23:33)**,
- an *"evil and adulterous generation"* **(Matthew 12:39)**,
- a *"wicked generation"* **(Matthew 12:45)**,
- a *"wicked and adulterous generation"* **(Matthew 16:4)**, and
- a *"faithless and perverse generation"* **(Matthew 17:17)**

Now, consider these seven summarized truths together:

- Each of these descriptions above found in Matthew simply refer to the *"children of this world"* **(Luke 16:8)**. In the context found in Matthew chapter 23, Christ asked THIS GENERATION (of vipers) *"how can ye escape the damnation of hell?"* **(Matthew 23:33)**. His reference to *"this generation"* was focusing upon the unconverted and unbelieving, not some generation of people alive on earth during some limited period of time.
- According to Luke's Gospel, Jesus said THIS GENERATION will be held accountable for all the innocent blood throughout time. It makes no sense to assume that the Lord referred only to those within a single generation, whether the first or the twenty-first century. This generation (the children of Satan) will be held accountable for all innocent blood shed **(Luke 11:51)**. The Lord was referring to an evil and adulterous, faithless and perverse generation of vipers throughout time.
- The first verse of the New Testament offers a definition of *"generation"* that deals more with a registry rather than only those alive at a certain point in time **(Matthew 1:1)**. The word *generation* in this context deals with a genealogy or people from the same race or progeny, not one generation existing at a particular point in time.
- The *"chosen generation"* found in **1 Peter 2:9** certainly does not refer only to those alive at a certain point in time but to all within

that *"lineage"* and grouping—a chosen group of people with similar characteristics.
- At the Second Coming, all the lost will be destroyed *(Luke 21:32)*—this is obviously the generation to whom Jesus referred: children of this world, the children of pride, and the children of the night, etc.
- Proverbs *(see **Proverbs 30:11-14**)* offers another example where generation refers, not to a group of people living at the same time, but a group of people demonstrating similar characteristics—*"There is a generation that curseth their father, and doth not bless their mother … that are pure in their own eyes, and yet is not washed from their filthiness … whose teeth are as swords, and their jaw teeth as knives, to devour the poor from off the earth, and the needy from among men."*
- First John contrasted the evil works of the children of the devil with the righteous works of the children of God. The key to discerning to which generation a person belongs is to consider his works and most especially how he loves others. We are warned not to be as Cain who was said to be of the wicked one and slew his brother Abel. Cain killed his brother because his works were evil—similar to the evil works of the wicked and adulterous generation to whom Jesus referred *(1 John 3:10-12)*.

The fact is that *"this generation"* in the Olivet Discourse does NOT refer to all those alive at one period of time. Instead, it refers to those who share a common lineage resulting from similar wicked attributes. The apostle John alluded to that when he recorded that those who sought the Lord were Abraham's seed by natural birth *(John 8:37)*, but that their father was the Devil *(John 8:44)*. Instead of being linked solely to one's physical lineage, this concept of a generation is demonstrable by one's works *(John 8:37-44 and Genesis 3:15)*.

The only consistent solution to correct Bible interpretation is to never allow one's preconceived notions to inadvertently influence one's eschatology. Learn and heed the admonition, *"God forbid: yea, let God be true, but every man a liar"* *(Romans 3:4)*. Unfortunately, many prophetic teachers have simply parroted what they were taught in this matter rather than going back to the scripture to test these long-held beliefs. The eschatological divisions within the body of Christ are taking place because God's people are confused by all the noise. It is time to turn down the rhetoric and turn to the truth.

The Church desperately needs prophecy teachers who are willing to critically question every long-held, accepted teaching that sounds good but fails the TRUTH TEST. Yet, far too many teachers are more concerned with what others will think rather than *"What saith the scripture?"* We do not need more prophecy teachers looking for the next sensationalistic concept but rather those willing to abide by God's FIRST admonition to any individual wanting to teach prophecy.

2 Peter 1:20 *Knowing this first, that* ***no prophecy of the scripture is of any private interpretation.***

It is time to rethink our long-held teachings and reject all the private interpretations that have caused the confusion and contradictions amongst those who sincerely want to know the truth, the whole truth, and nothing but the truth. Agreed?

> "The prophetic plan *applicable to the Jews* had not been **superseded** but would be **preceded** by a prophetic plan unknown to past generations."

[Excerpt from ***"Reviving the Blessed Hope,"*** page 21]

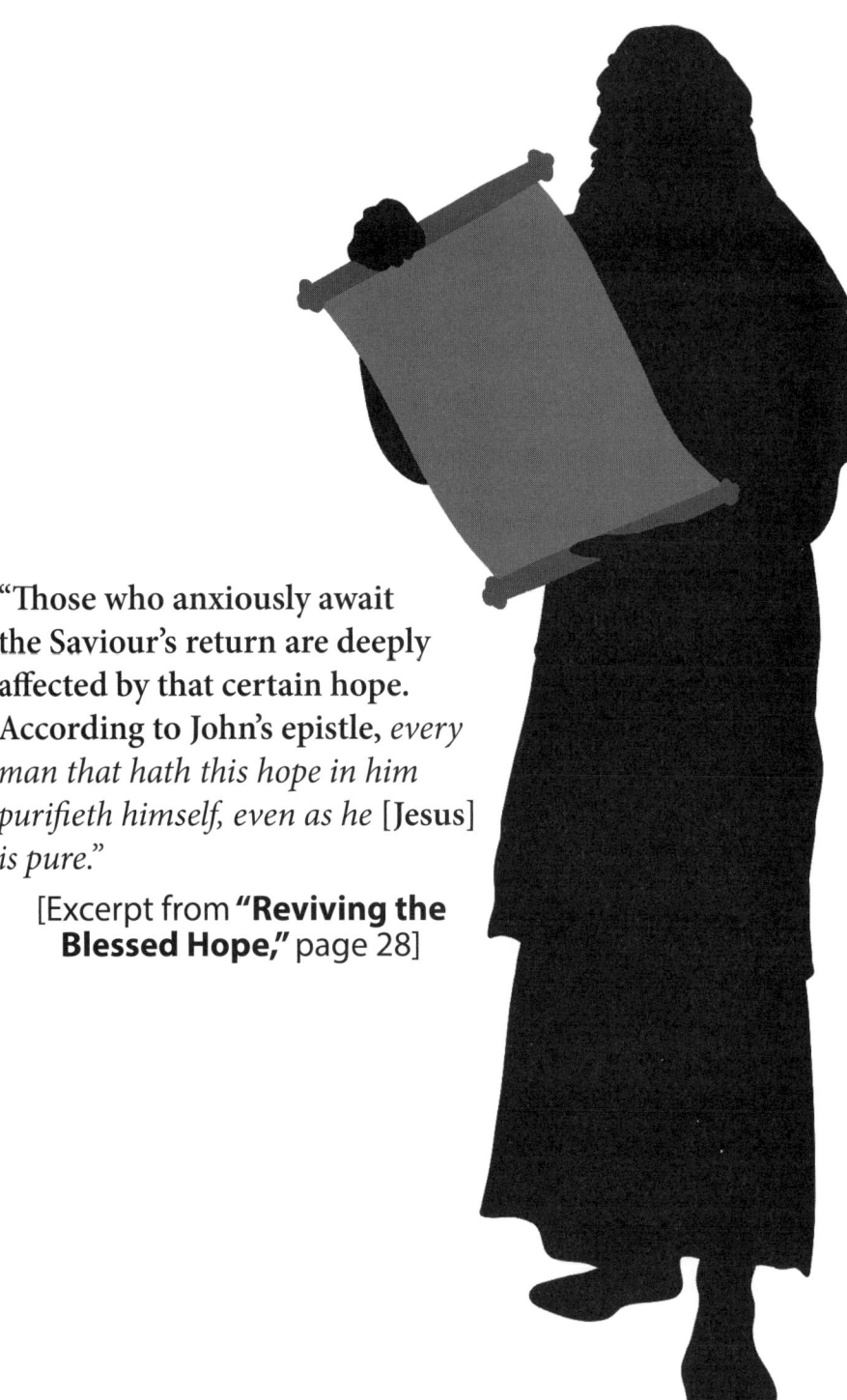

"Those who anxiously await the Saviour's return are deeply affected by that certain hope. According to John's epistle, *every man that hath this hope in him purifieth himself, even as he* [**Jesus**] *is pure.*"

   [Excerpt from **"Reviving the Blessed Hope,"** page 28]

2

The Temple Distraction

(Matthew 24:1-3)

The Parenthetical Matter Concerning the Temple

Only those who recognize the time period and context of the statements in the three Synoptic Gospels have any hope of grasping the overall understanding and comprehension of the specific details. As discussed earlier, the New Testament Church at this time had yet to be purchased with Christ's shed blood *(see Acts 20:28)* and therefore its formative years were yet future.

Matthew chapter 24 opens with the Lord departing from the *Jewish* temple with His *Jewish* disciples after having spoken a *Jewish* message (recorded in the previous chapter—Matthew chapter 23). Each of the synoptic writers opens his account by revealing a **DIVERSION** from the End-Times dialog to a question regarding the temple's magnificence.

> *Matthew 24:1 And Jesus went out, and **departed from the temple**: and his disciples came to him for to shew him **the buildings of the temple**.*
>
> *Mark 13:1 And as he went **out of the temple, one of his disciples** saith unto him, **Master**, see what manner of stones and what **buildings** are here!*
>
> *Luke 21:5 And as **some spake of the temple**, how it was adorned with **goodly stones** and gifts, he said,*

It is important to understand that the disciples genuinely expected their *Jewish* Messiah, Jesus Christ, to be enamored with the temple's grand splendor. After all, the Bible points out that the temple *"was adorned with goodly stones and gifts"* **(Luke 21:5)**. The Jewish people likely saw the grandeur of the temple as a monument of praise toward their Lord, yet Jesus obviously remained both unmoved and unimpressed. What did this infer?

Even a superficial understanding of the truths expressed in scripture would have led the Lord's followers to appreciate His lack of zeal for this magnificent edifice. Isaiah provides insight into God's perspective of being more concerned with man's heart than any attempts to show off any of man's supposed accomplishments:

> **Isaiah 66:1** *Thus saith the LORD, The heaven is my throne, and the earth is my footstool:* **where is the house that ye build unto me? and where is the place of my rest? 2 For all those things hath mine hand made, and all those things have been,** *saith the LORD: but to this man will I look, even to him that is poor and of a contrite spirit, and trembleth at my word.*

The Lord answered his disciples' comments concerning the temple's splendor with a sobering prophecy—one that would soon be fulfilled. The apostles must have instinctively understood the Lord's lack of reverential appreciation although they initially expected Him to agree with them. He stated that the beautiful buildings of the temple would all too soon become a heap of rubble. Again each of the Synoptic Gospels offers an account on what the Lord said:

> **Matthew 24:2** *And Jesus said unto them, See ye not all these things? verily I say unto you,* **There shall not be left here one stone upon another, that shall not be thrown down.**

> **Mark 13:2** *And Jesus* **answering** *said unto* **him, Seest thou these great buildings? there shall not be left one stone upon another, that shall not be thrown down.**

> **Luke 21:6** *As for these things which ye behold,* **the days will come, in the which there shall not be left one stone upon another, that shall not be thrown down.**

The context of the question along with the Lord's answer addressed only the temple buildings. These prophetic words were fulfilled in AD 70 when Titus and the Roman army systematically slaughtered the Jews and destroyed Jerusalem and the temple structures.[1] This stark revelation of the Lord's pronouncement seemed to fall upon deaf ears because the context of His earlier discussion on the End-Times quickly became the focus. This is clearly seen in that four of the apostles privately approached Jesus wanting further details of His earlier comments without addressing His comments on the temple's destruction.

The Context and Groundwork for the Teaching That Followed

Unlike much of the Lord's teaching during His earthly ministry, the contents of Matthew chapter 24 were *not* proclaimed to the masses. Instead, these comments were the Lord's private response to a series of questions asked by Peter, James, John, and Andrew (His *Jewish* disciples).

> ***Matthew 24:3** And as he sat upon **the mount of Olives,** the disciples came unto him **privately**, saying, Tell us, when shall these things be? and what shall be the sign of thy coming, and of the end of the world?*

> ***Mark 13:3** And as he sat upon **the mount of Olives** over against the temple, **Peter** and **James** and **John** and **Andrew** asked him **privately**,*

The Lord's response was strategic in nature down to the minutest details. Even the location of this exchange was evidently by divine design rather than mere happenstance. The location was *"the mount of Olives"* **(Matthew 24:3; Mark 13:3).**

> ***Acts 1:9** And when he had spoken these things, while they beheld, **he was taken up; and a cloud received him out of their sight**.*

> ***Acts 1:12 Then returned they** unto Jerusalem **from the mount called Olivet**, which is from Jerusalem a sabbath day's journey.*

The Bible points to the Mount of Olives as the location for several important events both historically and prophetically. The most significant future event concerns its selection as the exact spot for the Lord's Second Coming to earth. This is the spot where two of the primary purposes for Christ's physical visible return to the earth take place—He defeats the enemies of Israel and establishes His earthly millennial kingdom.

---

[1] According to the historian Josephus, the Romans torched the magnificent temple. He wrote that the fires burned so hot that the gold fittings and gilding on the walls ran into the cracks between the stones. The Romans wanted this gold so they broke apart these stones to get at the gold, thus fulfilling Jesus' prophecy that not one stone of the temple would remain upon another.

It was the Mount of Olives where the Lord heard His disciples' questions concerning *"the sign of thy [Christ's] coming, and of the end of the world."*

Matthew 24:3 *And as he sat upon the mount of Olives, the disciples came unto him privately, saying, Tell us, when shall these things be?* and **what shall be the sign of thy coming, and of the end of the world?**

From this location, the Lord Jesus briefly spoke to His disciples just prior to His ascension back into Heaven (see Acts chapter 1) when He was asked about restoring *"again the kingdom to Israel."* In fact, the *timing* of future events was the subject matter that most intrigued the disciples. Specifically, they wanted to know if He would immediately set up His kingdom.

Acts 1:6 *When they therefore were come together, they asked of him, saying, Lord,* **wilt thou at this time restore again the kingdom to Israel?**

None of these elements are coincidental but each aspect was divinely orchestrated just prior to Christ's ascension. The Lord's highly specific prophecies will be fulfilled with God-ordained precision. Old Testament prophets, like Zechariah, testified specifics concerning Christ's return, oftentimes providing additional details. Zechariah pointed out that God would gather the nations *"against Jerusalem to battle"* **(Zechariah 14:2)** only to see the Lord return to *"fight against those nations"* **(Zechariah 14:3)**. Zechariah also identified the location of Christ's return as the *"mount of Olives"* where His *"feet shall stand"* **(Zechariah 14:4)**. Christ's words to His disciples in the book of Acts simply confirm the ancient Old Testament prophecies concerning this event.

Zechariah 14:2 *For* **I will gather all nations against Jerusalem to battle**; *and the city shall be taken, and the houses rifled, and the women ravished; and half of the city shall go forth into captivity, and the residue of the people shall not be cut off from the city. 3* **Then shall the LORD go forth, and fight against those nations**, *as when he fought in the day of battle. 4* **And his feet shall stand in that day upon the mount of Olives**, *which is before Jerusalem on the east, and the mount of Olives shall cleave in the midst thereof toward the east and toward the west, and there shall be a very great valley; and half* *of the mountain shall remove toward the north, and half of it toward the south.*

Zechariah's prophecy continued by offering even more detail including the purpose of Christ's return. When Christ returns to the Mount of Olives, He will *"be king over all the earth."* This is the true divine Monarchy that will offer the world the best and perfect government.

Zechariah 14:9 And the LORD shall be king over all the earth: *in that day shall there be one LORD, and his name one.*

For all those truly seeking the truth, these passages teach an undeniable certainty. As described in these and other prophecies, it is readily apparent why the Second Coming CANNOT possibly be the Rapture of the Church and why the Rapture of the Church CANNOT possibly be the Second Coming. While many of the more distinctive details will be highlighted later in this work, it should be noted and understood that the Second Coming occurs AFTER Daniel's Seventieth Week *(Revelation 19:11-16)* and prior to the onset of Christ's earthly millennial kingdom *(Revelation 20:4-6)*.

Furthermore, it is imperative to understand that Christ's Second Coming serves as the long-awaited deliverance of the nation of Israel. The Rapture of the Church, on the other hand, takes place BEFORE the commencement of Daniel's Seventieth Week and serves as the supernatural deliverance and physical and spiritual transformation of all New Testament Church believers. Every diligent Bible student recognizes and accepts that the purpose for each return does not overlap nor can they be the same event. One return (for the Church) stops in the clouds for a gathering and the Second Coming shows Christ setting foot again upon the earth for judgment.

The opening verses of Matthew chapter 24 (after the parenthetical diversion in the first two verses) dramatically set the stage for the teaching and further revelation concerning the Second Coming. The context in no way refers to the as yet undisclosed Rapture of the Church. These revelations were not made known until the apostle Paul was led to reveal them to the New Testament Church. The context in Matthew is most assuredly when national Israel turns to the Lord. The questions themselves concern Israel and not the undefined entity—the Church.

The Disciples' Questions

Their questions point back to the End-Times discussion in the previous chapter

Matthew 23:34-39 *"Not see me"* till Israel says: *"Blessed is he that cometh in the name of the Lord"* (at thy Coming) and end of the world

[Not Here]
Matthew 24:1-2 *"and his disciples came to him for to shew him the buildings of the temple. ... There shall not be left here one stone upon another, that shall not be thrown down."*

Matthew 24:3 *"And as he sat upon the mount of Olives, the disciples came unto him privately, saying, Tell us, when shall these things be? and what shall be the sign of thy coming, and of the end of the world?"*

70th Week — 7 Years — Second Advent

© www.KJB1611.com   [Chart 2.10]

It All Points to the Second Coming

> **Matthew 24:3** *And as he sat upon the mount of Olives, the disciples came unto him privately, saying, Tell us, when shall **these things** be? and what shall be **the sign** of **thy coming**, and of **the end of the world**?*

This passage contains four key phrases that, when considered together, pinpoint the Second Coming as the context and only proper interpretation of the events mentioned. Those phrases are:

1) "these things"

2) "the sign" (Consider *1 Corinthians 1:22*)

3) "thy coming"

4) "the end of the world"

1) These Things

The *"these things"* of **Matthew 24:3; Mark 13:4; Luke 21:7** refer to circumstances to be accomplished upon a specified generation delineated in the chapter in Matthew previous to the Olivet Discourse. Only by considering these elements can one gain an understanding of the context.

> **Matthew 23:36** *Verily I say unto you, **All these things shall come upon this generation**.*

The Bible ties the *"these things"* to the abomination of desolation, the period of great tribulation, the end of the world, and the coming of the Lord Jesus Christ with power and great glory mentioned later in the Olivet Discourse. Regrettably, because of the diversion created by the comments concerning the temple and Christ's pronouncements of its complete destruction, there are some teachers who want to lump all the discourse into a single *past* fulfillment during the first century. Yet, Christ pinpoints the timing as the time when Israel will turn to the Lord.

Matthew 23:39 For I say unto you, ***Ye shall not see me henceforth, till ye shall say, Blessed is he that cometh in the name of the Lord.***

Some may suppose this narrative speaks of the Triumphal Entry, but it must be remembered that the Triumphal Entry had already occurred when Christ spoke these words. That being said, it is quite evident that this has not as yet happened. Israel, nationally, has not yet looked upon Christ, nor have they accepted Him and called Him *"Blessed"* (above) or as the prophesied *"Emmanuel" **(Matthew 1:23)***. This will not take place until after the betrayal and deception by the incarnate Devil and his desecration of Israel's future temple. After that time, their eyes will be collectively opened and God will reside with them. At this present time, they remain blinded ***(Romans 11:25)***.

These Things

The *"these things"* found in Matthew chapters 23 & 24 carry different meanings depending upon their context: End-Times versus the stones of the Temple

[End-Times Events]	[Stones]	[End-Times Events]
Matthew 23:36 Verily I say unto you, All **THESE THINGS** shall come upon this generation.	Matthew 24:1-2 ... shew him the **buildings** of the temple. ... See ye not all **THESE THINGS**? ... There shall not be left here one **stone** upon another, that shall not be thrown down.	Matthew 24:3 when shall **THESE THINGS** be? Matthew 24:6 all **THESE THINGS** must come to pass, but the end is not yet. Matthew 24:33 So likewise ye, when ye shall see all **THESE THINGS** ... Matthew 24:34 This generation shall not pass, till all **THESE THINGS** be fulfilled.

© www.KJB1611.com   [Chart 2.20]

Note: Sometimes people are fooled when the Bible uses identical wording with differing applications. Ignoring or missing context can make Bible study fatally flawed and misleading. The *"these things"* is an outstanding example. ***Matthew 23:36*** and ***Matthew 24:3, 6, 33, 34*** refer to a case in point. All these refer to the events of the End-Times and Christ's return. Yet, the *"these things"* mentioned in the comments concerning the Temple *(Matthew 24:2)* refers to the stones of the Temple and not the return of Christ or His End-Times judgments.

2) The Sign

This future fulfillment precedes and leads up to the Lord's Second Coming, a coming that will be signified by a particular sign identified as *"the sign"* of His coming.

> ***Matthew 24:3*** *And as he sat upon the mount of Olives, the disciples came unto him privately, saying, Tell us, when shall these things be? and what shall be **the sign** of thy coming, and of the end of the world?*

> ***Mark 13:4*** *Tell us, when shall these things be? and what shall be **the sign** when all these things shall be fulfilled?*

> ***Luke 21:7*** *And they asked him, saying, Master, but when shall these things be? and **what sign** will there be when these things shall come to pass?*

The specifics of this particular sign will be explored more fully within its context later in the chapter when we delve into the specifics of ***Matthew 24:30***. At this point, it is important to recognize that signs generally point directly to events relating to the Jews because of how they grew accustomed to walking *by sight* and not by faith.

> ***1 Corinthians 1:22 For the Jews require a sign***, *and the Greeks seek after wisdom:*

The Bible reflects that God confirmed His word *to the Jews* through the use of signs. In fact, Moses set the precedent of not accepting God at His word apart from verifying signs *(Exodus 4:1-30)*. This explains why the Lord Jesus sent forth His apostles with **signs** *"confirming the word"* they preached *(Mark 16:20)*.

From the time of Moses through the time of Christ and His apostles, God constantly and consistently used signs to deal with His chosen nation. Interestingly, following the death of the apostles (toward the end of the first century AD), those signs diminished until they became nonexistent. After the departure of the Church, the signs will be revived in association to the renewal of God's dealings with Israel. The *Jewish* signs will culminate with one final sign announcing the Second Coming of the Son of God.

3) Thy Coming

This coming IS NOT the return of Christ for the Church at the Rapture, but Christ's Second Coming to earth for Israel. It is the singular event where every eye shall see Him and every person wail because of Him. This will not happen at the Rapture of the Church.

> **Revelation 1:7** *Behold, he cometh with clouds; and* **every eye shall see him**, *and they also which pierced him: and* **all kindreds of the earth shall wail because of him**. *Even so, Amen.*

> **Matthew 24:30** *And then shall appear* **the sign of the Son of man in heaven:** *and* **then shall all the tribes of the earth mourn**, *and they shall see the Son of man coming in the clouds of heaven with power and great glory.*

Israel, in particular, shall mourn for Christ *"as one mourneth for his only son, and shall be in bitterness for him, as one that is in bitterness for his firstborn"* **(Zechariah 12:10)**. This is the only future coming of Christ preceded by and immediately introduced by signs similar to Christ's first coming to earth. It is important to note that the apostle Paul never mentions any signs associated to the Rapture of believers. The Second Coming remains distinct from Christ's return for His Church.

> **Zechariah 12:10** *And I will pour upon the house of David, and upon the inhabitants of Jerusalem, the spirit of grace and of supplications: and* **they shall look upon me whom they have pierced, and they shall mourn for him, as one mourneth for his only son, and shall be in bitterness for him, as one that is in bitterness for his firstborn.**

4) The End of the World

The Second Coming of Christ back to the earth ushers in an observable shift from the *permissive* power of Satan to the *absolute* power of Christ. This return fulfils the proclamation given during Daniel's Seventieth Week: *"The kingdoms of this world are become the kingdoms of our Lord, and of his Christ; and he shall reign for ever and ever"* **(Revelation**

11:15). This time also bears a strong scriptural association with prophecy concerning the *"end of the world."*

> *Matthew 13:39 The enemy that sowed them is the devil;* **the harvest is the end of the world;** *and the reapers are the angels. 40 As therefore the tares are gathered and burned in the fire;* **so shall it be in the end of this world.** *... 49* **So shall it be at the end of the world: the angels shall come forth, and sever the wicked from among the just,**

The Rapture of the Church prophesied by Paul does not indicate any type of severing of the wicked. It simply reflects a catching away of believers with only the unbelievers left behind upon the earth. Additionally, this prophecy is not the same event as the severing of the wicked from those who *"endured unto the end"* **(Matthew 24:13)** of Daniel's Seventieth Week. At the end of Daniel's Seventieth Week, Christ will send His angels to supernaturally protect the Elect. The wicked are severed from them and completely destroyed by the Lord. His coming ushers in the end of Satan's influence **(Revelation 20:3)** with the Lord beginning His reign upon this earth.

> *Matthew 24:3 And as he sat upon the mount of Olives, the disciples came unto him privately, saying, Tell us, when shall these things be? and what shall be the sign of* **thy coming, and of the end of the world?**

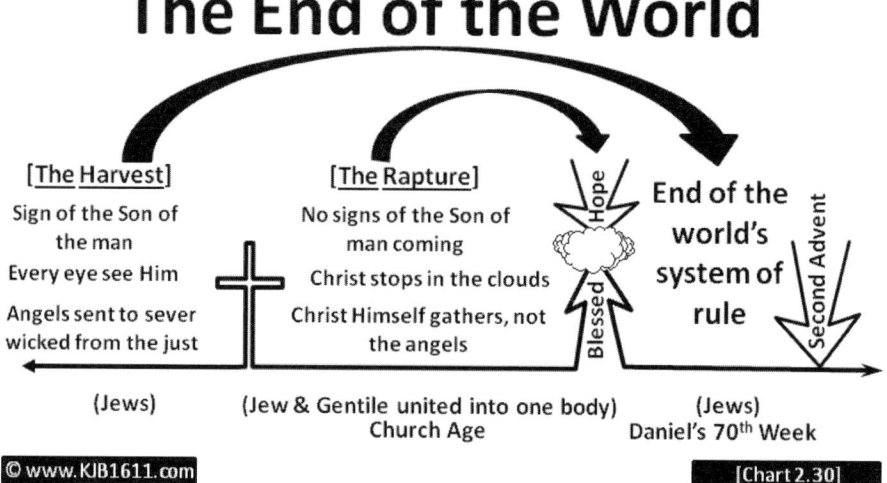

[Chart 2.30]

Destruction of Heaven and Earth

At this point, it is important to distinguish Christ's Second Coming at the end of Daniel's Seventieth Week from the physical destruction of the present heaven and earth that takes place 1,000 years later at the end of the Day of the Lord. Peter wrote that the heavens and the earth will be destroyed at the end of the period called the Day of the Lord (also specifically referred to as the Day of God).

> *2 Peter 3:10 But **the day of the Lord** will come as a thief in the night; in the which **the heavens shall pass away with a great noise, and the elements shall melt with fervent heat, the earth also and the works that are therein shall be burned up**. 11 Seeing then that all these things shall be dissolved, what manner of persons ought ye to be in all holy conversation and godliness, 12 Looking for and hasting unto **the coming of the day of God, wherein the heavens being on fire shall be dissolved, and the elements shall melt with fervent heat**?*

The destruction of the heaven and earth is specifically designated as *"the day of God"* and occurs at the end of the 1,000-year reign of Christ. John wrote that he saw a Great White Throne and then mentioned that the present heaven and earth fled away prior to the commencement of the Great White Throne Judgment.

> *Revelation 20:11 And I saw **a great white throne**, and him that sat on it, from whose face **the earth and the heaven fled away**; and there was found no place for them.*

The current earth and its heaven will be burned up. The new heaven and earth show up in the first verse of chapter 21 because the others passed away.

> *Revelation 21:1 And I saw a new heaven and a new earth: for **the first heaven and the first earth were passed away**; and there was no more sea.*

All this being said, it is important to note that the *"end"* spoken of in Matthew chapter 24 is *not* the destruction of the heaven and earth 1,000 years later. **It is the *end* of the world's system of rule replaced with the establishment of Christ's everlasting government.** It marks the initial judgment of the wicked upon the earth (which occurs at Christ's Second

Coming). This initial judgment will find its consummation at the Great White Throne Judgment (which occurs at the end of the millennial kingdom 1,000 years later).

Context, Context, Context

The context of the prophecy of Matthew chapter 24 is crystal clear! Only those approaching the Bible with preconceived biases can and will miss that Matthew chapter 24 speaks of Christ's Second Coming to deliver the *Jewish* people and their allies (Matthew chapter 25) and establish His earthly millennial kingdom.

The Church's Rapture is not even once mentioned nor even alluded to within the entire chapter or context! Rather, *Jewish* disciples desired to know about the judgment of **Matthew 24:3** and the timing for the restoration of their kinsmen according to the flesh—the Jewish people *(Acts 1:6).* The Lord answered their inquiries within the context of their questions. If Bible students would simply believe the Bible in its immediate context and *rightly divide* the scripture, the confusion and divisiveness would be drastically minimized.

*2 Timothy 2:15 Study to shew thyself approved unto God, a workman that needeth not to be ashamed, **rightly dividing** the word of truth.*

This is not a matter of opinion! This is not a matter of private interpretations. Instead, it is a God-given commandment to *"study"* given to every Christian. The same verse continues with an explanation as to the only proper method of effective Bible study. The Bible student must allow the Bible to correct his theology and doctrine and never force personal thoughts and biases into any text. As Jesus continued His Olivet Discourse, He did so by warning of great deception that will prove quite characteristic of Daniel's Seventieth Week.

God never intended for the questions and short discussion of the Temple and Christ's prophecy of its destruction to be associated with the End-Times, Daniel's Seventieth Week, or the Second Coming! This diversion by the disciples' comments has caused incalculable confusion.

3

The Beginning of Sorrows

(Matthew 24:4-8)

The Tribulation Period is more accurately referred to as Daniel's Seventieth Week, but what is Daniel's Seventieth Week? Daniel chapter 9 records a vision given to Daniel. In that vision, the angel Gabriel appeared to Daniel and gave to him the infamous prophecy of Daniel's Seventy Weeks. The prophecy of the seventy weeks of years (490 years) and especially that final seven years (the seventieth week) has perplexed many a Bible scholar. In a nutshell, these years were years of judgment against the nation of Israel because of their faithlessness.

Daniel's Seventieth Week *(Daniel 9:24-27)* is a time when *trouble* is compounded by greater troubles, *sorrow* by greater sorrows, and *tribulation* by greater tribulation. Those still living upon the earth will *not* escape this worldwide trouble, sorrow, and tribulation. In many ways, Daniel's Seventieth Week aligns with Amos' description of the Day of the Lord. The escalation of troubles described by Amos is likened to running from a lion only to be met by a bear, escaping from the lion into the safety of a house only to be bit by a serpent. This description reveals the absolute futility of man's resistance of God.

> ***Amos 5:18*** *Woe unto you that desire the day of the LORD! to what end is it for you?* ***the day of the LORD is*** *darkness, and not light. 19 As if a man did flee from a lion, and a bear met him; or went into the house, and leaned his hand on the wall, and a serpent bit him*.

Although there is some overlapping toward the end of Daniel's Seventieth Week, the Day of the Lord does NOT extend over the entirety of

Daniel's Seventieth Week. At the same time, there are some descriptive similarities due to this overlapping. The description above of the Day of the Lord seems to match the account of Daniel's Seventieth Week as laid out in the Synoptic Gospels. Descriptive phrases such as *"the beginning of sorrows" (Matthew 24:8; Mark 13:8)* and *"then shall be **great** tribulation" (Matthew 24:21)* suggest that Daniel's Seventieth Week opens with troubles or sorrows but increasingly worsens until the heavens open *(Revelation 19:11)* revealing Christ's Second Advent.

The Threat of Deception

The opening days of Daniel's Seventieth Week will be days of deception, particularly as it applies to a false covenant and false prophets. Deception is one of the Devil's most often used and effective weapons against the truth. Implemented incrementally since the garden in Eden, the Devil's lies will be fully displayed during Daniel's Seventieth Week. Simultaneously, the one who *"is a liar, and the father of it" (John 8:44)* will have his share of false prophets doing his bidding. Imagine the time of peril and change to this world following the departure of the Church!

In order to effectively deceive the multitudes into believing his lie at the Abomination of Desolation *(2 Thessalonians 2:4)*, the Man of Sin will impersonate God. Prior to that point, Satan must create doubt as to the identity and location of the Son of God. For those who suppose the Church will be present during Daniel's Seventieth Week, this makes no sense. After all, when Christ comes for the Church, He comes *in the clouds* and we meet Him *in the air (1 Thessalonians 4:17)*. No Church Age saint with any Bible sense would look for Christ **upon the earth**. No matter a person's position on the Rapture, everyone teaches that all believers will be caught up to meet Christ BEFORE HIS RETURN to earth.

When Christ comes at His Second Advent, He will return TO EARTH as a judge, a king, and as the captain of a great and mighty host. He will not come as a redeemer of men's souls. Christ came as the redeemer during His first advent and that aspect is finished *(John 19:30)*. In the Church's absence from earth, EVERY major religion will be highly susceptible to deception, looking for a coming redeemer. This is the type of deception warned against, because they all will seek an earthly deliverer. The following are a few examples to illustrate religious groups looking for their own anointed one:

- The orthodox **Jews** are looking for a great charismatic political leader in the end of days (during the *Olam Ha-Ba*—the Messianic Age). He will be well versed in Jewish law and observant of its commandments and called *"Mashiach ben David"* (Messiah, son of David).
- The **Shiite Muslims** are looking for their messiah called the *"12th Imam"* (the Mahdi) who was born in AD 868 and placed into hiding by Allah until the Day of Judgment. They believe he is **Mohammed ibn Hasan**, the 12th in the line of imams who were descendants of the prophet Mohammed.[1]
- The **Sunni Muslims** are looking for the first appearance of Mahdi.
- The **Buddhists** are looking for their savior, the "Maitreya," as the moral degradation and societal deterioration reaches an all-time low.
- The **Hindus** are looking for the tenth and final incarnation of Vishnu called the Kalki.

Many other world religions would add their "christs"[2] to this list through the same pattern of unbelief and rejection of the true Christ. One commonality amongst each of these religions is that they are all looking for a savior, deliverer, and redeemer to show up UPON THE EARTH. The Bible says that MANY will come in Christ's name and they will effectively deceive MANY. The dogmas taught by these religions and others are setting their followers (and the world) up for the acceptance of a false messiah who will come to deceive the world. This situation will be so unimaginable without any Christians here to warn of the deception.

---

[1] Iran's past president Mahmoud Ahmadinejad belongs to the mainstream Shi'a Islam group known as the *"Twelvers."* He believes that the Mahdi's return is near and that it is the responsibility of the Iranian government to prepare the world for his return. According to Ahmadinejad, the Mahdi will come and *"administer ultimate justice"* and he will bring order from chaos and righteousness from unbelief.

The Shi'a Muslims believe that Israel must be destroyed before the Mahdi can return and also highly esteem the date of August 22nd which could prove pivotal at some point. They also want to trigger a series of cataclysmic events which would precipitate the return of the 12th Imam. It must be understood that neither death nor the commonly accepted "mutual assured (nuclear) destruction" serves as a deterrent to this radical Islamic philosophy.

[2] Christ simply means *"the anointed."*

Matthew 24:4 And Jesus answered and said unto them, **Take heed that no man deceive you.** *5 For* **many shall come in my name, saying, I am Christ; and shall deceive many.**

Mark 13:5 And Jesus answering them began to say, **Take heed lest any** *man* **deceive you:** *6 For* **many shall come in my name, saying, I am Christ; and shall deceive many.**

Luke 21:8 And he said, **Take heed that ye be not deceived:** *for* **many shall come in my name, saying, I am** *Christ;* **and the time draweth near:** *go ye not therefore after them.*

Clearly, Daniel's Seventieth Week brings with it the highest levels of deception. After all, *"many shall come"* with a false message *"and shall deceive many."* Obviously, there will be many deceivers and many being deceived. The false gospel is basically threefold:

- *"I am Christ"* **(Matthew 24:5; Mark 13:6; Luke 21:8)**,
- *"the time draweth near"* **(Luke 21:8)**, and
- follow me—noted by the admonition: *"go ye not therefore after them"* **(Luke 21:8)**

Should any Christian, even if only possessing a basic understanding of scripture, be the least bit concerned over the possibility of this described deception? Christians, no matter their stance upon the timing of the Rapture, will not be looking for an earthbound deliverer. **The Pre-tribulation Rapture** believer looks to meet Jesus in the air before

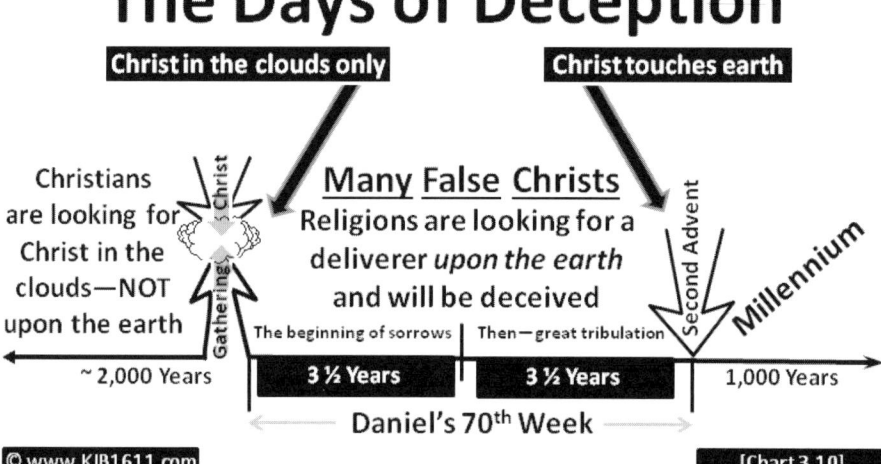

Daniel's Seventieth Week, not upon earth during it. **The Post-tribulation Rapture** teacher should be instructing his unfortunate followers to be looking for the angels sent to deliver those who have endured unto the end of Daniel's Seventieth Week *(Matthew 24:31)*. Neither of these groups should be fooled by someone on earth claiming to be Christ.

Deceptive Successes

Whether or not the deceptive satanic messengers bark out threatenings when their appeals are refused is not necessarily known, but what is known is that their appeals result in a high rate of success. In this capacity, these messengers, or *"antichrists,"* pave the way for the final Antichrist to follow.

> *1 John 2:18 Little children, it is the last time: and as ye have heard that **antichrist shall come, even now are there many antichrists**; whereby we know that it is the last time.*

Unfortunately, the Church Age has experienced its share of those claiming to be the Christ, yet these atrocities pale in comparison to the extent of the worldwide deception that will take place during Daniel's Seventieth Week. In fact, God warned that during Daniel's Seventieth Week the hordes of hell will implement signs and wonders attempting to draw away *"the elect"* (believing Israel).

> *Matthew 24:24 For there shall arise **false Christs**, and false prophets, and **shall shew great signs and wonders; insomuch that, if it were possible, they shall deceive the very elect**.*

> *Mark 13:22 For **false Christs** and false prophets shall rise, and **shall shew signs and wonders, to seduce, if it were possible, even the elect**.*

There should be no dispute as to who are the elect referred to in Matthew chapter 24. The context undeniably references the same group of the elect mentioned in the Old Testament[3] because the Lord was addressing a group of Jews prior to the establishment of the New Testament Church. Simply comparing scripture with scripture (also considering context) in obedience to God always supplies the right answer.

---

[3] *Isaiah 45:4 For **Jacob my servant's sake, and Israel mine elect**, I have even called thee by thy name: I have surnamed thee, though thou hast not known me.*

During this heightened time of deception, there will be many competing voices, some pointing in the same direction, but all pointing in the wrong direction. Similar to the garden in Eden, the introduction of multiple "authorities" causes confusion from God's explicit commands. During Daniel's Seventieth Week, the multitude of voices will overwhelm the masses.

Some counterfeiters will claim to be Christ *(Matthew 24:5; Mark 13:5-6; Luke 21:8)*. Others will claim to have seen Christ *(Matthew 24:23; Mark 13:21)*. To make matters worse, these imposters will have false signs to confirm their false messages *(Matthew 24:24; Mark 13:22)*. Understandably so, the serious nature of the time calls for a warning to *"Take heed"* or pay close attention.

> ***Matthew 24:4*** *And Jesus answered and said unto them,* ***Take heed*** *that no man deceive you. 5 For many shall come in my name, saying, I am Christ; and shall deceive many.*

> ***Mark 13:5*** *And Jesus answering them began to say,* ***Take heed*** *lest any man deceive you: 6 For many shall come in my name, saying, I am Christ; and shall deceive many.*

> ***Luke 21:8*** *And he said,* ***Take heed*** *that ye be not deceived: for many shall come in my name, saying, I am Christ; and the time draweth near: go ye not therefore after them.*

The Threat of Wars

If the concern for deception and the lack of spiritual soundness were not bleak enough, the earth's inhabitants will also be overwhelmed by the unrelenting threat of wars. Although Daniel's Seventieth Week opens with the Jews enjoying a confirmation of a covenant of peace with the Antichrist *(Daniel 9:27)*, they will be constantly bombarded by the news of *existing* wars and the threats of *possible* wars.

> ***Matthew 24:6*** *And* ***ye shall hear of wars and rumours of wars****: see that ye be not troubled: for all these things must come to pass, but the end is not yet.*

> ***Mark 13:7*** *And when* ***ye shall hear of wars and rumours of wars****, be ye not troubled: for such things must needs be; but the end shall not be yet.*

***Luke 21:9** But when **ye shall hear of wars and commotions**, be not terrified: for these things must first come to pass; but the end is not by and by.*

These tumultuous events should not trouble those who know and understand the timing of each prophecy. After all, these events must all come to pass, but the end is not yet. The current description of events takes place prior to the nations unleashing their hatred against Jerusalem.

***Zechariah 14:2** For **I will gather all nations against Jerusalem to battle**; and the city shall be taken, and the houses rifled, and the women ravished; and half of the city shall go forth into captivity, and the residue of the people shall not be cut off from the city.*

The Bible says that God will gather the nations to battle against Jerusalem. Yet, prior to the nations being gathered to fight against Jerusalem, they will wage war amongst themselves. Imagine, if you can, the pending danger when the United Nations will be even more inept and powerless to thwart the onslaught. Simply put, no global council will thwart the fulfillment of prophecy.

***Matthew 24:7** For **nation shall rise against nation, and kingdom against kingdom**: and there shall be famines, and pestilences, and earthquakes, in divers places.*

***Mark 13:8** For **nation shall rise against nation, and kingdom against kingdom**: and there shall be earthquakes in divers places, and there shall be famines and troubles: these are the beginnings of sorrows.*

***Luke 21:10** Then said he unto them, **Nation shall rise against nation, and kingdom against kingdom**:*

These wars and commotions will not necessarily be limited to one nation warring against another. Likely, the wars will involve many civil wars and much internal strife. Leaders will simply become obsessed with the lust for power, control, and oppression.

***Isaiah 19:2** And **I will set the Egyptians against the Egyptians**: and **they shall fight every one against his brother, and every one against his neighbour; city against city, and kingdom against kingdom**.*

On cue, the nations will eventually find a common enemy—the Jews. This same way of thinking has been prevalent in most every generation of the past. Israel, specifically the destruction of this tiny nation, is the one common enemy and one common cause that can bring together even the bitterest foes.

The Threat of Physical Disturbances

As we have seen, the earth's inhabitants will be haunted by wars (trouble from man to man), but they will also be bombarded by physical disturbances (trouble from God toward man). In fact, one of the most significant distinctions between the Church's last days and the last days of the Jews is the circumstances highlighting those two distinct periods. The Jews are a physical, earthly people seeking a physical, earthly kingdom. The Church, on the other hand, is a spiritual body born into God's family by a spiritual birth and looking for a spiritual, heavenly kingdom. This is why the last days of each group will reflect earthly versus spiritual distinctions.

The Church's Last Days

The last days, as they pertain to the Church, are highlighted by *spiritual* turbulence. During the Church's last days, believers will *"depart from the faith"* (or apostatize)[4] like no other time in history. This will happen by giving heed to seducing spirits and doctrines of devils. Furthermore, this apostasy will cause the perpetrators to have their consciences seared. This damaged conscience causes them to speak lies in hypocrisy.

> ***1 Timothy 4:1*** *Now the Spirit speaketh expressly, that **in the latter times some shall depart from the faith**, giving heed to seducing spirits, and doctrines of devils; 2 Speaking lies in hypocrisy; having their conscience seared with a hot iron;*

The description offered in Timothy's second epistle offers even greater details of the rampant apostasy. According to Second Timothy, men in the final days of the Church are plagued by self-love, covetousness, pride, disobedience, unthankfulness, trucebreaking, fierceness, despising holy living, arrogance, and an inordinate love of pleasure. Read of the Church's last days in context:

---

[4] This departing from the faith (or apostasy) can only take place amongst those who have first believed. This description is not one concerning unbelievers, but the detestable spiritual condition of the Church.

> ***2 Timothy 3:1** This know also, that **in the last days** perilous times shall come. 2 For **men shall be lovers of their own selves, covetous, boasters, proud, blasphemers, disobedient to parents, unthankful, unholy,** 3 **Without natural affection, trucebreakers, false accusers, incontinent, fierce, despisers of those that are good,** 4 **Traitors, heady, highminded, lovers of pleasures more than lovers of God;***

Consider what is noticeably absent from Paul's descriptions of the Church's last days—there is no mention by the apostle Paul of wars, earthquakes, and famines![5]

The clock started on the Church's last days at its inception. This rings especially true considering that the New Testament Church was a mystery. From man's perspective, the Church Age is a type of parenthetical insertion into the Lord's overall prophetic plan. From the beginning, the New Testament Church was a temporary vehicle by which the Lord would provoke the Jews to jealousy **(Romans 10:19; Romans 11:11)**. As such, Paul considered the days in which he lived to be the last days **(Hebrews 1:2)** and fully anticipated being alive at the Lord's return for the Church—as noted by his inclusion in *"**we** which are alive"* and exclusion from *"**them** which are asleep"* **(1 Thessalonians 4:15)**.

We know that the Church's last days likely began shortly after the crucifixion of Christ while the Jewish last days were temporarily suspended. The book of Acts clearly chronicles the transition from the Jews to the Gentiles as God's primary means of evangelization **(Acts 13:46; Acts 18:5-6; Acts 28:28)**. Additionally, the book of Romans explains that *"blindness in part is happened to Israel, until the fulness of the Gentiles be come in"* **(Romans 11:25)**. God broke off the nation of Israel **(Romans 11:17-20)** so that He could use the Gentiles to provoke the nation to jealousy.

> ***Romans 11:11** I say then, Have they stumbled that they should fall? God forbid: **but rather through their fall salvation is come unto the Gentiles,** for **to provoke them to jealousy.***

The time of the crucifixion marked the end of Daniel's first sixty-nine weeks with Daniel's Seventieth Week not beginning until after

---

[5] This is not to imply that these natural disasters will not be on the increase on a *localized* level prior to the Rapture or that they are not now on the rise. Simply put, our primary focus needs to be on the spiritual disintegration and apostasy of the believers.

the parenthetical period of the Church Age comes to an abrupt close at the Rapture. The Jewish last days will, no doubt, include some of the spiritual problems that have plagued the Church, but the overriding emphasis turns from *spiritual* to *physical* elements—famines, pestilences, earthquakes, and other fearful SIGHTS.

> ***Matthew 24:7*** *For nation shall rise against nation, and kingdom against kingdom: and **there shall be famines**, and **pestilences**, and **earthquakes**, in divers places.*
>
> ***Mark 13:8*** *For nation shall rise against nation, and kingdom against kingdom: and **there shall be earthquakes** in divers places, and there shall be **famines and troubles**: these are the beginnings of sorrows.*
>
> ***Luke 21:11*** *And **great earthquakes** shall be in divers places, and **famines**, and **pestilences**; and **fearful sights** and **great signs** shall there be from heaven.*

The Church is not to be focused upon supposed signs and fearful sights from the heavens taking place simply because they are prophesied on a worldwide scale after our departing. According to the Synoptic Gospels, three categories of physical disasters will manifest themselves in epic proportions during Daniel's Seventieth Week: (1) famines, (2) pestilences, and (3) great earthquakes.

Even today, these disasters strike fear into the hearts of people, yet they are more *localized* rather than the massive disasters described during Daniel's Seventieth Week. In fact, there has not been a worldwide physical calamity since Noah's flood covered the entire earth. The change will be drastic, fearful, and virtually unprecedented. In the last days described in the Synoptic Gospels, the devastation will be take place simultaneously *"in divers places"* (***Matthew 24:7; Mark 13:8; Luke 21:11***).

One can only imagine the escalating fear associated to the simultaneous breakout of diseases, famines, and earthquakes—both on a national and a transcontinental scale. In fact, many Bible students have pontificated concerning what could be the driving force for a worldwide unity in the last days. Nothing unites enemies like fear of the unexpected from the *"fearful sights and great signs ... from heaven"* (***Luke 21:11***). This sense of things spiraling out of control could easily serve as the momentum behind people completely turning against God as they look for a hell-sent savior promising them the world's greatest desire—peace and safety.

The Threat of Fear

In the midst of these fears and apprehensions, the Lord admonished His people not to fear *(Matthew 24:6; Mark 13:7; Luke 21:9)*. After all, these occurrences will not signify the end, but merely t*he beginning of sorrows*.

*Matthew 24:8 All these are the **beginning of sorrows**.*

*Mark 13:8 For nation shall rise against nation, and kingdom against kingdom: and there shall be earthquakes in divers places, and there shall be famines and troubles: these are the **beginnings of sorrows**.*

With all of this truth *from the New Testament scriptures* intended for future Jews, one can easily recognize the purpose for the Devil's onslaught at discrediting the New Testament. The Devil wants to keep the Jews blinded so that they believe on the false Christ and reject the Lord Jesus Christ *(2 Corinthians 4:4)*. The Devil wants them to remain oblivious to the details about their future predicament and the oncoming mass deception.

The initial question set forth by the *Jewish* disciples concerned *"the end of the world" (Matthew 24:3)*. For this reason, the Lord informed the disciples of signs preceding the end but encouraged them not to be overcome by fears associated to those calamities. After all, Christ pointed out that *"these things must come to pass, but the end is not yet"* **(Matthew 24:6)**.

Such information may seem insignificant to the Church Age believer and rightfully so. Yet, physical survival during the physical troubles of Daniel's Seventieth Week places all of these issues at the forefront of one's daily mind-set. Fear will only increase as the troubles and deception rise. These things increasingly add to the Jews' vulnerability to either losing their lives or believing the most reprehensible of lies.

The Hijacked Future Warning

The Jews are not the only group the Devil desires to blind concerning the wars and disturbances to come. The average prophecy teacher is likewise confused concerning these End-Times events. Every time it appears a new war is about to ensue, or a new disease threatens man's well-being, or a new physical disturbance demonstrates its destructive potential, the prophecy "expert" pontificates about these fulfilling the signs of the times. Unfortunately, little is learned from his last failed prophetic prognostication.

He uses the newfound fear to rally the troops, convincing them once again that the end is near and the sky is falling. He appeals to them for financial assistance to help *"spread the word."* For further confirmation, he reminds his followers that the present days are just like *the days of Noah* **(Matthew 24:37-38; Luke 17:26-27)** and *the days of Lot* **(Luke 17:28)**: (1) people eat and drink, (2) people marry and give in marriage, (3) people buy and sell, (4) people plant, and (5) people build. This is simply the typical misapplication of scripture. Sound familiar?

Yet, the astute Bible student understands the folly of such thinking. It is equivalent to suggesting that a toothpick and a dinner table are the same because they are both made of wood. Present-day events may demonstrate some qualities of the future prophetic fulfillment, but this does not mean that these events are the actual fulfilled prophecy. The wars, commotions, rumors of wars, famines, earthquakes, and pestilences during Daniel's Seventieth Week will make every present and past calamity seem like child's play in comparison.[6]

Twenty-first Century doom-and-gloom pontificators simply underscore the real danger of how easily man can abuse modern technology to gain a following. A man no longer has to be a true student of the Bible in

---

[6] Of course, this is with the exception of Noah's worldwide flood and the destruction of Sodom and Gomorrah.

order to garner his following. In fact, the more sensationalistic his style and message, the more people he will potentially influence—with the proverbial "click and share" mentality. We need a prophetic "fact check" system. The reader should be reminded that we do have one—it is the Bible!

The novice and the unlearned man, or worse yet, the wolf in sheep's clothing, find it increasingly easy to access a gullible audience. Most anyone of these undesirables build their audience by first building a website, starting a television or internet broadcast, uploading videos online, or posting opinions on social media platforms. Those ignorant of the scriptures will always fall for the next false teacher and "prophet" because of man's inward desire to know the truth and believe the worst.

In other words, you do not have to know God or know the Bible to gain popularity or garner a huge following. Many false teachers are securing a dedicated following in today's *perilous times* **(2 Timothy 3:1)**. Paul warned about these false teachers long before technology provided the efficient means and far-reaching platform.

> **Acts 20:29** *For I know this, that after my departing shall* **grievous wolves enter in among you, not sparing the flock.** *30 Also of your own selves shall men arise, speaking perverse things,* **to draw away disciples after them.**

Fortunately, a time of reckoning is also on the horizon. Unfortunately, it will impact more than just the false teachers with their false messages. It will also harm the unfortunate sheep who have rejected the truth of God's word for man's opinions. The world does not need more prophetic sensationalism; it needs teaching that points people to the Saviour and His return—first for the Church **(1 Thessalonians 4:16-17)** followed by His return with the armies of heaven seven years later **(Revelation 19:11)**. Between Christ's return to the clouds and His return to earth, as love increasingly grows cold, there will be an outpouring of hatred unseen since the days of Noah. The only way to insure that you will not be here is by trusting in the Lord for salvation **(Ephesians 1:13)**.

The simple salvation chart on the next page is provided for those wanting to know more about how to be saved from the eternal penalty of sin. The left column shows the **Scriptural Declarations** and the right column contains the **Personal Acknowledgements** to help guide in the most important decision in any person's life.

For all have sinned, and come short of the glory of God (Romans 3:23).	**1. Realize that you are a sinner:** "I know that I have broken the laws of God and am a sinner, and my sin causes me to come short of God's perfect standard."
He that believeth on him is not condemned: but he that believeth not is condemned already, because he hath not believed in the name of the only begotten Son of God (John 3:18). *He that believeth on the Son hath everlasting life: and he that believeth not the Son shall not see life; but the wrath of God abideth on him (John 3:36).*	**2. Recognize that you are currently under God's wrath and deserve to end up in hell because of your sin:** "I believe the Bible which says that I am currently under the wrath of God and condemned to hell. I justly deserve to be eternally punished for my sin and know that I am simply awaiting the execution of my sentence by the eternal Judge once I die. Thankfully, the Son of God has paid my sin debt by dying and shedding His blood in my place so that I could have eternal life by believing on Him."
But God commendeth his love toward us, in that, while we were yet sinners, Christ died for us (Romans 5:8).	**3. Believe that the Lord Jesus Christ died for your sins:** "I believe that Christ died for my sins and also rose from the dead for my justification" (see I Corinthians 15:1–4).
Or despisest thou the riches of his goodness and forbearance and longsuffering; not knowing that the goodness of God leadeth thee to repentance? But after thy hardness and impenitent heart treasurest up unto thyself wrath against the day of wrath and revelation of the righteous judgment of God (Romans 2:4, 5).	**4. Repent of trusting in anything else to save you:** "In believing on Jesus Christ, I know that I must trust in Him and Him alone. If I try to add anything (good works, baptism, church membership, etc.) to Christ's payment then I am saying to God that His Son's sacrificial death and blood shed on the cross was not sufficient to pay for my sin."
For the wages of sin is death; but the gift of God is eternal life through Jesus Christ our Lord (Romans 6:23).	**5. Accept God's gift of salvation:** "I believe that Jesus died for my sin and I accept His gift of salvation freely given to me based on the promise of God."
That if thou shalt confess with thy mouth the Lord Jesus, and shalt believe in thine heart that God hath raised him from the dead, thou shalt be saved. For with the heart man believeth unto righteousness; and with the mouth confession is made unto salvation (Romans 10:9, 10). *For whosoever shall call upon the name of the Lord shall be saved (Romans 10:13).*	**6. Ask the Lord to save you by simply trusting in Him and His word:** "I believe that God wants to forgive my sins and has graciously provided the way for me to receive that payment on my behalf." **Now in your own words, if you are ready to trust in Christ, ask Him to forgive you and save you. Ephesians 1:13 says:** "In whom ye also trusted, after that ye heard the word of truth, the gospel of your salvation: in whom also, after that ye believed, ye were sealed with that holy Spirit of promise."

4

The Outpouring of Hatred

(Matthew 24:9-13)

The Bible repeatedly states that *God is love* **(1 John 4:8, 16)**! The less that man understands and knows God, the less he comprehends love. Bible prophecy points to a dire time when most love grows completely *cold*. In fact, Daniel's Seventieth Week, with the absence of Christians and true Christianity, ushers in an unparalleled hatred for one another.

During that time, few people will be able to be trusted, whether friend or foe, family or stranger, religious or abject heathen. This inability to trust others will, in turn, produce an unprecedented fear and paranoia. In fact, the intense hatred chronicled during Daniel's Seventieth Week serves as a logical path for the complete departure from truth and the utter despairing of life.

Hatred from Without

Abject hatred puts love to its ultimate test. During this future period, the Jews will first experience the dire threats originating from *without* before turning against each other. Darwinian philosophies rule the day and many of the Jews will further forsake the religion of their fathers' God as they adopt the philosophy of *survival of the fittest*. The contrast taking place between truth and error is a major difference between man-made humanism and biblical religion *(James 1:27)*. Humanism says love thyself first, yet biblical religion says love others first and love them always above oneself.

Historically, the Jewish people have been persistently persecuted—more than any other people group. Yet, during Daniel's Seventieth Week, they will experience an ever-increasing level of hatred. This hatred originates from those without—from non-Jews. This truth is easily confirmed by simply noting the pronoun distinctions used in our subject passage (i.e., notice how it is THEY/THEM who deliver and kill YOU/YE).

> **Matthew 24:9** *Then shall **they** deliver **you** up to be afflicted, and shall kill **you**: and **ye** shall be hated of all nations for my name's sake.*
>
> **Mark 13:9** *But take heed to yourselves: for **they** shall deliver **you** up to councils; and in the synagogues **ye** shall be beaten: and **ye** shall be brought before rulers and kings for my sake, for a testimony against **them**.*
>
> **Luke 21:12** *But before all these, **they** shall lay **their** hands on **you**, and persecute **you**, delivering **you** up to the synagogues, and into prisons, being brought before kings and rulers for my name's sake.*

The pronouns serve distinct and useful purposes referring to those who will seek to persecute and destroy the Jews. Unfortunately, most modern bible versions produced by men frequently blur and distort the important pronoun distinctions. In fact, those who fail to emphasize the importance of every word of God generally have no appreciation for the simpler things of God's word—like the importance of pronouns. However, pronoun usage within scripture is extremely important. This truth bears similarities to how the *"they"* versus *"ye"* is contrasted in First Thessalonians chapter 5.[1]

The phenomenon in Thessalonians demonstrates that Christians will ***not*** be on the receiving end of the Day of the Lord. Similarly, the contrast of *"they"* versus *"you/ye"* in the verses above also provides an important function. The pronouns clearly indicate that the hatred of the Jews will be instigated from WITHOUT (the *"they"* and *"them"*) and not from amongst the Jews themselves.

Why Synagogues and Not Churches?

Students of history recognize that history is both cyclical and repetitive, yet men rarely learn the true lessons of history. This is especially

---

[1] See the extensive discussion of the pronouns contained in First Thessalonians chapter 5 in *"Reviving the Blessed Hope"* by the same authors, pages 64-67.

true of the history that involves spiritual or moral truths. Here is a case in point. In the first century, those who believed in Christ (the believers) were delivered up to the religious leaders (in the synagogues). The same scenario will take place following the Rapture, only this time the whole world will unite against those Jews who refuse to get on board with the new one-world system and religion. Many Bible passages teach the principle of repetitive history, but Ecclesiastes goes much further. It also provides insight into how the Bible intertwines the past, the present, and the future.

> **Ecclesiastes 3:15** *That which **hath been** is **now**; and that which is **to be** hath already **been**; and God requireth that which is past*

History repeats! Ecclesiastes refers to the past *("hath been")* revealing that past events also take place in the present *("now")* and in the future *("to be")*. In other words, that *"which is to be hath already been."* That is why *"there is no new thing under the sun"* **(Ecclesiastes 1:9)**. Bible students, especially the Preterists, force passages into a single historical context when many of them can have dual or triple applications.

Jesus said those who do not participate in this new religion are delivered up to the *synagogues* and not churches. In the first century, Jewish believers were delivered up to the synagogues; the same will be true in the future. The synagogues existing prior to the Rapture will again exist following the Rapture (rejecting Jesus Christ). After the Rapture, with all believers gone, every religious institution existing will be full of the unbelieving and the apostate.

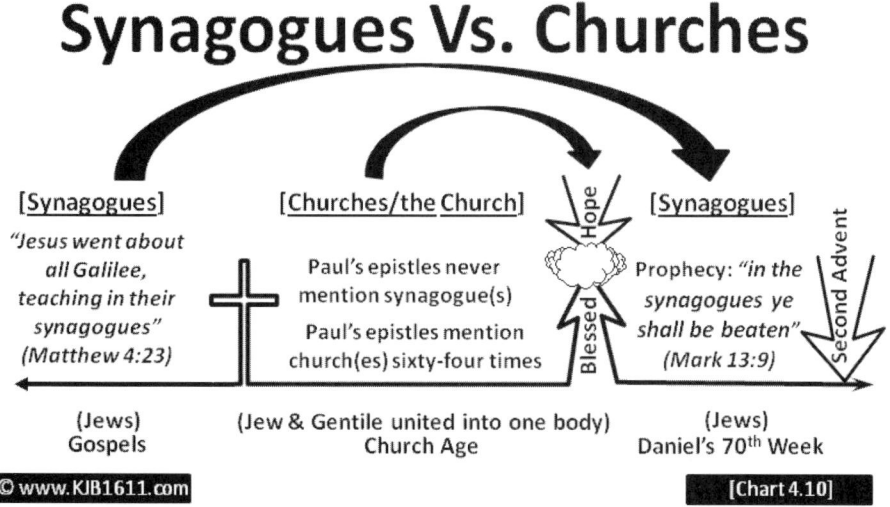

[Chart 4.10]

The primary focus will be squarely upon Israel and her synagogues. All Jews refusing to submit to the world system put in place by Satan's minions will be in grave danger. These Jews who refuse to participate will *not* be delivered to some apostate church but to the unbelieving who infiltrate the Jewish synagogues which will again become the focus of false worship and an intense persecution of believers.

The greatest hindrance for understanding these future events is the prevailing Western mind-set fixated upon the "here and now" that refuses to focus upon how dramatically things change after the Rapture. The world's persecution will be redirected primarily toward the Jews who refuse the obvious pagan worship. The synagogues during Daniel's Seventieth Week (the synagogues of Satan—**Revelation 2:9 and Revelation 3:9**) are not going to be transformed into a place of true worship but a means to persecute all those who refuse to submit.

Who Are "You"?

Before considering the identity of the people group addressed as *"they"* and *"them,"* it must first be understood that the *"you"* or *"ye"* does not refer to the NEW TESTAMENT CHURCH. If the reader has skipped ahead to this point in the book, you have missed an essential section dealing with the fact that the New Testament Church was not presently in existence at the time of the Olivet Discourse.

Even a simple cursory reading of the introduction to the Gospel of John offers enough proof as to whom these truths were directed. John pointed out that Christ *"came unto **his own**,"* and these JEWISH BRETHREN rejected Him ***(John 1:11)***. Additionally, Jesus pointed out that He was sent to the *"lost sheep of the house of Israel"* **(Matthew 15:24)**.

The *"you"* or *"ye"* in context refers to the Jews on the earth just prior to the Lord's Second Coming and *"the end of the world"* **(Matthew 24:3)**.

Who Are "They"?

As always, the context of the passage identifies those referenced, in this case by the pronouns of *"they"* and *"them."* As a general rule, a pronoun refers back to a noun (the antecedent) found previously within the context but now replaced by the appropriate pronoun. The people group mentioned in the Synoptic Gospels prior to these particular pronouns is *nations* and *kingdoms*. This is further confirmed when this group is again identified in **Matthew 24:9**.

*Matthew 24:7 For **nation** shall rise against nation, and **kingdom** against kingdom: and there shall be famines, and pestilences, and earthquakes, in divers places. 8 All these are the beginning of sorrows. 9 Then shall **they** (the unbelieving nations and kingdoms) deliver you up to be afflicted, and shall kill you: and ye shall be hated of all **nations** for my name's sake.*

*Mark 13:8 For **nation** shall rise against nation, and **kingdom** against kingdom: and there shall be earthquakes in divers places, and there shall be famines and troubles: these are the beginnings of sorrows.*

*Luke 21:10 Then said he unto them, **Nation** shall rise against nation, and **kingdom** against kingdom:*

During Daniel's Seventieth Week, the nations and kingdoms will gather together against a common foe. The severity of that hatred toward Israel seems almost incomprehensible by any standard of imagination. This intensity of hatred for the Jews amongst the other nations and kingdoms helps the reader grasp the resultant actions and reactions taken by those who are vehemently persecuted.

The Jews will witness their loved ones cast into prisons only to be brought before the kings and rulers of these nations. The Jews will be afflicted and beaten with many killed. As the Jews see their loved ones delivered for interrogation to the councils and synagogues, they become overwhelmed by the resultant fear. Unfortunately, the Jews will not withstand the onslaught and eventually turn upon each other.

*Matthew 24:9 Then shall **they deliver you up to be afflicted**, and **shall kill you**: and ye shall be hated of all nations for my name's sake.*

*Mark 13:9 But take heed to yourselves: for **they shall deliver you up to councils**; and **in the synagogues ye shall be beaten**: and **ye shall be brought before rulers and kings** for my sake, for a testimony against them.*

*Luke 21:12 But before all these, **they shall lay their hands on you**, and **persecute you, delivering you up to the synagogues**, and **into prisons**, being **brought before kings and rulers** for my name's sake.*

This persecution of the Jews will ultimately serve as a testimony against the nations and kingdoms. Regardless of the people's ignorance, the promises of God and His pronounced curses remain true and unwavering: God pronounced: *"I will bless them that bless thee, and curse him that curseth thee"* **(Genesis 12:3)**. In fact, when the nations stand before the Lord at the Judgment of the Nations (after the Second Advent) the criteria for judgment will reflect each nation's treatment of the Jews **(Matthew 25:31-46)**. These distinctions concerning Jew and Gentile during Daniel's Seventieth Week make no sense if the Church remains upon the earth during that time since national distinctions are temporarily eliminated within the body of Christ **(Galatians 3:28; Colossians 3:11)**.

The Jews will endure horrific and unspeakable acts against themselves and their families. In fact, the Bible offers an ominous description of the troubles faced in Daniel's Seventieth Week. The persecution will be *"such as was not since the beginning of the world … nor ever shall be"* **(Matthew 24:21)**.

In other words, the Holocaust's devastation will pale in comparison with Daniel's Seventieth Week. However, in the end, all that the Jews will endure will be *"for my* [Jesus'] *name's sake"* (**Matthew 24:9**; see also **Mark 13:9; Luke 21:12**). At some point during this period, the Jews will no longer be identified by their rejection of the Lord Jesus Christ, but by their acceptance of Him and obedience to Him. Most Post-tribulationists miss the fact that the Jews will be directly identified as having the *"testimony of Jesus Christ"* **(Revelation 12:17)**.

The Blessings or Cursings?

The rise or fall of any nation or people group has historically been tied to its walk with God and frequently attributable to its treatment of the Jews. For example, America's greatness has paralleled its close relationship with the nation of Israel. If and when America turns its back to Israel, this will further seal America's ultimate demise.

Throughout the history of the New Testament Church, a Christian remnant has always unwaveringly stood with Israel. These Christians were often identified as Baptists, but more so today as *Bible-believers* since many Baptist groups have been led astray by the wolves. This is especially true today since many Baptists have now lost sight of their rich heritage. An increasing number of Bible-believing Baptists are accepting the Preterist's position[2] of replacement theology. See the appendix that addresses the land of Israel and the legitimacy of its current occupants.

There is a resurgent movement amongst uninformed Christians suggesting that the Jews are simply cursed of God and receiving their just recompense. These groups teach that the Jews have been and continue to be deserving of extra punishment because of their words during the crucifixion.

*Matthew 27:25 Then answered **all the people,** and said, **His blood be on us, and on our children**.*

Yet, this assessment of the continuing Jewish condemnation has a major glaring flaw amongst its many flaws. First, the honest Bible student would have to acknowledge that the context refers to *"all the people"* present which could have included the Romans and not just those of Jewish descent. If the Jews were held accountable and judged for this vow, all Gentile descendents would also have to be held accountable. *"All the people"* made this foolish vow so it could have conceivably extended beyond the Jewish people. Fortunately for us all, even this point, regardless of the application, is moot because of Christ's display of mercy and grace while being crucified. In fact, the Lord's words while hanging upon the cross cancelled the people's vow.

*Luke 23:34 Then said Jesus, **Father, forgive them; for they know not what they do**. And they parted his raiment, and cast lots.*

Christians who proclaim their unwavering belief in the complete infallibility of the scriptures need to be as equally diligent to study the scriptures within their full and complete context. When this is done, the diligent Bible student realizes that Jesus' prayer on the cross completely negated the vow recorded in *Matthew 27:25*.[3]

---

[2] Preterism teaches that some or all of the biblical prophecies concerning the Last Days (or End-Times) refer to events which actually happened in the first century. In other words, the Olivet Discourse is not yet to be fulfilled prophecy but is past history. Some Preterists teach that Nero was the Antichrist, and since the destruction of the Temple was fulfilled in AD 70, all of the prophecies were likewise fulfilled. Therefore, they conclude that the Great Tribulation took place almost two millennia ago. Granted some of the events that took place in the first century do parallel what Jesus foretold but this does not mean that God intended for the first century to be considered a fulfillment of the prophecy. Rome was in power during the first century and will be in power following the Rapture.

[3] This forgiveness of the vow was based upon the spirit and application of Numbers chapter 30 which refers to the disallowing of a vow. (Continued)

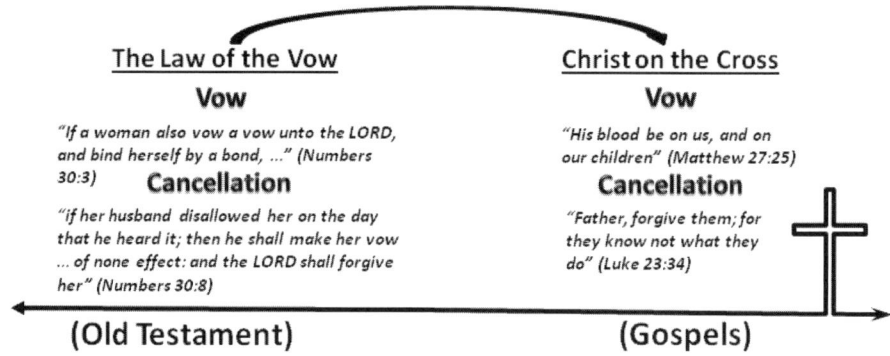

Christians (and especially Bible-believing Christians) should reject and repudiate any movement that suggests any degree of justification for disparaging the Jews. The Jews have not been forever thrown upon the trash heap and they will receive the promises given to them of the Lord. Historically, every group that has turned against Israel has paid dearly for such an unwise decision. God still has a sword whetted and ready to use against all those who choose Israel as an enemy worthy of destruction and damnation. The nations in Daniel's Seventieth Week will learn this lesson the hard way.

Clearly, those faithful Jews during this fateful time are again reminded by the Lord of His presence and help in the midst of their trials. Although they will be delivered up to the ruling elite, the faithful are told not to fear. In fact, they are told not even to premeditate a response to their judges' inquiries. The Lord promised (through the Holy Ghost) to give His saints a faithful message to testify in their most dire time of need.

Numbers 30:3 If a woman also vow a vow unto the LORD, and bind herself by a bond, being in her father's house in her youth; ... 6 And if she had at all an husband, when she vowed, or uttered ought out of her lips, wherewith she bound her soul; 7 And her husband heard it, and held his peace at her in the day that he heard it: then her vows shall stand, and her bonds wherewith she bound her soul shall stand. 8 But if **her husband disallowed her on the day that he heard it;** *then he shall make her vow which she vowed, and that which she uttered with her lips, wherewith she bound her soul,* **of none effect: and the LORD shall forgive her.**

***Mark 13:11** But when they shall lead you, and deliver you up, **take no thought beforehand what ye shall speak, neither do ye premeditate: but whatsoever shall be given you in that hour, that speak ye:** for it is not ye that speak, but the Holy Ghost.*

***Luke 21:14 Settle** it therefore in your hearts, **not to meditate before what ye shall answer**: 15 **For I will give you a mouth and wisdom,** which all your adversaries shall not be able to gainsay nor resist.*

This brings up another point that must be addressed within this context. Since Christians are Spirit indwelled, far too many have erroneously taught that when we are gone, the Spirit leaves this earth with us. However, nowhere does the Bible teach that God's Spirit (the Holy Ghost) leaves the earth when the Church departs at the Rapture. This common misconception comes from the misapplication of *2 Thessalonians 2:7* and teaching that the Holy Ghost is the restrainer who is *"taken out of the way."* [4] Read the end of *Mark 13:11* again which states that *"whatsoever shall be given you in that hour, that speak ye: for **it is not ye that speak, but the Holy Ghost.***"

The Lord will continue to have a people (the Jews) to guide, empower, and use. They will be the ones pointing willing listeners to the Lord Jesus Christ. Similar to the record found concerning Stephen in Acts chapter 7, the adversaries will not be able to gainsay or resist the unwavering testimony of these Jews. Yet, these miraculous interventions are not intended to prevent persecution any more than Stephen's protection meant that he would not die for his Lord. The Bible says that Stephen was a man *"full of the Holy Ghost" (Acts 7:55)* and those who are given the words to speak will likewise be filled with Him too!

Hatred from Within

Fear of the unknown frequently motivates men to stoop to unfathomable new lows. Due to the threats made by the nations and kingdoms during Daniel's Seventieth Week, the Jews will grow increasingly apprehensive. As a result, they will take extreme measures to protect themselves. These defensive maneuvers will progressively decline in morality. They begin with personal offences before spiraling into a complete betrayal and hatred for even those of their own families.

---

[4] See **"Reviving the Blessed Hope"** by the same authors which covers this issue in detail along with the prophetic portions of First and Second Thessalonians.

*Matthew 24:10 And **then shall many be offended, and** shall **betray** one another, **and** shall **hate one another**.*

The word *offended* is often simply defined as hurt feelings or anger in response to something said or done by another person. However, both scripturally and historically this is not always the case. Uniquely, the makeup of the word broken down into its component parts, *off-ended*, gives insight into its true meaning. The word can mean "to strike against" but also entails stumbling or falling from one's steadfastness.

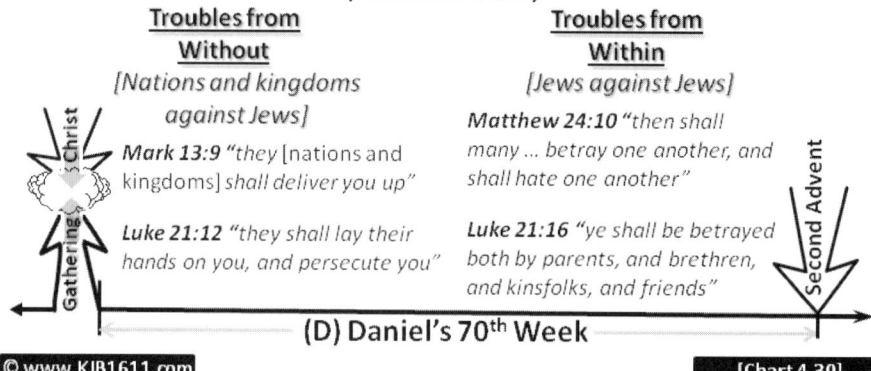

We are told that men's hearts will fail them because of fear during Daniel's Seventieth Week *(Luke 21:26)*. Any soundness of heart and stability of mind will be completely replaced with paranoia, anxiety, confusion, and mass hysteria. This scenario causes men to turn against each other in unimaginable ways.

The threats that started from without will now deprive families and communities of any peace even within their once protected environments. This environment will lead to a betrayal with no one immune. This betrayal will include friends but eventually extends to both distant and immediate family members.

*Mark 13:12 Now **the brother shall betray the brother** to death, and **the father the son**; and **children shall rise up against their parents**, and shall cause them to be put to death.*

***Luke 21:16** And **ye shall be betrayed both by parents**, and **brethren**, and **kinsfolks**, and **friends**; and some of you shall they cause to be put to death.*

This terrible state of affairs is virtually inconceivable for any Westerner to comprehend. Our present circumstances of relative peace, safety, and security make it hard to imagine that such horrific practices will become so commonplace worldwide. A good example of those who have failed to learn from history would include the failed attempts by communist takeovers in the Soviet Union, China, the French Revolution, Cambodia, Vietnam, etc., in addition to the debauchery of the Nazis of the Third Reich. Yet, the Jews in the future will be willing to watch their brothers, fathers, mothers, sons, daughters, aunts, uncles, grandparents, grandchildren, cousins, and friends be put to death so long as the suffering assures their own personal safety, physical preservation, and immediate survival.

Hatred of Truth and Righteousness

For those who find this scenario impossible to accept or believe, consider the circumstances surrounding the early church. The apostle Paul (an unsaved Pharisee named Saul at the time) removed men and women from their homes, compelling them to blaspheme or die **(Acts 8:3; Acts 26:10-11)**. Why? Simply because of Saul's intense hatred for those Jews who had trusted Christ! This same type of division seems to appear during Daniel's Seventieth Week. After all, the Lord Jesus offered the following context stating all this will be *"for my* [Jesus'] *name's sake"* **(Matthew 24:9; Luke 21:12)**. Since the Church is gone, this necessitates that some Jews will proclaim the name of Christ.

Any outward acknowledgement of the truth becomes increasingly dangerous *and deadly*. The desire for alternatives reaches an all-time high. As demand for false truths arise, the Devil has a sufficient supply of false teachers at his disposal. Historically, the Bible chronicles many periods in Israel's history that will simply be repeated on a grander scale during Daniel's Seventieth Week.

For instance, Jeremiah's day reveals many commonalities to Daniel's Seventieth Week. The people during Jeremiah's day had no desire to hear the truth. They wanted soothing messages that made them feel better about themselves and their present circumstances. They simply wanted to hear messages containing a false peace, offering them a false hope. The Devil eagerly provided every willing messenger with what became the popular message of the day—*"peace, peace."*

> **Jeremiah 6:13** *For from the least of them even unto the greatest of them every one is given to covetousness; and* **from the prophet even unto the priest every one dealeth falsely**. *14 They have healed also the hurt of the daughter of my people slightly,* **saying, Peace, peace; when there is no peace**.

> **Jeremiah 8:10** *Therefore will I give their wives unto others, and their fields to them that shall inherit them: for every one from the least even unto the greatest is given to covetousness,* **from the prophet even unto the priest every one dealeth falsely**. *11 For they have healed the hurt of the daughter of my people slightly,* **saying, Peace, peace; when there is no peace**.

> **Jeremiah 5:31** **The prophets prophesy falsely, and the priests bear rule by their means**; *and* **my people love to have it so**: *and what will ye do in the end thereof?*

These same types of false messages—of peace and safety—will flourish in the days just prior to the Day of the Lord *(1 Thessalonians 5:3)*. Yet, these messages actually begin quite early in Daniel's Seventieth Week. Those Jews who put their faith in the words of God early in this prophetic Week of years, will be much like king Josiah when he heard the words from *"the book of the law"* found *"in the house of the LORD" (2 Kings 22:8)*. He reacted with shock and amazement and wanted to know the whole truth *(2 Kings 22:13)*.

The hearts of believing Jews will remain tender towards Christ as they are truly sorry for their sins and the sins of their fathers. They will be aware of the impending judgment. Yet, many of their brethren (in the flesh) will choose to reject Christ and reject the message of the forthcoming judgment. Instead, they will be looking for alternatives to this impending calamity. The Devil will happily oblige them with such falsehoods and deception—especially in the spiritual realm.

> **Matthew 24:11** *And* **many false prophets shall rise, and shall deceive many**.

It is important to note that truth and righteousness are inseparable! As lies supplant truth, iniquity replaces righteousness. Unfortunately, no one controls how far things spiral out of control. As iniquity abounds and escalates, love simply dies—or waxes cold and indifferent.

Matthew 24:12 *And **because iniquity shall abound, the love of many shall wax cold**.*

Man has not witnessed a time (on a worldwide scale) when no semblance of love existed outside a small remnant—that is, since before Noah's flood *(Genesis 6:5)*. This is why a time destitute of love seems unfathomable and even unimaginable to Christians today.

We simply find it hard to conceive a time when the masses will gladly betray one another to death with no remorse. Some perspective would help. No matter how bad things get concerning the sanctity of life before the Rapture (with abortions—or murder as it stands in God's eyes, senicide, geronticide, assisted suicides, etc.), Christians today still impact many societies. Now, imagine a future world without any Christian influence—a world where love has completely waxed cold—that's Daniel's Seventieth Week! As love waxes cold, life is no longer precious and loses its significance. People's consciences will be seared.

Hatred of Life

Isaiah offered a vivid description of these future times when he said, "I [the LORD] *will make a man more precious than fine gold; even a man than the golden wedge of Ophir*" *(Isaiah 13:12)*. As man continues to devalue human life, murder and other deviant criminal activities escalate out of control. The taking of life will be commonplace and easily justifiable in these last days.

For those who have carefully paid attention to the context of the Olivet Discourse, the next passage further reveals this truth. The salvation[5] mentioned simply refers to the physical salvation and preservation of one's life. Those who *physically* endure without taking the Mark of the Beast are ultimately *physically* delivered to enter *physically* into the Millennium.

---

[5] Enduring to the end of the Seventieth Week period in the context has nothing to do with being born again or a soul's salvation. It refers to those who refuse the Mark of the Beast but also flee for their lives day after day, hour by hour, and minute by minute. Three scenarios: they endure, get caught, or give up and give in to the lie.

*Matthew 24:13 But **he that shall endure** unto the end, the same shall be saved.*

The sad truth is that far too many Bible teachers view *saved* and *salvation* in the Bible as always referring to one's soul, like that found in *Acts 4:12*. Yet, the Matthew passage is speaking of physical elements—enduring physically and being physically saved. The widespread incorrect application of this verse has led to some questionable teachings and unfortunate contradictions.

Misinterpretations by the Arminians, Calvinists and Dispensationalists

Consider these three groups that fail to see the forest for the trees.[6]

Arminians: For four and one-half centuries, the strict *Arminian* (follower of Jacobus Arminuis' teachings) has been persuaded by the incorrect teaching and application of **Matthew 24:13**. He has been taught to use this verse along with several others as "proof verses" that someone can lose his soul's salvation by failing to endure unto the end of his life.

Not only is this a gross misapplication of the verse, but the Arminian has also lifted **Matthew 24:13** completely out of God's intended context. If that is you, hopefully a certain fear is setting in as you realize that the context teaches something different from what you have been taught. Hopefully, you are taking things one step further and wondering, "What if much of what I have been taught in this line of thinking is actually wrong?"

It is important to realize that one of the greatest tools for spiritual growth involves overcoming the fear and trepidation from admitting that you could be wrong. EVERYONE has beliefs that are wrong and only those sincerely willing to admit their fallibility have any hope of moving from error to truth.

Calvinists: The *Calvinist* (follower of John Calvin's teachings) has a whole different matter of contention with this verse and its application.

---

[6] The saying that someone *"can't see the forest for the trees"* simply means that the individual is so engrossed in the details of any situation that he loses sight of the larger issue. In the United Kingdom, the expression usually goes something like: *"you can't see the wood for the trees."* In either case, the individual needs to step back from the situation a bit to regain a wider perspective on the problem.

Since he balks at any notion that the so-called elect can do anything but remain "saved," he simply ignores the truth conveyed.[7]

Simply put, they believe that the ELECT will endure because their physical salvation could never depend upon anything they do or choose not to do. The correct application of this verse is even more ominous for the Calvinist when he comes to the fearful realization that his doctrinal system is completely flawed. Since the typical Calvinist is Post-millennial, and believes that all the promises God gave to Israel were assumed by the New Testament Church, then he/she is presented with a problem. In these passages, could salvation really be predicated upon man's freewill and freedom to choose whether to endure or cave into the deceitful ways of the Antichrist during this perilous period?

Dispensationalists: Some *dispensationalists* find themselves upon shaky ground too. Many of them have been taught to believe that this passage refers to a soul's salvation during Daniel's Seventieth Week rather than mere physical salvation during that period. These believers innocently, ignorantly, or even blatantly ignore the context. They know no better or can ill afford to lose this "proof verse" that "Tribulation saints" must endure to the end to be saved (i.e., to go to heaven)!

Once people are enlightened to any truth, accepting such truths as taught in this verse serves as the proving ground for those desiring to remain true Bible-believers. Those who elevate the doctrines and precepts of any man above the word of God simply fail to believe the scripture. Unfortunately, far too many Christians would rather continue to believe a false teaching than to admit that their teachings must change to remain true to what the Bible actually teaches.

The context proving the type of salvation is plainly given in Matthew chapter 24, Mark chapter 13, and Luke chapter 21—this salvation is obviously *physical* in nature. Jesus refers to a man's flesh ***(Matthew 24:22;***

---

[7] Calvinists point to all non-Calvinists as Arminians, yet the middle ground is that Jesus is *"the Way, the Truth, and the Life"* and the Bible is to be one's sole authority. It is very dangerous to define God, His plan, and His nature by the understanding and interpretation of two fallible men and then insist on naming yourself after one of them. Our finite minds will never be able to fully understand God's ways and all the "isms" fall short of perfection. It is best to speak (with absolute certainty about doctrine) when the Bible speaks and be silent when the Bible is silent.

Mark 13:20), even including the preservation of the hairs upon one's head *(Luke 21:18)*. Read the context:

> **Matthew 24:22 And except those days should be shortened, there should no flesh be saved**: *but for the elect's sake those days shall be shortened.*

> **Mark 13:20 And except that the Lord had shortened those days, no flesh should be saved**: *but for the elect's sake, whom he hath chosen, he hath shortened the days.*

> **Luke 21:18 But there shall not an hair of your head perish.**

God promised to shorten the days in order to preserve physical life. If those days are not shortened in some fashion, the Bible says that none of the elect (believing Israel) would be able to physically endure to the end. The shorter the days, the more that will be saved (physically spared).

If this salvation mentioned in the Olivet Discourse referred to a **spiritual salvation or birth** (which it does not), the shortening of days would produce the opposite outcomes. With less time, fewer would be reached with the message of salvation. The longer time continues, the more people could have an opportunity to be birthed into God's family. This passage simply does not refer to a spiritual birth, but it does refer to a **physical escape**.

The end result of this physical salvation, for those who endure, is entrance into an earthly kingdom with natural bodies—the millennium. The word *saved* used to describe a physical deliverance is quite common in scripture. In fact, this usage (physical versus spiritual) is its more frequent application within the entirety of the scripture. Unfortunately, Bible teachers read the soul's salvation into most references to saved or salvation and come to the wrong conclusions.

Even the New Testament Church believer has two applications of salvation. Each believer experiences a new birth (quickened spirit, redeemed soul) and in the future will experience another salvation (the adoption, or redemption of the body). In order to understand the latter use of saved and salvation even today, here are three points to consider concerning this salvation/adoption:

1. This adoption involves the redemption of the body.

Romans 8:23 *And not only they, but ourselves also, which have the firstfruits of the Spirit, even we ourselves groan within ourselves,* ***waiting for the adoption, to wit, the redemption of our body.***

2. This adoption (or salvation) is nearer than when we first believed.

Romans 13:11 *And that, knowing the time, that* **now *is our salvation nearer than when we believed.***

3. This adoption ushers believers into a heavenly kingdom at death or at the Rapture.

2 Timothy 4:18 *And* **the Lord shall deliver me** *from every evil work, and* will **preserve me unto his heavenly kingdom***: to whom be glory for ever and ever. Amen.*

These truths concerning salvation, redemption, and deliverance apply to the New Testament Christian. The Jews, however, are looking to receive an earthly kingdom promised to them as far back as Abraham in Genesis chapter 12. God's promises to Israel were not superseded by the Church, nor does the Church replace Israel. God's promises to Israel simply will not be thwarted by all the error being taught, nor by the fiery darts of the wicked.

Understanding the Confusion

"But he that shall endure unto the end, the same shall be saved."
(Matthew 24:13)

[Arminians Teach]	[Dispensationalists Teach]	[Calvinists Teach]
Salvation is dependent upon a man enduring unto the end.	Tribulation saints must endure in order to keep their salvation.	The elect cannot do anything but remain "saved" and will endure because they are elect.

(D) Daniel's 70th Week

© www.KJB1611.com [Chart 4.40]

God makes many promises *"for the elect's sake" **(Matthew 24:22)**.* As noted in the circumstances concerning the Judgment of the Nations (see **Matthew 25:31-46**), Jews will be deprived of food, drink, housing, clothing, healthcare, and freedom. The nations will be rewarded for having provided these things. Yet, God shortened the days to ensure some could and would survive the onslaught from every side.

Physical survival during Daniel's Seventieth Week for a Jew and others refusing the Mark of the Beast will be like running a gauntlet with danger around every corner. The believers will be sandwiched between the wrath of their enemies, the wrath of their friends, and that of their families. Additionally, the wrath of the unholy trinity will rise, followed by the unleashing of the full wrath of Almighty God. Apart from God's assistance and protection, no one will endure unto the end. No flesh in its own power will be saved, spared, or preserved! None!

The next chapter will consider the gospel of the kingdom in great detail. Once this gospel has gone into all the world, then the end shall come. Anyone trying to claim that the gospel of the kingdom in the first century **(Matthew 4:23; Matthew 9:35; Matthew 24:14)** included the death, burial, and resurrection has simply failed to rightly divide the scripture **(2 Timothy 2:15)**. It is true that the Bible says that the apostles went out preaching *"the gospel" **(Luke 9:1, 6)**,* but they did not yet understand that Christ must go to the cross, die, and be resurrected **(Luke 18:31-34)**. In fact, these truths concerning Christ's death, burial, and resurrection were hidden from them PRIOR TO THE CROSS. Simply look up the scriptures and read and believe what they say.

This all makes sense when one considers that the apostles, even following Christ's resurrection, did not believe the eyewitness accounts from the women who had seen the angels at the empty tomb **(Luke 24:11)**. Peter then ran to the tomb and seeing it empty, he wondered what had happened **(Luke 24:12)**. If he had been preaching about the death, burial, and resurrection, his reaction to the empty tomb certainly indicated otherwise. How could anyone reconcile these facts with the gospel clearly delineated in Paul's epistles **(1 Corinthians 15:1-4)**? The next section will discuss the gospel of the kingdom in greater detail.

5

The Gospel of the Kingdom

(Matthew 24:14)

Matthew 24:14 And **this gospel of the kingdom** *shall be preached in all the world for a witness unto all nations; and then shall the end come.*

There has never been a time in history when Bible study was as "easy" as it is today. The mass influx of resources has reduced seemingly insurmountable tasks to a couple of keystrokes on a computer or smart device. However, with this ease of access, many sloppy and unsavory tactics have crept into theological studies and been falsely identified as Bible study. One such reckless practice involves applying the same definition to every instance of a word found in scripture. Sadly, this practice is quite common among far too many Bible teachers.

This misapplication limits the Lord's intended diversity of meaning and usage. This is not only unwise but sometimes results in some disastrous outcomes! It must always be kept in mind that the CONTEXT of any given passage always determines the true meaning and the intent of a word.

For instance, we have already discussed how the context of the word *salvation* is the most significant factor for determining its meaning and God's intended usage. This word carries a more *general* definition (i.e., deliverance) applicable to every instance. However, the *specifics* (i.e., whether physical deliverance or spiritual deliverance) may vary from the Old Testament to the New, from the Gospels to the Epistles, and even from one single verse to another (sometimes within the same book of the Bible or section of scripture). In fact, sometimes the varied meanings apply to a single reference within a verse to another reference within the same verse! Here is a great example of deliverance from hell along with deliverance from current and future troubles.

> ***2 Corinthians 1:10*** *Who **delivered** us from so great a death, and **doth deliver**: in whom we trust that he will **yet deliver** us;*

Consider the following illustration that effectively demonstrates this truth. The larger circle represents the *general* definition of any given word. That definition, when correctly understood, applies to every usage of the word in scripture. However, more specific definitions (those narrower in scope) appear throughout scripture as the context dictates usage and application. These *specific* definitions vary from each other but never contradict the overall *general* definition of the word. The illustration below shows the individual specific definitions represented by the smaller circles existing within the larger circle (the general definition).

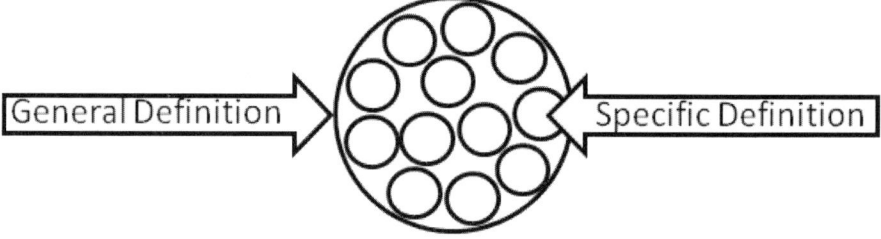

As we have seen, this principle certainly applies to words like *salvation* and *saved*. The general definition of these two words is *deliverance*, yet the context reveals the specific definition for each usage. This same principle applies to other extremely important words in scripture. Another example pertaining to our discussion is the word *gospel*. Its *general* definition applies universally to every usage, while the particular context within scripture maintains more specific individualized definitions.

> ***Matthew 4:23*** *And Jesus went about all Galilee, teaching in their synagogues, and preaching **the gospel** of the kingdom, and healing all manner of sickness and all manner of disease among the people.*

Matthew 4:23 serves as a good case in point as it records the first appearance of the word *gospel* in the Bible. Yet, this verse in Matthew is not the first instance when *gospel* is **discussed** within the pages of scripture.

Through Bible study, we learn that the Old Testament refers to the gospel prior to the word appearing in scripture. This truth is confirmed by comparing scripture with scripture especially when the New Testament quotes Old Testament passages. The next passage from Romans gives a good starting point for understanding this truth.

> **Romans 10:15** *And how shall they preach, except they be sent?* **as it is written,** *How beautiful are the feet of them that preach* **the gospel** *of peace, and bring glad tidings of good things!*

It is important to notice the bolded word *gospel*, but equally important to notice that the verse uses a phrase *"as it is written."* This phrase demonstrates that something being written generally or specifically refers back to the Old Testament. It could indicate that word *gospel* occurs in the original source quoted by **Romans 10:15**, but we know that it does not because the first appearance of the word *gospel* is found in **Matthew 4:23**. So, we next refer back to two Old Testament books being referenced by Romans.

> **Isaiah 52:7** *How beautiful upon the mountains are the feet of him that bringeth* **good tidings**, *that publisheth peace; that bringeth* **good tidings** *of good, that publisheth salvation; that saith unto Zion, Thy God reigneth!*

> **Nahum 1:15** *Behold upon the mountains the feet of him that bringeth* **good tidings**, *that publisheth peace! O Judah, keep thy solemn feasts, perform thy vows: for the wicked shall no more pass through thee; he is utterly cut off.*

Because we have the New Testament, we understand that both Isaiah and Nahum are referring to the gospel. Additionally, it is important to note how the Bible can be used in this fashion to define words by considering cross-reference contexts. Any honest and open-minded Bible student immediately notices that the word *gospel* directly connects to the phrase *good tidings* or *glad tidings*. In fact, the verse from Romans clearly associates the word *gospel* with its intended definition found in Isaiah.

> **Romans 10:15** *And how shall they preach, except they be sent? as it is written, How beautiful are the feet of them that preach the* **gospel** *of peace, and bring* **glad tidings** *of good things!*

Based on this passage alone, one might assume that the word *gospel* is defined, in a general sense, as good or glad tidings. Yet, this association and definition is further enhanced and confirmed when one considers the direct correlation between *Isaiah 61:1* and *Luke 4:18*.

> *Isaiah 61:1 The Spirit of the Lord GOD is upon me; because* **the LORD hath anointed me to preach good tidings unto the meek**; *he hath sent me to bind up the brokenhearted, to proclaim liberty to the captives, and the opening of the prison to them that are bound;*

> *Luke 4:17 And there was delivered unto him the book of the prophet Esaias. And when he had opened the book, he found the place where it was written, 18 The Spirit of the Lord is upon me, because* **he hath anointed me to preach the gospel to the poor**; *he hath sent me to heal the brokenhearted, to preach deliverance to the captives, and recovering of sight to the blind, to set at liberty them that are bruised,*

Every true student of the Bible should readily see and accept that the word *gospel* simply means good or glad tidings. This definition might seem foreign to those with preconceived notions or ill-conceived biases. Yet, understanding this simple truth ensures that all the pieces fit together, especially when one considers some of the various mentions of gospel within scripture.

Does every reference refer to the exact same thing? No! For instance, consider each of these expressions: *"the gospel of the kingdom"* (*Matthew 4:23*), *"the gospel of the grace of God"* (*Acts 20:24*), *"the gospel unto Abra-*

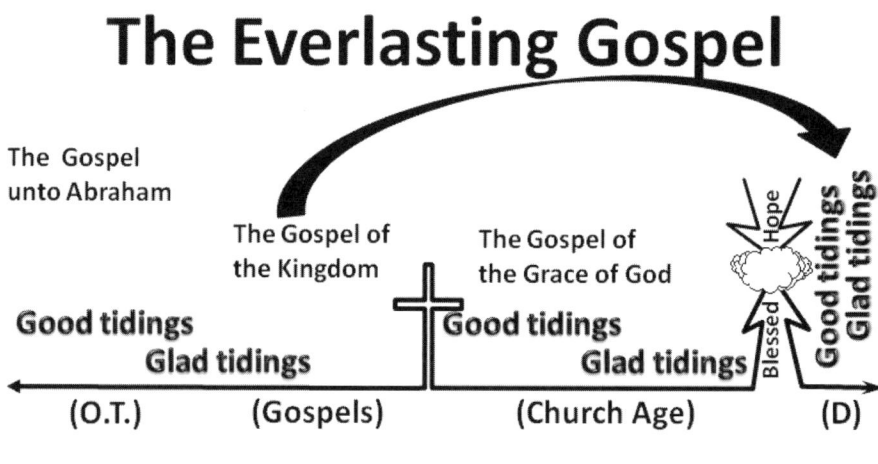

[Chart 5.10]

*ham" **(Galatians 3:8),** "the gospel" preached unto Jews in the wilderness **(Hebrews 4:2),** and "the everlasting gospel" **(Revelation 14:6).*** The general meaning indicates that the gospel is a message of good or glad tidings. Yet the specifics of the intended gospel are defined and distinguished by the CONTEXT surrounding their particular mention.

At this point, the reader finds himself at a very important crossroads. For a few of the astute Bible students, the content just discussed was met with a yawn of familiarity. Yet, for others, the sirens are sounding and voices inside your head are crying out to reject something so foreign to what you have always believed. Why is that? What could possibly be misconstrued up to this point as unscriptural or unsavory? Why is man so filled with fear and trepidation when confronted with doctrinal positions outside our proverbial comfort zones?

One can liken this scenario to the boy who had parents who could not swim. These parents therefore always instructed the boy concerning the dangers of water. Surely, water can be dangerous, but so can air, cars, bicycles, etc. One day, the boy became a man and his son asked to go swimming. Should the boy, now turned adult, fear because those whom he loved and trusted warned concerning the dangers of water? Or should he reconsider the unreasonableness of his man-made fears and learn to swim himself so that he can, in turn, teach his own children to do likewise? Men simply fear the unknown and feel most comfortable when they keep tradition thereby refusing to accept any change in the status quo.

The Christian's fearfulness concerning the idea that varying gospel messages exist within scripture is both expected and completely understandable. This is especially true today considering Paul's dire warning against those who preach another gospel during this age *(**Galatians 1:8**)* or seek to pervert the gospel of the grace of God *(**Galatians 1:7**).*

Unfortunately, this fear concerning "the gospel" results from Bible ignorance and the long-held shame associated with going against the religious dogma.

In addition, false teachers cultivate fear by making affiliation with their religious institutions a necessity for salvation. Unfortunately, people tend to hold onto long-held beliefs even in the face of overwhelming evidence to the contrary. Anyone denying the existence of multiple gospels in the Bible should do so based solely upon the truth of scripture, not because of fear associated with those he has known, trusted, and loved. The truth should trump all else.

Fear causes people to accept and retain doctrines that are both non-scriptural and unscriptural. This same type of fear of the unknown has led people to falsely ASSUME that Adam and Eve knew about the death, burial, and resurrection of Jesus Christ. Fear has also led people to ASSUME that Lot knew about the gospel of Christ. Fear also leads people to ASSUME that the gospel believed by Abraham is the same gospel we preach today, but these beliefs have no basis in scripture. In fact, *"the gospel"* (or the good tidings) preached to Abraham was clearly delineated in scripture. The gospel was that *"in thee shall all nations be blessed."*

Galatians 3:8 And **the scripture**, *foreseeing that God would justify the heathen through faith,* **preached** *before* **the gospel unto Abraham, saying, In thee shall all nations be blessed.**

This point bears repeating! Galatians unmistakably identifies the gospel preached to Abraham. What were these good tidings preached to Abraham? The same verse defines it: all nations would be blessed in him. The existence of multiple *gospels* (good or glad tidings) within scripture is one of those indisputable truths, yet this teaching is completely foreign to the majority of Bible teachers and students. Yet, every one of these gospels required a single response of FAITH.

With these foundational principles in place, it is time to consider our subject passage. The particular gospel mentioned in Matthew chapter 24 is clearly referred to as the *"gospel of the kingdom."*

Matthew 24:14 And **this gospel of the kingdom** *shall be preached in all the world for a witness unto all nations; and then shall the end come.*

The Content of This Particular Gospel

For years, far too many believers with advanced degrees from well-known seminaries fell into the ditch of allowing their "learning" to trample upon God's precious word. Unfortunately, on the other side of the road lies another ditch. In it are all those who proudly wear their willful ignorance on their sleeves as though it serves as a badge of honour. They reference Paul's assertion that he *"determined not to know any thing …*

save Jesus Christ, and him crucified" ***(1 Corinthians 2:2)*** as proof for the spirituality of simplistic Bible preaching resulting from their paltry Bible study.

Those with a willful ignorance who look for a second witness will look no further than the testimony of Peter and John. After all, they will point to Peter and John of whom the Bible says the religious leaders *"perceived that they were unlearned and ignorant men"* ***(Acts 4:13)***. Neither of these passages justifies the spiritual ignorance of those who desire to know and teach God's word. In fact, the latter passage serves to prove just the opposite. Those men had never been taught in the classrooms of the scribes, Pharisees, or Sadducees, but their knowledge caused others to marvel and to take note of their association with Jesus.

We too are admonished to STUDY ***(2 Timothy 2:15)***, but study what? Since those reading this book likely speak English, it might be wise to study the English language with its sentence construction in the English Bible. Yet, we need to go beyond everyone's forced elementary grammar lessons (which most people would rather forget!). We need to examine some of the grammatical rules and guidelines. With that being said, a review of some prepositional phrase rules would be most helpful to the present study.

Sometimes Bible study involves the study into the meanings of words, phrases, sentences, and whole paragraphs. ***Matthew 24:14*** emphasizes a gospel and identifies it by the prepositional phrase *"**of** the kingdom."* The purpose of a prepositional phrase is to modify or offer clarity concerning other words found within any particular sentence. In the case of our passage from Matthew, the prepositional phrase *"of the kingdom"* is meant to offer clarity to the identity of a particular gospel. The prepositional phrase is made up of three component parts: *of* (preposition) *the* (modifier) *kingdom* (noun). In other words, the gospel to which the passage refers particularly pertains to *"the kingdom"* gospel.

Simply put, a kingdom is the domain of a king. However, this particular kingdom (yet future) was the subject emphasized during the life and ministry of the Lord Jesus Christ. That is why *the gospel of the kingdom* preached by Jesus and the apostles referred specifically and directly to the good or glad tidings of the kingdom. This truth can be made no plainer but we will delve into some additional proofs.

According to scripture, *"The law and the prophets were until John: since that time **the kingdom** of God is preached" (**Luke 16:16**)*. This statement certainly emphasizes and confirms a shift in message, but to what does the gospel of the kingdom specifically apply?

The glad tidings of the kingdom included news that the kingdom was *"at hand"* and that men should *"repent"* and *"believe"* to enter into it *(**Mark 1:14-15**)*. The gospel message incorporated men's responsibilities and the ensuing benefits of their obedience *(**Matthew 5:1-48**)*. The tidings introduced the nature of this kingdom by ascribing its likeness to earthly events and practices *(**Matthew 13:1-52; Matthew 18:23-35; Matthew 20:1-16; Matthew 22:2-14; Matthew 25:1-30**)*, and the message was confirmed by signs, wonders, and the healing of *"all manner of sickness and all manner of disease" (**Matthew 4:23; Matthew 9:35; Luke 9:2**)*.

It is important not to ASSUME that the gospel of the kingdom in the first century included the message of the death, burial, and resurrection. The scriptures plainly teach otherwise and it is paramount to let them speak for themselves. As early as chapter 4 of Matthew's gospel, the Lord Jesus Christ began preaching the kingdom of heaven. Immediately thereafter, the Lord sought out disciples to follow Him.

> ***Matthew 4:17** From that time **Jesus began to preach, and to say, Repent: for the kingdom of heaven is at hand**. 18 And Jesus, walking by the sea of Galilee, saw two brethren, Simon called Peter, and Andrew his brother, casting a net into the sea: for they were fishers. 19 And he saith unto them, **Follow me,** and I will make you fishers of men. 20 And they straightway left their nets, and **followed him.** 21 And going on from thence, he saw other two brethren, James the son of Zebedee, and John his brother, in a ship with Zebedee their father, mending their nets; and he called them. 22 And they immediately left the ship and their father, and **followed him.***

Jesus and His apostles travelled together as He preached *"the gospel of the kingdom."* The Bible repeatedly confirms this truth.

> ***Matthew 4:23** And Jesus went about all Galilee, teaching in their synagogues, and **preaching the gospel of the kingdom**, and healing all manner of sickness and all manner of disease among the people.*

*Matthew 9:35 And Jesus went about all the cities and villages, teaching in their synagogues, and **preaching the gospel of the kingdom**, and healing every sickness and every disease among the people.*

*Matthew 11:5 The blind receive their sight, and the lame walk, the lepers are cleansed, and the deaf hear, the dead are raised up, and the poor have **the gospel preached** to them.*

Later, along with others, these men were sent forth on their own missionary journeys to preach the gospel of the kingdom *(Matthew 10:1-42)*. Yet, none of these men preaching the gospel given them to preach heard or understood the death, burial, and resurrection until after this gospel they preached had been spread far and wide.

*Matthew 16:21 **From that time forth began Jesus to shew unto his disciples**, **how** that **he must** go unto Jerusalem, and **suffer** many things of the elders and chief priests and scribes, **and be killed, and be raised again the third day**.*

Bible assumptions run rampant as it pertains to these men and their understanding of the gospel of the death, burial, and resurrection. Many Bible teachers wrongfully suggest that these men had already known of the death, burial, and resurrection, but to assume such is to deny the authority of scripture which states, "***From that time forth began** Jesus to shew unto his disciples, how that he must ... suffer ... be killed, and be raised again the third day*" *(Matthew 16:21)*. Even after this initial revelation of the will of God concerning the cross, the Bible states that the disciples "*understood not that saying* [the death, burial, and resurrection—see **Mark 9:31**], *and were afraid to ask him* [Christ]" *(Mark 9:32)*. In fact, Luke proclaimed that their lack of understanding was because "*it* [the death, burial and resurrection] *was hid from them*" (**Luke 9:45**; see also **Luke 18:34**).

Secondly, many assume that the disciples willingly and joyfully received the news when they heard that Christ was going to the cross, but to do so is to again deny the authority of the scripture when it states, *"Then* [after hearing of the death, burial, and resurrection] *Peter took him* [the Lord Jesus Christ], *and began to rebuke him, saying, Be it far from thee, Lord: this* [the death, burial, and resurrection] *shall not be unto thee" (Matthew 16:22)*.

The reality presented by scripture is that the disciples did not understand and believe in the death, burial, and resurrection until AFTER Christ was raised from the dead. Therefore, it stands to reason that although the disciples preached the gospel of the kingdom, they did not preach the death, burial, and resurrection UNTIL after the resurrection had taken place.

> **John 20:8** *Then went in also that other disciple [John], which came first to the sepulchre, and* **he saw, and believed.**

> **Mark 16:14** *Afterward* **he** *[Jesus Christ]* **appeared unto the eleven** *as they sat at meat,* **and upbraided them with their unbelief** *and hardness of heart, because* **they believed not them which had seen him after he was risen.**

> **John 20:25 The other disciples therefore said** *unto him [Thomas],* **We have seen the Lord. But he** *[Thomas]* **said unto them, Except I shall see in his hands the print of the nails, and put my finger into the print of the nails, and thrust my hand into his side, I will not believe.**

It is likely that the message of the death, burial, and resurrection became intertwined with the message of the coming kingdom but certainly not until after the Lord rose from the dead. In fact, after Christ's resurrection when the Lord commanded his followers to *"preach the gospel,"* they interpreted that to mean they were *"to be a witness ... of his* [Christ's] *resurrection."*

> **Mark 16:15** *And he said unto them, Go ye into all the world, and* **preach the gospel** *to every creature.*

> **Acts 1:22** *Beginning from the baptism of John, unto that same day that he was taken up from us, must one be ordained to be* **a witness** *with us* **of his resurrection.**

A primary qualification for Judas' replacement as one of the twelve apostles was that that individual was a witness of Christ's resurrection. This scenario would have existed until the message of the earthly and promised kingdom completely transitioned to a focus upon a heavenly and spiritual *kingdom*. However, the Lord has not intended for the kingdom of heaven (as emphasized in the Gospel books) to be an element in the gospel as preached by any true New Testament believer for the past 1,900+ years.

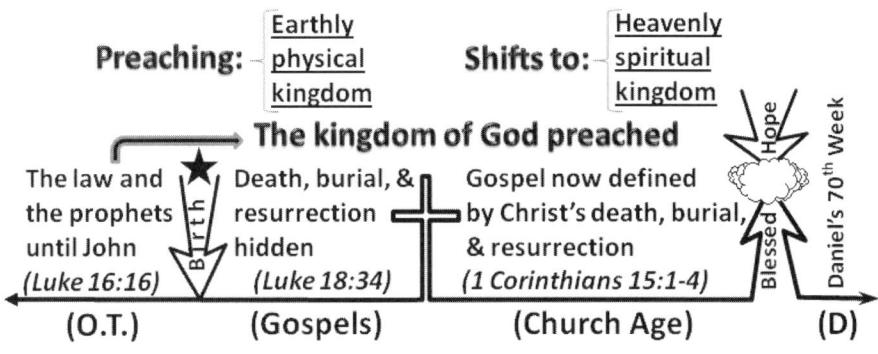

[Chart 5.20]

The Course of This Gospel

The *gospel of the kingdom* is distinguishable from the gospel we preach today in at least three major areas: (1) in its content, (2) in its intended audience, and (3) in its outcome. We have already explored the issue of the distinction in the *content* of the gospels.

We will address the distinction in its outcome later, but we must first consider the targeted audience to whom the gospel of the kingdom was initially directed. Prophetically, the future intended audience to whom the gospel of the kingdom *will be* preached is likewise of paramount importance. The unquestionable future importance of this gospel becomes crystal clear simply by considering the prophetic nature of our subject passage.

> *Matthew 24:14 And this gospel of the kingdom* **shall be preached** *in all the world for a witness unto all nations; and* **then shall the end come.**

The audience of today's gospel has NEVER been limited by God in any way! However, the same fact does not hold true concerning those commissioned to preach *the gospel of the kingdom*. In fact, their audience was originally limited in both a negative sense (neglected audience) and positive sense (intended audience). Simply read and believe what the Bible clearly says:

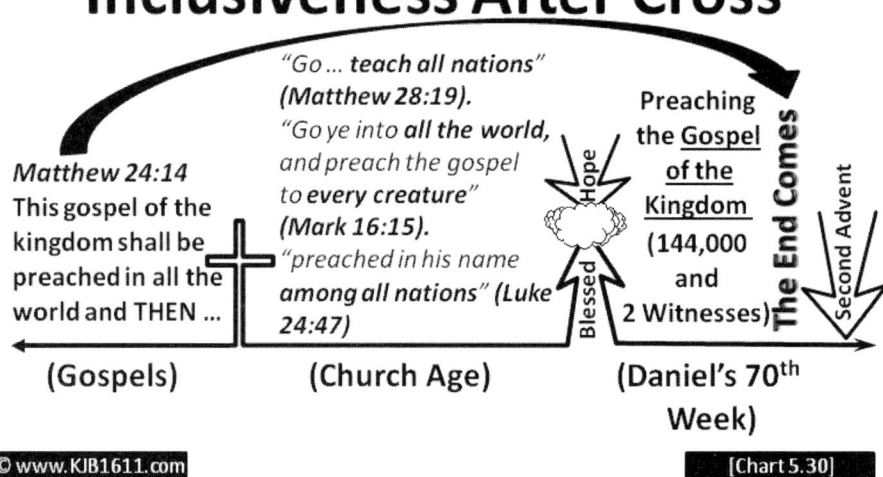

*Matthew 10:5 These twelve Jesus sent forth, and commanded them, saying, **Go not** into the way of the Gentiles, and into any city of the Samaritans **enter ye not**: 6 **But go** rather to the lost sheep of the house of Israel.*

When the disciples were initially commissioned to preach their God-given gospel message, they were specifically told, "GO NOT" to any that were Gentiles (non-Jews) or Samaritans (half-Jews). Instead, they were commanded to "go" and only go *"to the lost sheep of the house of Israel."*

For many Bible teachers, this truth proves quite inconvenient. They know that God never changes in character *(Hebrews 13:8)*, yet they fail to account for the fact that God's message, methods, and intended audiences have changed several times throughout history. Instead of seeking for some means to reject these obvious truths, we should seek to embrace them and fully understand why these things are so. We need to become more like the faithful Bereans who searched the scriptures to see if these things were so *(Acts 17:11)*. The choice is simple: become like the studious Bereans or reject any teaching that makes you rethink what you think you already know about the Bible.

The Bible is plain. God sent twelve disciples (Jews) to preach the kingdom of heaven (a Jewish message) to the lost sheep of the house of Israel (Jews)! Why did God limit the message and outreach? The answer is quite simple: the Jews were God's focus for that message at that time. While it is true that the intended audience eventually broadened to include the Gentiles, yet those specifically targeted with the gospel of the kingdom were undeniably the Jews. Any exceptions to this fact merely serve to prove the rule and reinforce the reality!

After Christ's death, burial, and resurrection, the commission was expressed in the final chapter of each of the three Synoptic Gospels. Its general inclusiveness can be easily ascertained. Matthew wrote: *"Go ye therefore, and **teach all nations**."* Mark wrote: *"Go ye into **all the world, and preach the gospel to every creature.**"* Luke wrote: *"repentance and remission of sins should be preached in his name **among all nations**, beginning at Jerusalem."*

> **Matthew 28:19** *Go ye therefore, and **teach all nations**, baptizing them in the name of the Father, and of the Son, and of the Holy Ghost:*

> **Mark 16:15** *And he said unto them, Go ye **into all the world**, and preach the gospel **to every creature**.*

> **Luke 24:47** *And that repentance and remission of sins should be preached in his name **among all nations, beginning at Jerusalem**.*

At this juncture in history, some teachers might squabble over whether or not the kingdom remained an integral part of the message.

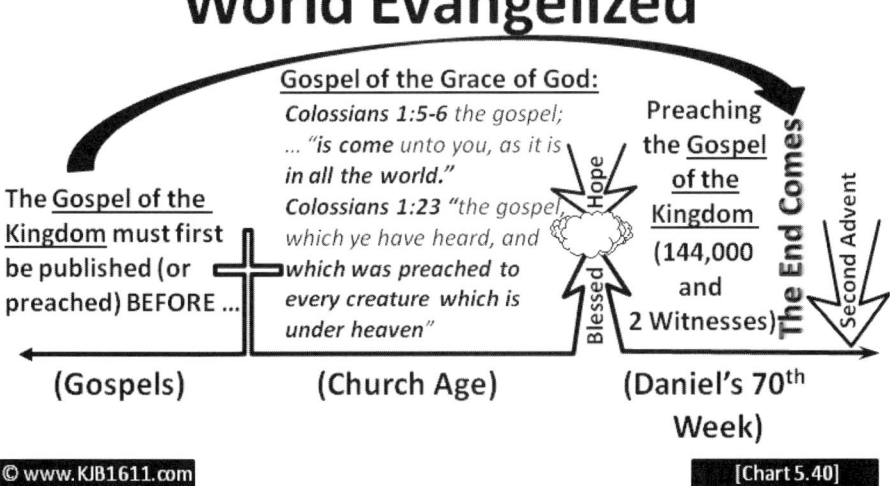

that the kingdom was still on the minds of the Jews. In fact, it was so prevalent to the Jews' thinking that it was the focal point of their final question prior to Christ's ascension.

> ***Acts 1:6*** *When they therefore were come together, they asked of him, saying, Lord, wilt thou at this time* **restore again the kingdom to Israel?**

No doubt the apostles remained clearly focused upon the restoration of the kingdom. Yet by the time the apostle Paul began his gospel ministry, the transition from the gospel of the kingdom to the gospel of the grace of God had begun. Paul championed this transition until the transition was completed. By the end of Paul's ministry, anybody preaching the gospel of the kingdom would have preached the wrong gospel. This is why any true Bible believer resolutely focuses upon proclaiming the gospel of the grace of God. But what can the world anticipate upon the Church's departure and the oncoming restoration of the nation of Israel?

At the church's departure, God's attention will again return to the Jewish people. As such, the Lord will once again call and empower some Jewish messengers (for instance, consider the 144,000—see Revelation chapter 7, and the two witnesses—see Revelation chapter 11). These Jewish messengers will boldly proclaim a message concerning the coming kingdom with its rightful King ruling. Unlike the first century limitations, the audience will be indiscriminate both geographically (*"in all the world"*) and nationally (*"unto all nations"*).

> ***Matthew 24:14*** *And this gospel of the kingdom shall be preached* **in all the world** *for a witness* **unto all nations**; *and then shall the end come.*

> ***Mark 13:10*** *And the gospel must first be published* **among all nations**.

The Conclusion of This Gospel

To those who pay close attention to the context and verb tense of our subject passages, it is quite obvious that the promise of ***Matthew 24:14*** and ***Mark 13:10*** is prophetic or futuristic in nature. The Bible says that the gospel of the kingdom *"must first be published"* or *"shall be preached"* before the end comes. In short, the worldwide proclamation of the gospel of the kingdom was—and still is—a future event. The same does not hold true concerning the gospel of the grace of God. According to the scripture, the gospel that Paul expounded, the gospel of the grace of God, was already preached *"in all the world"* and *"to every creature which is under heaven"* before the canon of scripture was fully penned in the first century.

> **Colossians 1:6** *Which [gospel—see* **Colossians 1:5***]* ***is come*** *unto you, as it is* ***in all the world****; and bringeth forth fruit, as it doth also in you, since the day ye heard of it, and knew the grace of God in truth:*

> **Colossians 1:23** *If ye continue in the faith grounded and settled, and be not moved away from the hope of the gospel, which ye have heard, and* ***which was preached to every creature which is under heaven****; whereof I Paul am made a minister;*

Those who fail to esteem the truths taught in God's word might miss or even dismiss this distinction, but be assured that these truths were important enough to be included in the Bible. Furthermore, those who dismiss this crucial distinction create for themselves a contradiction in God's word. Paul wrote that the gospel that he preached had gone into all the world during his ministry ***(Colossians 1:5-6)***, and yet Matthew wrote that when this happens, the end shall come.

> **Matthew 24:14** *And this gospel of the kingdom shall be preached in all the world for a witness unto all nations; and* ***then shall the end come****.*

Since the end did not come in Paul's day, this would mean one of two things. The Bible contains contradictions or Paul and Matthew were referring to two distinct gospels. If the gospel preached by Paul equaled the gospel of the kingdom, the end would or should have come in Paul's day. It didn't and God can't lie!

> **1 John 3:20** *For if our heart condemn us,* ***God*** *is greater than our heart, and* ***knoweth all things****.*

> **Titus 1:2** *In hope of eternal life, which* ***God****, that* ***cannot lie****, promised before the world began;*

In the context, *"the end"* ***(Matthew 24:14)*** is identified as the time of the Lord's *"coming, and of the end of the world"* ***(Matthew 24:3)***. This is why it is so important to rightly divide the scriptures ***(2 Timothy 2:15)***.

The end in Matthew chapter 24 is *not* the Blessed Hope or the Rapture of the Church! In fact, it is important to note that the Rapture is not on hold, as some teach, awaiting the evangelism of some remote heathen. Nothing, save the Father's timing, stands between the Lord Jesus Christ and His return to the clouds to meet the New Testament Church.

When all is said and done, the Bible student must understand that the Church is *not* Israel; the gospel of the kingdom is *not* the gospel of the grace of God; the end of the world is *not* the Rapture of the Church; Matthew chapter 24 is *not* a parallel passage for 1 Thessalonians chapter 4 or 1 Corinthians chapter 15. Yet, far too few are able to articulate these differences. With so many failing to make these distinctions, is there any wonder why so many Christians remain confused concerning eschatology? Far too many Bible teachers and students are either unaware of these distinctions or they are simply too fearful of the brethren to openly teach these truths.

> **Proverbs 29:25** *The fear of man* bringeth a snare: but whoso putteth his trust in the LORD shall be safe.

> "Faithful service and personal holiness *always* go hand in hand with an earnest expectation of the fulfillment of Bible prophecy and the expectant return of Christ."

[Excerpt from *"Reviving the Blessed Hope,"* page 29]

6

The Abomination of Desolation

(Matthew 24:15-20)

Daniel's prophecy, along with several other key passages, places the abomination of desolation around the midpoint of Daniel's Seventieth Week *(Daniel 9:27)*. In other words, this *abomination* is the hinge upon which the door of Daniel's prophetic Week of years swings. It is important to understand that troubles, sorrows, intense hatred, etc., exist both before and after the abomination. Likewise, judgment is poured out both before and after this event, but immediately following the abomination, God's word exclaims, *"then shall be great tribulation."* Simply put, the tribulation experienced during Daniel's Seventieth Week will be intensified greatly.

> *Matthew 24:15 When ye therefore shall see the abomination of desolation… 21 **For then shall be great tribulation**, such as was not since the beginning of the world to this time, no, nor ever shall be.*

Because of God's goodness, He never judges where He has not first instructed and facilitated a way of escape. In fact, Paul stated that *"sin is not imputed when there is no law" **(Romans 5:13)***. Paul later asked the question, *"How shall we escape, if we neglect so great salvation?" **(Hebrews 2:3)***. In other words, God's wrath is always preceded by the enlightenment of truth and provision for life and safety *(John 15:22-24)*. This is a testimony of God's character as noted by Abraham when he said, *"Shall not the Judge of all the earth do right?"*

> *Genesis 18:25 That **be far from thee** to do after this manner, **to slay the righteous with the wicked:** and that the righteous should be as*

the wicked, that be far from thee: **Shall not the Judge of all the earth do right?**

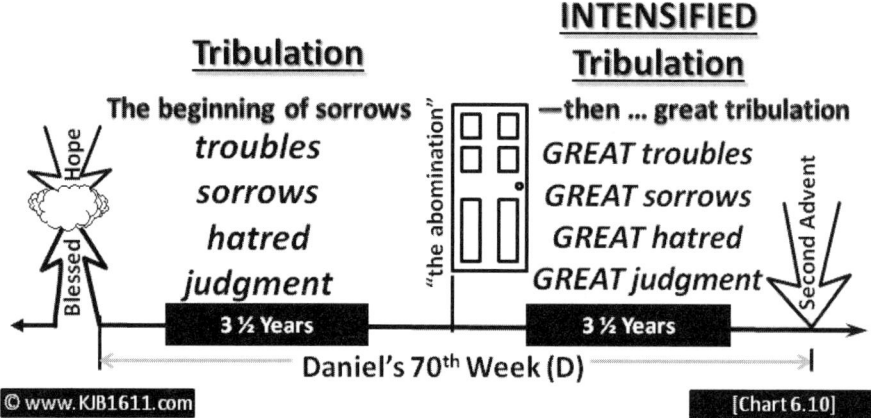

Before God's final gavel falls with His uninhibited wrath poured out upon the earth, the Lord will send His heralds to proclaim the gospel of the kingdom *"in all the world for a witness unto all nations"* **(Matthew 24:14)**. Just as God removed Lot prior to the outpouring of His wrath upon Sodom and Gomorrah, God will provide a way of escape during this period. Those Jews who believe His word will heed the admonition to *"flee into the mountains"* **(Matthew 24:16)**. The apostle John foresaw this event and stated, *"to the woman* [Israel] *were given two wings of a great eagle, that she might fly into the wilderness, into her place, where she is nourished for a time* [one year], *and times* [two years], *and half a time* [six months], *from the face of the serpent"* **(Revelation 12:14)**. This timing directly addresses the final three and one-half years of the seven-year period.

The abomination delineated in Daniel chapters 9, 11, and 12, Matthew chapter 24, and Mark chapter 13 is the event signifying the beginning of the end. These chapters each point to this event as the sign to the Jewish people (and believing nations) that all hell is about to break loose upon the earth. It is even referred to as *"the abomination that maketh desolate."* Read each of these parallel passages.

Daniel 9:27 *And he shall confirm the covenant with many for one week: and in the midst of the week he shall cause the sacrifice and the oblation to cease, and for* **the overspreading of abominations he shall make it desolate***, even until the consummation, and that determined shall be poured upon the desolate.*

Daniel 11:31 *And arms shall stand on his part, and they shall pollute the sanctuary of strength, and shall take away the daily sacrifice, and they shall place* **the abomination that maketh desolate***.*

Daniel 12:11 *And from the time that the daily sacrifice shall be taken away, and* **the abomination that maketh desolate** *set up, there shall be a thousand two hundred and ninety days.*

Matthew 24:15 *When ye therefore shall see* **the abomination of desolation***, spoken of by Daniel the prophet, stand in the holy place, (whoso readeth, let him understand:)*

Mark 13:14 *But when ye shall see* **the abomination of desolation***, spoken of by Daniel the prophet, standing where it ought not, (let him that readeth understand,) then let them that be in Judaea flee to the mountains:*

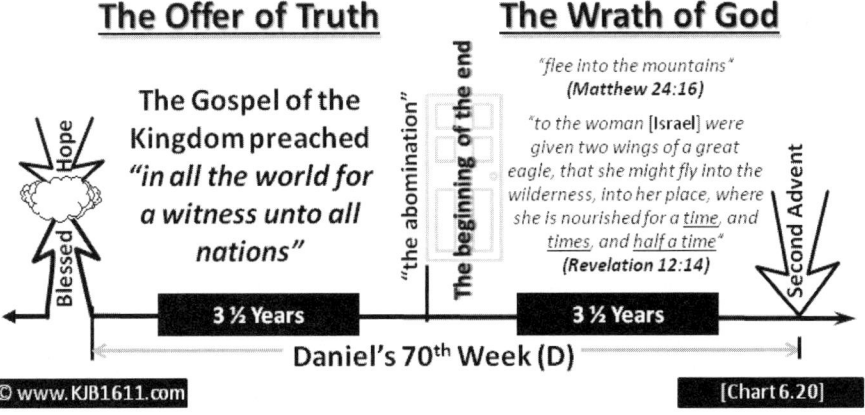

The Abomination's Precursors

This book has already chronicled several of the precursors (or forerunners) to this abomination, but there remain two more events needing attention: (1) the armies of Satan encompassing Jerusalem and (2) the Devil's arrival upon the earth after having been cast from heaven. Although we have not yet discussed the ministry of the two witnesses of Revelation *(Revelation 11:3-13)*, it is likely that their deaths and subsequent resurrection occur around the same time as the abomination that makes desolate.

During this time, imagine the Jews' heightened level of fear and uncertainty. They are bombarded on every side with threats: threats of deception, of wars, of physical disturbances, and of personal hatred from those without and from those within. Added to this is the sheer contempt for the truth. The masses rejoice at the death of the two witnesses by making merry and sending gifts to one another. The people are thrilled that they will no longer be tormented by the message and ministry of God's two witnesses.

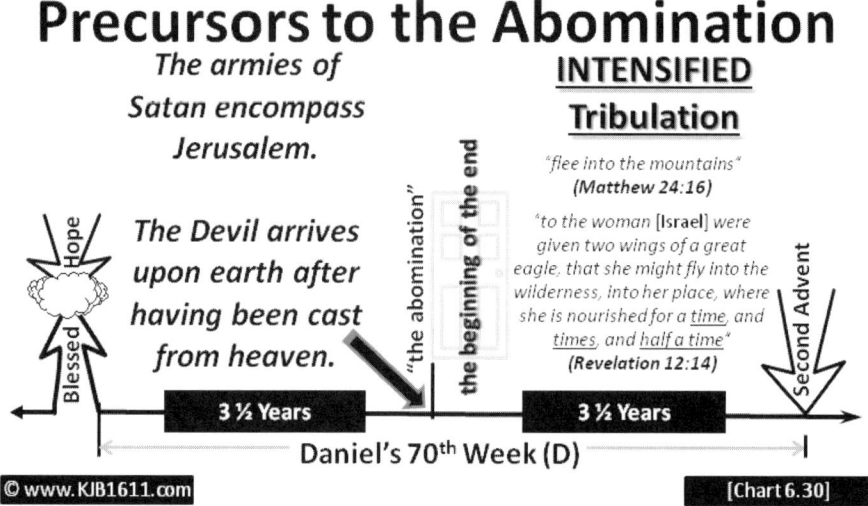

We know that the Jews seem to worship unhindered in their temple based upon the false covenant of peace with the man of sin—see **Daniel 9:27**. Yet, once Satan is cast from heaven, he seems to immediately claim this temple and demand man's worship *(2 Thessalonians 2:4)*. The Jews should know what is taking place because God warned Israel that the desolation is near when they see the armies surround Jerusalem.

> **Luke 21:20** And when ye shall see **Jerusalem compassed with armies**, then know that the **desolation** thereof **is nigh**.

Keep in mind that the Bible says that this is *"the time of Jacob's trouble"* ***(Jeremiah 30:7)*** and intended *"to finish the transgression, and to make an end of sins, and to make reconciliation for iniquity"* ***(Daniel 9:24)***. The sacrifices, resumed sometime after the confirmation of the covenant of peace and building of the temple, will probably be halted by the infiltrating armies or when Satan himself shows up. We do not know the exact time line but we do know that the sacrifices resume during the first half of the prophetic week of years only to cease again.

> **Daniel 9:27** *And he shall confirm the covenant with many for one week: and* ***in the midst of the week he shall cause the sacrifice and the oblation to cease****, and for the overspreading of abominations he shall make it desolate, even until the consummation, and that determined shall be poured upon the desolate.*

Another factor to keep in mind concerns Israel's protector—Michael. The Bible repeatedly tells us that Michael stands to defend Israel against her enemies, but he can only be in one place at a time—either in heaven or upon the earth, but not both simultaneously.

> **Daniel 12:1** *And at that time shall* **Michael** *stand up,* **the great prince which standeth for the children of thy people**: *and there shall be* **a time of trouble**, *such as never was since there was a nation even to that same time: and at that time* **thy people shall be delivered**, *every one that shall be found written in the book.*

While these events are unfolding upon the earth, Michael, the prince and protector of Israel, will be summoned to the third heaven to war against Satan. Unsurprisingly, Michael and his angels will be victorious resulting in the Devil being *"cast out into the earth."* The heavens will have reason to rejoice, but the earth then becomes completely exposed to Satan's *"great wrath."* More importantly, Israel will no longer have Michael to restrain the Devil's onslaught against them.

> **Revelation 12:7** *And* **there was war in heaven: Michael and his angels fought against the dragon; and the dragon fought and his angels**, *8 And prevailed not; neither was their place found any more in heaven. 9 And* **the great dragon was cast out, that old serpent, called the Devil, and Satan, which deceiveth the whole world: he was cast out into the earth**, *and his angels were cast out with him. 10 And I heard a loud voice saying in heaven, Now is come salvation,*

and strength, and the kingdom of our God, and the power of his Christ: for the accuser of our brethren is cast down, which accused them before our God day and night. 11 And they overcame him by the blood of the Lamb, and by the word of their testimony; and they loved not their lives unto the death. 12 ***Therefore rejoice, ye heavens, and ye that dwell in them. Woe to the inhabiters of the earth and of the sea! for the devil is come down unto you, having great wrath, because he knoweth that he hath but a short time.***

It is difficult to dogmatically assert the events above to the minutest details, but it is certain that they are all interrelated. Once cast from heaven, Satan's first act on earth may very well be to set up the abomination in the temple. Consider this plausible scenario: the armies of Satan encompass Jerusalem; the man of sin calls for the end of sacrifices offered to the God of heaven; and Satan himself is cast down to the earth. What would likely follow? The abomination that maketh desolate.

The Proceedings of the Abomination

After the Church's departure, the nation of Israel will live under a covenant of peace for forty-two months. This peace, or supposed peace, will fade as the armies of the Antichrist encompass Jerusalem and demand a cessation of the Jewish sacrifices. At such time, *"the sanctuary of strength"* **(Daniel 11:31)** or *"the temple of God"* **(2 Thessalonians 2:4)** will be defiled, becoming Satan's seat.

[Chart 6.40]

In order to fully understand this pivotal event and its ramifications, we must consider the various names and explanations for the *desolation* found within scripture. For example, although this event is named *"the abomination that maketh desolate"* in Daniel, the New Testament refers to it as *"the abomination of desolation."* The differences in wording, at least in part, result from the source of translation whether Hebrew (the language utilized by Daniel in these references) or Greek (the language used by Matthew and Mark). Because these references provide the necessary insight into understanding the foundational details of the event itself, we need to include them together:

Daniel 11:31 *And arms shall stand on his part, and they shall pollute the sanctuary of strength, and shall take away the daily sacrifice, and they shall place* **the abomination that maketh desolate***.*

Daniel 12:11 *And from the time that the daily sacrifice shall be taken away, and* **the abomination that maketh desolate** *set up, there shall be a thousand two hundred and ninety days.*

Matthew 24:15 *When ye therefore shall see* **the abomination of desolation***, spoken of by Daniel the prophet, stand in the holy place, (whoso readeth, let him understand:)*

Mark 13:14 *But when ye shall see* **the abomination of desolation***, spoken of by Daniel the prophet, standing where it ought not, (let him*

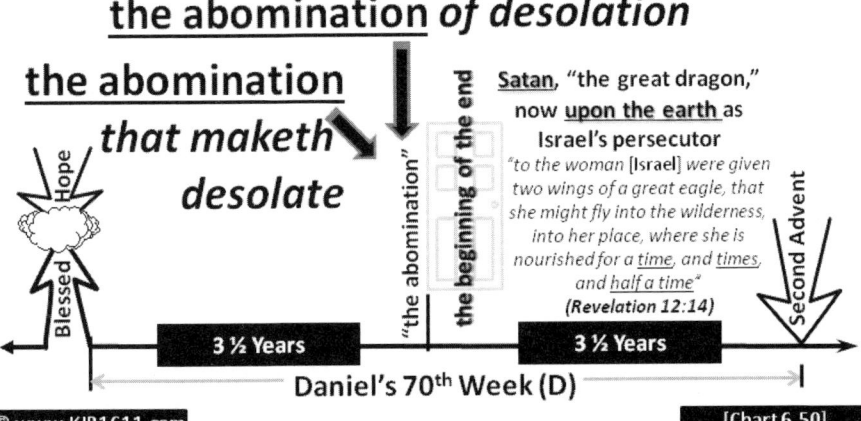

that readeth understand,) then let them that be in Judaea flee to the mountains:

Technically, the event is known simply as **"the** *abomination"* but it is further defined by descriptive phrases such as *"that maketh desolate"* or *"of desolation."* Although this distinction may seem quite insignificant, it may offer the very answer as to the focus of the event. The phrase *"the abomination"* is found thirteen times in scripture with the last four instances testifying specifically of the event now under consideration. It is important to realize that at least six of these occurrences involve an association between the word *goddess* or *god* and the phrase *"the abomination."*

> **1 Kings 11:5** *For Solomon went after Ashtoreth* **the goddess of the Zidonians,** *and after Milcom* **the abomination** *of the Ammonites … 7 Then did Solomon build an high place for Chemosh,* **the abomination** *of Moab, in the hill that is before Jerusalem, and for Molech,* **the abomination** *of the children of Ammon.*

> **2 Kings 23:13** *And the high places that were before Jerusalem, which were on the right hand of the mount of corruption, which Solomon the king of Israel had builded for Ashtoreth* **the abomination of the Zidonians,** *and for Chemosh* **the abomination** *of the Moabites, and for Milcom* **the abomination** *of the children of Ammon, did the king defile.*

"The abomination" that takes place in the midst of Daniel's Seventieth Week will assuredly involve the idolatrous actions connected with a false god. This will be accomplished in at least two major events: (1) the setting up of an image in the temple of God *(Daniel 11:31; Daniel 12:11; Matthew 24:15; Mark 13:14)* and (2) the presence of and worship of the man of sin in the temple of God *(2 Thessalonians 2:4).*

Image worship and false religion almost always take place in tandem. This is why the Lord warned both the Old Testament Jews *(Exodus 20:4)* and the New Testament Christians *(Acts 17:29; Romans 1:23)* concerning the wickedness and dangers of worshipping idols. During Daniel's Seventieth Week, every faithful Jew will understand the imminent peril when *"the abomination"* is placed *(Daniel 11:31)*, set up *(Daniel 12:11)*, and standing in the holy place *(Matthew 24:15)* where it ought not *(Mark 13:14)*. It is also likely at this point that the *"man of sin" (2 Thessalonians 2:3)* will present himself as God as he sits *"in the temple of God, shewing himself that he is God" (2 Thessalonians 2:4)*.

The Prophecy of the Abomination

Jews faithfully attending to the reading of either testament will have ample warning when they visibly see *"the abomination"* take place. As we are informed in the New Testament, this prophecy was initially *"spoken of by Daniel the prophet" (Matthew 24:15; Mark 13:14)*. In fact, Daniel spoke of these things repeatedly and recorded them in three separate chapters.

> ***Daniel 9:27*** *And he shall confirm the covenant with many for one week: and in the midst of the week he shall cause the sacrifice and the oblation to cease, and for* **the overspreading of abominations he shall make** it **desolate**, *even until the consummation, and that determined shall be poured upon the desolate.*

> ***Daniel 11:31*** *And arms shall stand on his part, and they shall pollute the sanctuary of strength, and shall take away the daily sacrifice, and* **they shall place the abomination that maketh desolate**.

> ***Daniel 12:11*** *And from the time that the daily sacrifice shall be taken away, and* **the abomination that maketh desolate set up**, *there shall be a thousand two hundred and ninety days.*

Much of our study has been focused, and rightly so, on *"the abomination,"* but one of Daniel's references also mentions specifically *"the overspreading of abominations" (Daniel 9:27)*. Apparently, *"the abomination"* that makes desolate will be only one among many different abominations that will take place in the midst of Daniel's final prophetic week of years.

Daniel's warning will be sufficient for those Jews with an understanding of their Old Testament. However, the prophecy with its warnings was also provided by both Matthew and Mark *(Matthew 24:15; Mark 13:14)*. God surely gave sufficient witness to the Jews and surrounding nations *(Deuteronomy 19:15)* with the combined prophecies of Daniel and those recorded by Matthew and Mark. Yet, God will provide additional witnesses establishing the validity of the coming events through the preaching of the two witnesses.

The Product of the Abomination

The outcome of *"the abomination"* is desolation! When *"the daily sacrifice"* is taken away and *"the sanctuary of strength"* polluted *(Daniel 11:31)*, the Jews are warned to flee for their lives. In fact, they are admonished both where to go and the speed at which to escape the coming onslaught.

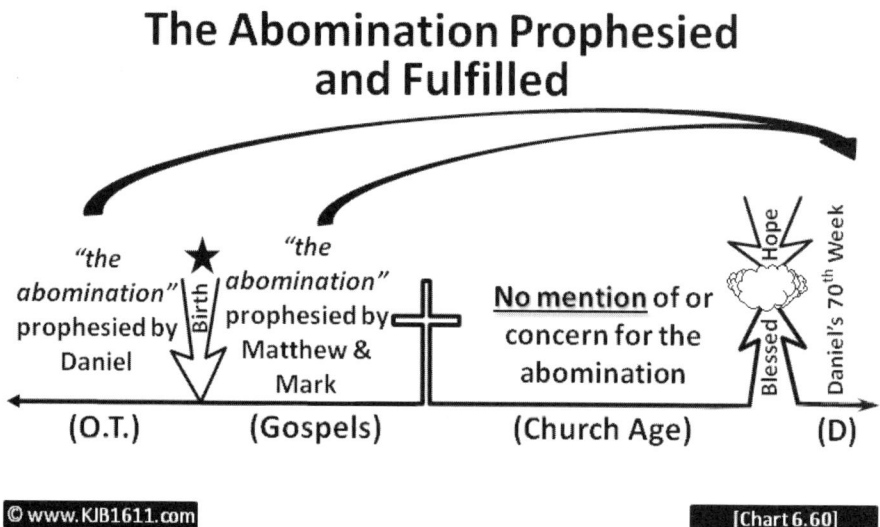

*Matthew 24:16 Then let them which be in Judaea **flee into the mountains**: 17 Let him which is on the housetop not come down to take any thing out of his house: 18 Neither let him which is in the field return back to take his clothes.*

*Mark 13:14 But when ye shall see the abomination of desolation, spoken of by Daniel the prophet, standing where it ought not, (let him that readeth understand,) then let them that be in Judaea **flee to the mountains**: 15 And let him that is on the housetop **not go down into the house**, neither enter therein, to take any thing out of his house: 16 And let him that is in the field **not turn back again** for to take up his garment.*

*Luke 21:21 Then let them which are in Judaea **flee to the mountains**; and let them which are in the midst of it depart out; and let not them that are in the countries enter thereinto.*

Those in Judaea are admonished to *"flee into the mountains."* Those *"in the countries"* are warned not to *"enter thereinto* [Judaea]*."* The sad and fearful truth is that during Daniel's Seventieth Week, physical endurance is paramount. As such, the Jews will swiftly shift from a covenant of peace to fearing and fleeing for their lives. In fact, the level of fear will be so high that the Jews on their housetops are told to leave their homes without concern for material goods. Those in their fields are instructed not to return home to gather even their clothing.

During this time, the Jews can ill afford delays, hindrances, or complications. Their lives depend upon their exiting the oncoming onslaught without delay. This is why the Lord set forth two major concerns that might exist for the Jews attempting to flee on the day when *"the abomination"* is set up: (1) the presence of infants or toddlers and (2) the limitations of travel due to weather or Sabbath day restrictions.

***Matthew 24:19** And woe unto them that are **with child**, and to them that **give suck** in those days! 20 But pray ye that your flight be not in the **winter**, neither on the **sabbath day**:*

***Mark 13:17** But woe to them that are with **child**, and to them that give suck in those days! 18 And pray ye that your flight be not in the **winter**.*

***Luke 21:23** But woe unto them that are with **child**, and to them that give suck, in those days! for there shall be great distress **in the land**, and wrath upon **this people**.*

Obviously, things quickly turn quite stressful for THIS PEOPLE (Israel) IN THE LAND (Israel). It is not hard to gauge how bad things become as the Lord suggests that children, previously known as *"his reward"* **(Psalm 127:3)**, have now become a hindrance and a burden! Yet, that is exactly what the Lord states concerning the dangers the Jews face as they attempt to flee for safety. In fact, younger children who must be carried will present a grave danger. Although not stated here, it is also likely that the elderly will present just as much difficulty as the smaller children.

The Bible also specifically addresses two other difficulties presenting their own unique set of difficulties. First, the Jews are told to *"pray"* that their flight (departure) is *"not in the winter."* Comparably, the weather is not terribly cold in this particular region, but winter includes the wet season. These wet conditions would certainly not be favorable for a mass exodus of Jews seeking refuge from the man of sin.

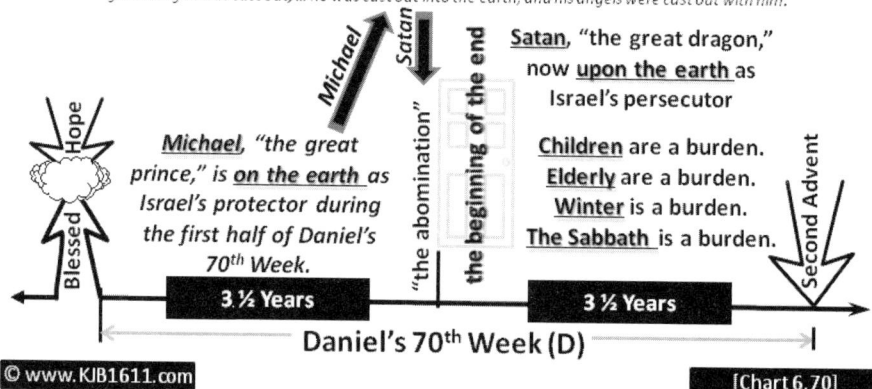

Furthermore, the Jews are encouraged to pray that their flight does not take place *"on the sabbath day."* Why is there a problem if *"the abomination"* occurs on this day? The answer, or at least the hint to the answer, is found in **Acts 1:12**. In this passage, the Lord reveals the Jews acceptable travel distances that separate the Sabbath day from any other day. Although we may not specifically know the exact acceptable distance in **Acts 1:12**, the distance would likely be limited to just over two and one-half miles.

> **Acts 1:12** *Then returned they unto Jerusalem from the mount called Olivet, which is from Jerusalem* **a sabbath day's journey.**

Those living today probably have little understanding of the fear the Jews will face once their safety has been removed in the midst of Daniel's Seventieth Week. The covenant of peace will be replaced by unfathomable fear. The already unstable global relations will crumble. The blessings of small children and elderly will turn to immense burdens. The joys of rain for crops will become a frustration as they flee to their hiding places. Perhaps all this is a reminder of why we, those of us living today, ought to:

> **Psalm 122:6** *Pray for the peace of Jerusalem: they shall prosper that love thee.*

7

The Time of Great Tribulation

(Matthew 24:21-28)

As we have seen, the Abomination of Desolation is the spiritual hinge upon which the door of Daniel's Seventieth Week swings: from a time of sorrows, hatred, gospel preaching, and false covenants to a time of increased trouble surpassing any other time in human history. The heightened dangers will consist of two major threats: (1) spiritual deception and (2) loss of life.

The threat upon human life (specifically that of the Jews) will be so severe that the Bible warns unless the days of this period are shortened, no flesh will survive. These assaults upon God's chosen nation will serve

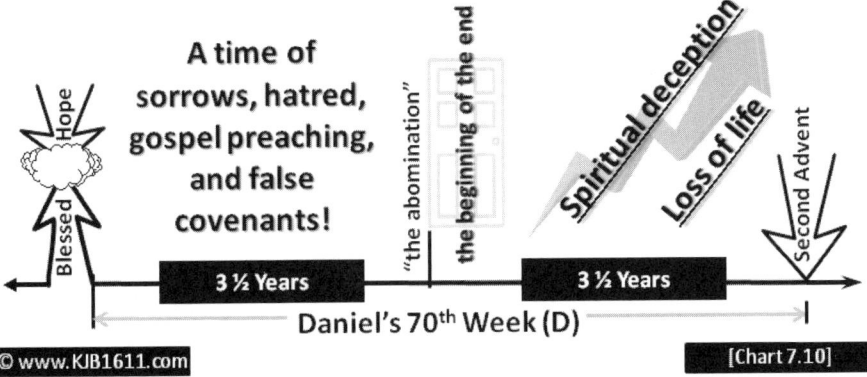

as the Devil's last great attempt to thwart God's will by robbing Israel of their promised blessings and promised kingdom.

Because of the Devil's immense pride, he simply does not know that he serves as one of God's pawns. In fact, the Bible prophesies that God will send the *"Assyrian, the rod of mine anger"* **(Isaiah 10:5)** *"against an hypocritical nation"* **(Isaiah 10:6)** *"to take the spoil, and to take the prey, and to tread them down like the mire of the streets"* **(Isaiah 10:6)**. The prideful Devil will assume he is in control and it will be *"in his heart to destroy and cut off nations not a few"* **(Isaiah 10:7)**.

Once finished with the Assyrian, the Lord *"will punish the fruit of the stout heart of the king of Assyria, and the glory of his high looks"* **(Isaiah 10:12)**. In fact, Satan's work is likened to an axe boasting *"itself against him that heweth therewith"* **(Isaiah 10:15)**. Out of these troubles will emerge a *"remnant of Israel, and such as are escaped of the house of Jacob"* and they *"shall stay upon the LORD, the Holy One of Israel, in truth"* **(Isaiah 10:20)**.

The Assyrian

First, God will ...
send the *"Assyrian" (Isaiah 10:5) "against an hypocritical nation" (Isaiah 10:6) "to take the spoil, and ... the prey, and to tread them down like the mire of the streets" (Isaiah 10:6)*

The Devil will ...
assume he is in control and it will be *"in his heart to destroy and cut off nations not a few" (Isaiah 10:7)*

Then, God will ...
"punish the fruit of the stout heart of the king of Assyria, and the glory of his high looks" (Isaiah 10:12)

"the abomination" | the beginning of the end | **3 ½ Years** | Second Advent

Latter Half of Daniel's Seventieth Week

© www.KJB1611.com [Chart 7.20]

In order to survive this most terrible time, the Jews will have to obey the words of the Lord in two specific commandments: (1) they will need to flee for their safety and (2) they will need to reject the deceptive ploys to get them to seek after any false Christs. Failure to abide by God's directives in either of these areas will likely result in the loss of life or the spiritual deception warned against.

The Fear of Safety

The time frame following the Abomination of Desolation is known as *"the times of the Gentiles" **(Luke 21:24)***. According to Revelation chapter 11, the Gentiles will *"tread under foot"* the holy city for forty and two months (or three and one-half years). This should not seem unusual when one understands the natural cruelty of Gentiles **(Matthew 20:19, 25; Luke 18:32; Galatians 2:15)**. In fact, the Lord quantified the severity of danger—it will be a period of GREAT tribulation.

> *Matthew 24:21 For then shall be **great tribulation**, such as was **not** since the beginning of the world to this time, no, nor ever shall be.*

> *Mark 13:19 For in those days shall be **affliction**, such as was not from the beginning of the creation which God created unto this time, neither shall be.*

The troubles during this time will surpass those of any period chronicled by God's word or in the annals of man. It may seem hard to comprehend, but the tribulation and affliction at this time surpasses even that which took place during Noah's worldwide flood. During the flood, all those living (Noah and his family) had the protection of the ark with the masses quickly perishing. However, during this time of GREAT tribulation, the physical and spiritual onslaught will be pervasive, persistent, and overpowering.

The average person has limited ability to comprehend such a magnitude of suffering and destruction. This time cannot be likened to a mere recession or some localized drought because the reality is far beyond that. According to the gospel of Luke, many of the Jews will *"fall by the edge of the sword"* and others *"shall be led away captive into all nations."*

> *Luke 21:24 And **they** (this people—verse 23) **shall fall by the edge of the sword, and shall be led away captive into all nations**: and Jerusalem shall be trodden down of the Gentiles, until the times of the Gentiles be fulfilled.*

Additionally, there will be an overhaul of the monetary system so *"that no man might buy or sell, save he that had the mark, or the name of the beast, or the number of his name."*

> *Revelation 13:17 And that **no man might buy or sell, save he that had the mark, or the name of the beast, or the number of his name**.*

These events are compounded when one considers the wars, famines, pestilences, and earthquakes that have already taken place and are yet to occur during this time.

> **Matthew 24:7** *For* **nation** *shall rise* **against nation***, and* **kingdom against kingdom***: and there shall be* **famines***, and* **pestilences***, and* **earthquakes***, in divers places.*

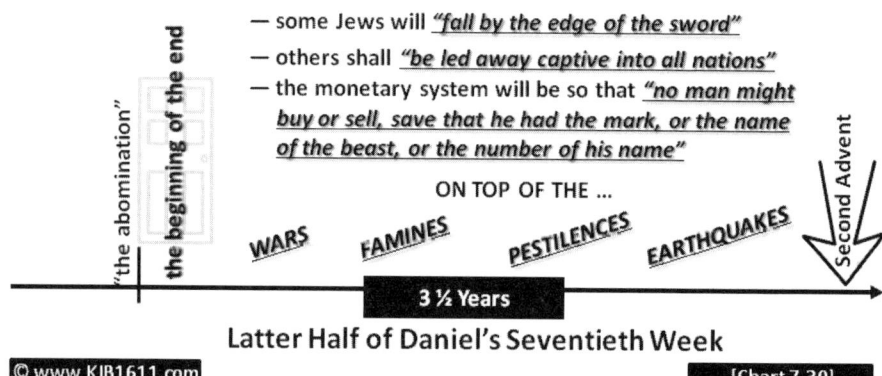

Consider for a moment the magnitude of this type of human suffering. Starving Jews will be unable to purchase the necessary food to feed their families unless they deny their God, worship the beast, and take his mark. Homes devastated by earthquakes cannot be repaired because only those who have the mark can purchase the necessary supplies for repair. People will fall ill but be unable to purchase the necessary medications to combat the onslaught of diseases. The only hope on earth for the Jewish people will be the aid of the stockpiles of the nations to which they are scattered.

Fortunately, this help from some of the nations is both prophesied and confirmed within the pages of God's word. First, Matthew chapter 25 chronicles the often misunderstood Judgment of the Nations. In doing so, the Bible identifies that a foundational basis for the judgment is whether or not the nations aided the Jews in their time of need (the time of Jacob's Trouble). To the helpful nations, the Lord will say, *"I was an hungered, and ye gave me meat: I was thirsty, and ye gave me drink: I was a stranger, and ye took me in: Naked, and ye clothed me: I was sick, and ye visited me: I was in prison, and ye came unto me"* **(Matthew 25:35-36)**. The nations flabbergasted by the remarks ask *"when"* **(Matthew 25:37-39)** they did such things to which the Lord will respond, *"Inasmuch as ye have done it unto one of the least of these my brethren* [the Jews], *ye have done it unto me"* **(Matthew 25:40)**.

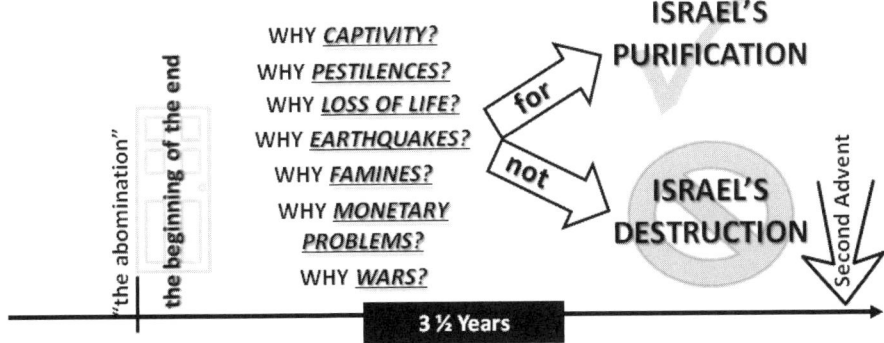

The borders, identities, and names of the nations may even vary in the future from what they are today, but the fact remains that nations will survive Daniel's Seventieth Week and enter into the Lord's earthly, millennial kingdom *(Isaiah 2:2)*. In fact, the Lord specifically named Egypt as one nation that will be present in the millennium *(Zechariah 14:16-20)*. A key to this entrance into the kingdom will be helping hungry, thirsty, naked, sick, and imprisoned Jews. The severity of the dangers is such that the Lord warned that the only way mankind, especially the Jews, could survive would be for the days to be shortened *(Matthew 24:22; Mark 13:20)*.

> Matthew 24:22 And *except those days should be shortened, there should no flesh be saved: but for* **the elect's sake** *those days shall be shortened.*

> Mark 13:20 And *except that the Lord had shortened those days, no flesh should be saved: but for* **the elect's sake, whom he hath chosen**, *he hath shortened the days.*

How these days will be shortened has been debated and the debate continues, but for whom they will be shortened is not open to debate. The shortening of the days is *"for the elect's sake" **(Matthew 24:22; Mark 13:20)***, defined as the ones *"whom he* [the Lord] *hath chosen" **(Mark 13:20)***. Both of these phrases clearly identify and point to the people of God's concern as a believing remnant of the seed and lineage of Jacob.

> **1 Chronicles 16:13** *O ye seed of Israel his servant,* **ye children of Jacob, his chosen ones.**

> **Psalm 105:6** *O ye seed of Abraham his servant,* **ye children of Jacob his chosen.**

> **Psalm 135:4** *For* **the LORD hath chosen Jacob** *unto himself, and Israel for his peculiar treasure.*

> **Isaiah 41:8** *But thou, Israel, art my servant,* **Jacob whom I have chosen***, the seed of Abraham my friend.*

> **Isaiah 44:1** *Yet now hear, O Jacob my servant; and* **Israel, whom I have chosen***: 2 Thus saith the LORD that made thee, and formed thee from the womb, which will help thee; Fear not, O* **Jacob***, my servant;* **and thou, Jesurun, whom I have chosen.**

> **Isaiah 45:4** *For Jacob my servant's sake, and* **Israel mine elect***, I have even called thee by thy name: I have surnamed thee, though thou hast not known me.*

The primary purpose of Jacob's Trouble is the purification of His people, not the destruction of His elect. In order to fulfil His promises to Abraham, Isaac, and Jacob, the Lord must preserve His earthly people unto their earthly kingdom. With this in mind, the Lord has promised to shorten the days of Jacob's Trouble. How He shortens the days is a matter over which many good people have been divided.

Some suggest that the ***number*** of days will be shortened, but this seems unlikely. According to scripture, Jacob's Trouble seems to be the last three and one-half years of Daniel's Seventieth Week defined three ways: *"a time, times, and an half" **(Daniel 12:7; Revelation 12:14)***, or *"forty and two months" **(Revelation 11:2)***, or *"a thousand two hundred and threescore days" **(Revelation 12:6)***. That being said, it seems unlikely that the Lord would be that specific in quantifying this period only to prophecy of His shortening them quantitatively.

Perhaps the best insight given on the subject matter is to consider an event from Israel's history when God **lengthened** a day in order to give Israel a great victory. In the days of Joshua, the sun stood still upon Gibeon until the Israelites *"had avenged themselves upon their enemies" (Joshua 10:12-13)*. Should nighttime have fallen and the earth turned dark, the enemy would have found solace and protection in the darkness. If the Creator was able and willing to lengthen a day in order to preserve, protect, and give victory to His people Israel, it is quite plausible that He could shorten the duration of a day during Jacob's Trouble to offer additional protection.

__Revelation 8:12__ And the fourth angel sounded, and the third part of the sun was smitten, and the third part of the moon, and the third part of the stars; so as the third part of them was darkened, and __the day shone not for a third part of it, and the night likewise.__

Those trying to hide would find solace if one third of the day and one third of the night were pitch black *(Matthew 24:29; Mark 13:24; Joel 3:15; Isaiah 13:10)*.

The Fear of Deception

In addition to all this, the Jews will be constantly bombarded with false information and false hope concerning their coming Messiah. To the Christian, it may seem foolish that the Jews could be duped into believing the lies concerning Christ's supposed presence upon the earth. However, people deprived of hope often cling to any glimmer of hope offered. Just as the introduction of a conflicting voice caused difficulty for Adam and Eve in the garden in Eden, so it will be difficult for Jews who have notoriously turned a blind eye toward their Messiah. God's truth and His words are the only effective means to combat the temptation of conflicting voices during the time of Jacob's Trouble.

__Matthew 24:23__ Then if any man shall say unto you, Lo, __here is Christ__, or there; believe it not. 24 For there shall arise __false Christs__, and __false prophets__, and shall shew great signs and wonders; insomuch that, __if it were possible__, they shall __deceive the very elect__. 25 Behold, I have told you before. 26 Wherefore if they shall say unto you, Behold, he is in the desert; go not forth: behold, he is in the secret chambers; believe it not.

> ***Mark 13:21*** *And then if any man shall say to you, Lo,* ***here is Christ****; or, lo, he is there; believe him not: 22 For* ***false Christs*** *and* ***false prophets*** *shall rise, and shall shew signs and wonders, to* ***seduce, if it were possible, even the elect***. *23 But take ye heed: behold, I have foretold you all things.*

The Bible points out that these false messengers will not be able to deceive or seduce the elect. Before proceeding further, it is important to clarify that in any given dispensation, Israel is made up of two parts: the elect (believing Jews) and the nonelect (unbelieving Jews). This truth is clearly indicated in Romans chapter 11. At first glance, it appears that Israel is contrasted with *"the election,"* but a closer look indicates that Israel is divided into two subsets: *"the election"* and *"the rest."* Only those who receive the truth become known as the elect and the remainder (or *"the rest"*) remains blinded.

> ***Romans 11:7*** *What then?* ***Israel hath not obtained that which he seeketh for;*** *but* ***the election hath obtained it****, and* ***the rest were blinded***

Those who did not believe were blinded from the truth. The truth concerning the elect and election within Israel has been a subject of much confusion for students and teachers of the Bible. On one hand, the Bible teaches that *"all Israel shall be saved"* **(Romans 11:26)**, and yet in other places, the scripture plainly confirms that a *"remnant of Israel"* **(Isaiah 10:20)** *"shall return, even the remnant of Jacob, unto the mighty God"* **(Isaiah 10:21)**. This remnant is the same group identified in other places as *"the very elect"* **(Matthew 24:24)**. Ultimately, it makes sense that a remaining remnant of any people group would then be seen as the *"all"* **(Romans 11:26)** of that people group. Part of Jacob's purification includes the removal of unbelieving Jews; those who choose to remain blinded.

Understanding this truth becomes crucial in light of the truths taught in Matthew chapter 24. The scripture boldly proclaims that it is impossible to deceive **(Matthew 24:24)** or seduce **(Mark 13:22)** the elect. It makes no sense to make an appeal to obey if disobedience to the appeal is impossible. Therefore, it stands to reason that there will be some Jews (unbelieving Jews) who can and will be deceived into believing the lies of the Antichrist. Hence the warning! Those believing Jews who have not been blinded will not be deceived or seduced.

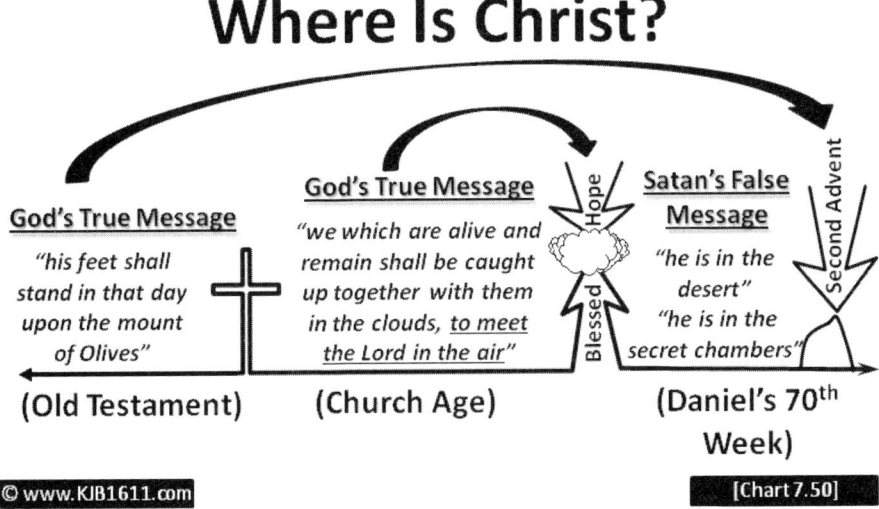

With hope for redemption growing dim, the voices appealing to the Jews continue to escalate. As such, it will become increasingly important for the Jewish people to have a working knowledge of God's word, especially as it pertains to Christ's coming to establish His kingdom. Failure to understand the *when* and *where* of Christ's return could cause unbelieving and ignorant Jews to accept the words of false prophets and false Christs doing everything to keep focus off of the true Messiah.

*Matthew 24:23 Then if any man shall say unto you, **Lo, here is Christ, or there**; believe it not.*

*Mark 13:21 And then if any man shall say to you, **Lo, here is Christ; or, lo, he is there**; believe him not:*

Bible-believing Jews will know perfectly and precisely the location of Christ's return—the mount of Olives. In fact, the Lord reminded them in **Mark 13:23**, *"behold, I have foretold you all things."* Included in the *"all things"* in Mark is that Christ would return to *"the mount of Olives."*

*Zechariah 14:4 And **his feet shall stand in that day upon the mount of Olives**, which is before Jerusalem on the east, and the mount of Olives shall cleave in the midst thereof toward the east and toward the west, and there shall be a very great valley; and half of the mountain shall remove toward the north, and half of it toward the south.*

Regardless of the dispensation, faith in the word of God is imperative. In this case, Jews who fail to accept and believe God's word concerning the precise location of Christ's return will be in danger of accepting the deception offered that Christ *"is in the desert"* or *"in the secret chambers."* He will not be in those places; He will return to the mount of Olives.

> **Matthew 24:26** Wherefore **if they shall say unto you, Behold, he is in the desert; go not forth: behold, he is in the secret chambers; believe it not.**

One of the greatest pitfalls for the Jews will be the fact that they are prone to trusting in signs. The Lord knew the Jews' need for signs and acknowledged it when He said, *"the Jews require a sign"* **(1 Corinthians 1:22)**. In the early church, the Lord compensated for this need *"confirming the word* [the message preached by the apostles] *with signs following"* **(Mark 16:20)**, but in the future, the Jews' dependence upon signs will be their downfall. The Antichrist will come *"with all power and signs and lying wonders"* **(2 Thessalonians 2:9)**, and false prophets will show *"signs and wonders"* to confirm their false message that Christ awaits them in the desert or in the secret chambers.

> **Matthew 24:24** For **there shall arise false Christs, and false prophets, and shall shew great signs and wonders**; *insomuch that, if it were possible, they shall deceive the very elect.*

> **Mark 13:22** For **false Christs and false prophets shall rise, and shall shew signs and wonders**, *to seduce, if it were possible, even the elect.*

The only remedy against this temptation and resulting deception will be to believe what God has already said. This is why the Lord said, *"take ye heed"* to what I have said and *"I have told you before."* A false perception might lead one to believe that the Jews' survival will be based upon works, but the reality is that their survival will be dependent upon their faith to believe God and His word. The works follow the faith and are the only true identifier of faith's existence *(James 2:18)*. God has provided the Jews with all the necessary information to know when, where, and how Christ will return. When confronted with false or conflicting information, the Jews are simply admonished to *"believe it not."*

> *Matthew 24:25 Behold, **I have told you before.** 26 Wherefore **if they shall say unto you, Behold, he is in the desert; go not forth: behold, he is in the secret chambers; believe it not.***

> *Mark 13:23 But take ye heed: behold, **I have foretold you all things.***

The Fierceness of Christ's Coming

The greatest fear for the Jews should not simply be the fear of deception, but rather the swiftness, fierceness, and power of Christ's return. In other words, the worst scenario would not be that the Jews were deceived, but that the Lord would return to find them in a state of deception. In fact, the Lord emphasized this concern when He asked, *"when the Son of man cometh, shall he find faith on the earth?" **(Luke 18:8)***. To illustrate the impact of His coming, the Lord relied upon man's understanding of two earthly scenarios: (1) the flashing of lightning and (2) the gathering of eagles upon carcasses.

> *Matthew 24:27 For as the **lightning** cometh out of the east, and **shineth** even unto the west; so shall also the coming of the Son of man be. 28 For wheresoever the **carcase** is, there will the **eagles be gathered together.***

Although both scenarios—the lightning and the carcasses attracting the eagles—are used to depict one single event, they present unique aspects of that same event. The illustration of lighting highlights the swiftness, fierceness *(Zechariah 9:14)*, and surprise of the Lord's return. This may not be readily understood by simply considering the passage as it appears in *Matthew 24:27*, but the context of Luke chapter 17 makes this abundantly clear.

> *Luke 17:24 For **as the lightning, that lighteneth out of the one part under heaven, shineth unto the other part under heaven; so shall also the Son of man be in his day.** 25 But first must he suffer many things, and be rejected of this generation. 26 And **as it was in the days of Noe, so shall it be also in the days of the Son of man.** 27 **They did eat, they drank, they married wives, they were given in marriage, until the day that Noe entered into the ark, and the flood came, and destroyed them all.** 28 Likewise also **as it was in the days of Lot; they did eat, they drank, they bought, they sold, they planted, they builded;** 29 But **the same day that Lot went out of Sodom it rained fire and brimstone from heaven, and destroyed***

***them all.** 30 Even thus shall it be in the day when the Son of man is revealed. 31 In that day, he which shall be upon the housetop, and his stuff in the house, let him not come down to take it away: and he that is in the field, let him likewise not return back. 32 Remember Lot's wife.*

Both Noah and Lot had to exercise faith prior to the execution of God's judgment. There was no time allotted for a change of mind once God's wrath fell from heaven. We do not read of any escaping God's judgment once the rain began or the brimstone fell. Likewise, the Lord's return will be like the flash of lightning—swift, fierce, and surprising! Failure to trust the warnings of God prior to the onset of judgment will first result in deception and ultimately in being on the receiving end of God's judgment. Once the lightning strikes—when Jesus comes—the Jews will have no opportunity for repentance.

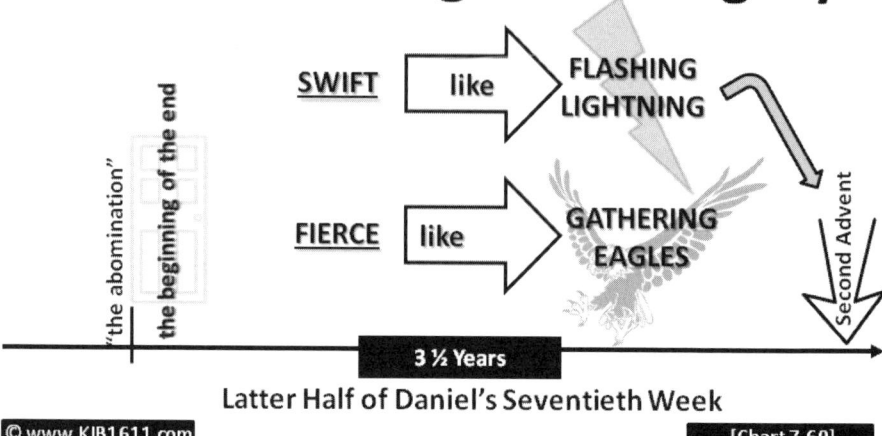

The purpose of Christ's coming serves as the second important and defining aspect of Christ's Second Coming. In order to make this point, the Lord pointed to eagles taking flight to pounce upon carcasses. This is an important point especially in offering clarity to those who suspect that the Olivet Discourse speaks of the Rapture of the church. An eagle pounces upon a carcass, not for the purpose of protecting the carcass, but for the purpose of feeding upon its flesh. Likewise, those taken in **Luke 17:34-36** are not taken to heaven for protection, but taken away in judgment. Similarly, those taken in the days of Noah and the days of Lot were those who died in judgment.

> ***Luke 17:34*** *I tell you, in that night there shall be two men in one bed; the **one shall be taken**, and the other shall be left. 35 Two women shall be grinding together; the **one shall be taken**, and the other left. 36 Two men shall be in the field; the **one shall be taken**, and the other left.*

When Christ returns, He will pounce upon His prey. He knows precisely the location of the wicked for He will *"gather all nations against Jerusalem to battle" **(Zechariah 14:2)*** only to *"go forth, and fight against those nations" **(Zechariah 14:3)***. He *"will smite all the people that have fought against Jerusalem" **(Zechariah 14:12)***. *"Their flesh shall consume away while they stand upon their feet, and their eyes shall consume away in their holes, and their tongue shall consume away in their mouth" **(Zechariah 14:12)***. This is the judgment on the Day of the Lord.

Obviously, nobody desires to be on the receiving end of the Lord's vengeance at His return. Yet, the Jews must heed the Lord's admonition not to be deceived. They must place their faith in the words of God and not trust the words of false prophets and false Christs that seek to deceive. The Jews must flee when told to flee and refuse to follow the false witnesses when warned against them. Failure to exercise faith in the words of God yields disobedience to the commandments of God resulting in receiving judgment from God.

The time of GREAT tribulation will be a time bombarded with decisions. In whom will men place their faith? Will men exercise faith in the Antichrist, his false prophets, and his false Christs, or will men choose to trust the Lord and His word? Who or what will men fear? Will men choose to fear the loss of life? Will they fear persecution? Or, will men choose to *"fear him which is able to destroy both soul and body in hell"* ***(Matthew 10:28)***? Those who choose to fear and trust the Antichrist will do so to their own demise when the Lord descends upon them. Yet, those at that time living by faith in the true and living God will have the power to resist the temptations and means of deception.

> "The New Testament Church lives together, serves together, loves together, reaps rewards together, and one day will leave together to meet Christ in the clouds."

[Excerpt from **"Reviving the Blessed Hope,"** page 33]

8

The Sign of Christ's Coming

(Matthew 24:29-31)

There are only two comings of the Lord Jesus Christ to earth (with the exception of the Old Testament preincarnate appearances—called Theophanies). These two earthly appearances are referred to as His first and second advent. The details of these appearances are only known to man through the word of God. Obviously, God wants man to know about the past, but equally as important, God wants man to be forewarned and prepared concerning future events. For instance, God's word provides enough details for the Jews to avoid being surprised by Christ's Second Coming.

Two of the primary purposes of Christ's Second Advent are to judge the earth and to ultimately deliver believing Israel. Yet, Israel has a problem with walking by faith. The Bible points out that the Jews grew accustomed to—and dependent upon—signs ***(1 Corinthians 1:22).*** God, therefore, in His infinite wisdom and boundless mercy, will provide three distinct and visible precursors announcing the return of His Son. These three forerunners are

- Cosmic and earthly disturbances,
- The sign of the Son of man, and
- Christ's sending His angels for the purpose of gathering the elect.

Although no one can be completely certain concerning the duration of the cosmic and earthly disturbances, the second and third precursors seem to provide no time for the unbelieving to repent. We will consider each of these three precursors in greater detail.

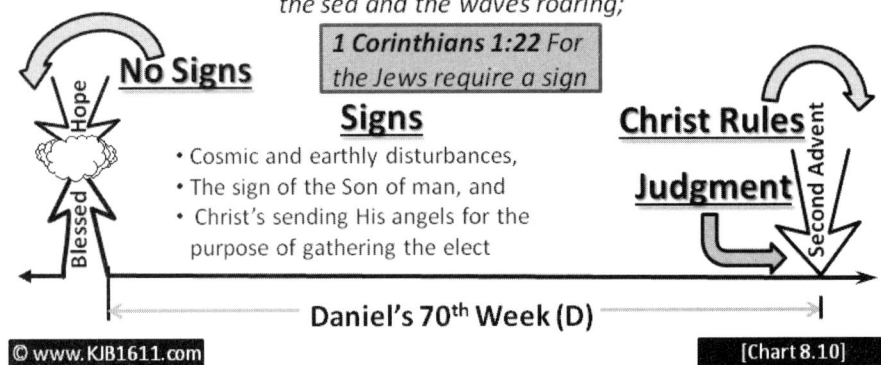

(1) The Cosmic and Earthly Disturbances *(Matthew 24:29)*

Unfortunately, many prophecy teachers fail to recognize the distinguishing features between the Rapture of the Church and Christ's Second Coming. The Rapture, involving the Church's gathering to the clouds, promises no visible precursors. However, this is certainly not the case concerning the Second Coming. Christ's return to earth begins with judgment soon followed by the blessings of His ruling in an earthly kingdom.

This Second Coming to earth is preceded by visible evidence, especially natural disturbances, or what the world refers to as "natural disasters." Every "real" Rapture passage noticeably excludes any indicators of these physical precursors. Yet, these types of disturbances are prevalent and dramatic just prior to Christ's Second Coming. In fact, the anxiety caused by the worldwide upheavals will cause men's hearts to fail them. These events consist of at least five specific types of catastrophic events:

(a) the sun will be darkened *(Matthew 24:29)*

(b) the moon will stop shining *(Matthew 24:29)*

(c) the stars will fall from heaven *(Matthew 24:29)*

(d) the powers of the heavens will be shaken *(Matthew 24:29)*

(e) the sea and the waves will roar *(Luke 21:25)*

Matthew 24:29 Immediately after the tribulation of those days **shall the sun be darkened**, *and* **the moon shall not give her light**, *and* **the stars shall fall from heaven**, *and* **the powers of the heavens shall be shaken**:

Mark 13:24 But in those days, after that tribulation, **the sun shall be darkened**, *and* **the moon shall not give her light**, *25 And* **the stars of heaven shall fall**, *and* **the powers that are in heaven shall be shaken**.

Luke 21:25 And **there shall be signs in the sun, and in the moon, and in the stars**; *and upon the earth distress of nations, with perplexity;* **the sea and the waves roaring**; *26 Men's hearts failing them for fear, and for looking after those things which are coming on the earth: for* **the powers of heaven shall be shaken**.

Luke refers to these events as signs. This is important because God's use of signs always points to Israel.

1 Corinthians 1:22 For the Jews require a sign, and the Greeks seek after wisdom:

Some scoffers have pointed to the unfathomable magnitude of the destruction as their so-called "proof" for the scripture's illegitimacy. Yet,

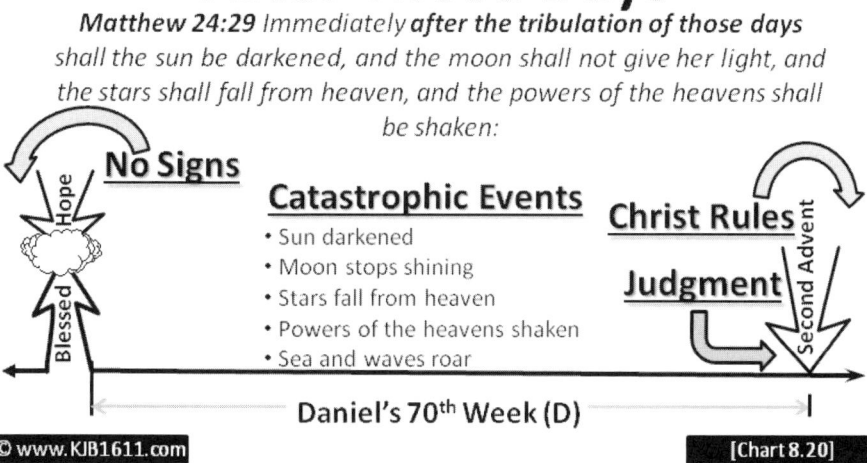

the same God who spoke the heavens and the earth into existence can just as easily use elements within His creation for His purposes of divine warning and divine judgment. These cataclysmic events are not limited to the writings of the New Testament followers of Christ alone, nor did they originate with Christ's earthly min'istry. Instead, these catastrophes were prophesied by several Old Testament prophets like Isaiah, Ezekiel, Joel, Amos, and Haggai.

Unfortunately, most men today choose to ignore and reject the truths of scripture. A natural by-product of this ignorance is man's current educational system. It seems purposefully designed to lead students away from the truths of scripture. When educated men seek to exclude God from the *truth equation*, the outcome produces some of the greatest scientific pitfalls. Yet, when man finally runs out of possible answers, he simply creates new hypotheses which produce what the Bible refers to as *"science falsely so called"* **(1 Timothy 6:20)**.

Interestingly, very few scientists realize that their rejection of God as the originator and sustainer of all things involves a greater level of "faith" than accepting Him as the Almighty. Additionally, those scientists who have read the described events could offer in-depth explanations how the utter chaos described in the last days of Jacob's Trouble could take place through natural means or by man's use of nuclear weapons, etc. Yet, only an honest scientist familiar with the Bible would ever suggest that it could—and will—happen at the direction and leading of Almighty God.

These events not only announce the coming of Israel's Messiah; they also declare the onset of the Day of the Lord. The Day of the Lord lasts approximately 1,000 years **(2 Peter 3:8)**. This period begins just prior to the Lord's Second Coming and continues until the dissolving of the present heaven and earth **(2 Peter 3:10)**. According to scripture, the arrival of the Day of the Lord and the Lord's arrival are announced by the heavens. The Lord's arrival as a conquering King is a terrible day!

> ***Isaiah 13:10*** *For* **the stars of heaven and the constellations thereof shall not give their light: the sun shall be darkened in his going forth,** *and* **the moon shall not cause her light to shine.**
>
> ***Joel 2:10*** *The earth shall quake before them; the heavens shall tremble:* **the sun and the moon shall be dark,** *and* **the stars shall withdraw their shining**:

*Joel 2:31 The sun shall be turned into darkness, and the moon into blood, **before the great and the terrible day of the LORD come**.*

*Joel 3:15 The sun and the moon shall be darkened, and **the stars shall withdraw their shining**.*

The recent "blood moon" phenomenon (or fiasco)[1] has happened, at least in part, because of a misunderstanding concerning the timing of the Day of the Lord. However, a good analogy to help visualize the scriptural series of events would be to consider what has been characterized as the "domino effect." In other words, the occurrence of one event triggers and sets in motion the next event which will, in turn, set in motion the event which follows it.

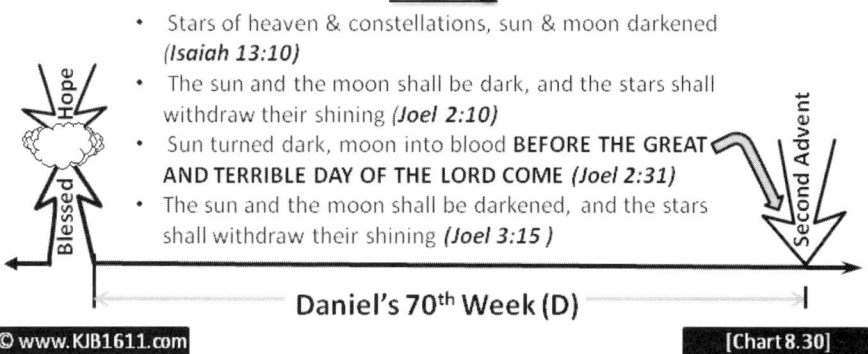

For instance, we are told that the sun and moon will go dark and the stars will fall from heaven. Included in this or added to it will be the shaking of the powers of the heavens.

Most likely resulting from these dramatic changes to the sun and moon, the sea and its waves will roar. It is important to realize that the moon stabilizes the earth's axial tilt and both the sun and moon affect the solar and lunar tides. Any change in the sun and moon can cause

---

[1] The moon will be turned into blood at the sixth seal **(Revelation 6:12)**; this phenomenon did not take place on 4/15/14, 10/8/14, 4/4/15, or 9/28/15, nor will it take place until sometime after the midpoint of Daniel's Seventieth Week (to date no earlier than the year 2021).

unpredictable and catastrophic results. For instance, multiple worldwide tsunamis caused by the changes described in the text may only be the tip of the iceberg.

Understandably, these events cause great apprehension in the minds and hearts of the earth's inhabitants. The book of Luke says that the fear will be so severe that men's hearts will fail them. The book of Revelation points out that the emotional and mental anguish will cause men to say to the mountains and rocks, *"Fall on us, and hide us from the face of him that sitteth on the throne, and from the wrath of the Lamb"* **(Revelation 6:16)**.

(2) The Sign of the Son of Man *(Matthew 24:30)*

When the world turns pitch black, earth's inhabitants will not expect what is about to take place, nor how drastically things will soon change. The Day of the Lord will be introduced with the sun and moon being darkened, but this phenomenon of darkness is only temporary. Upon Christ's return, things instantaneously swing to the opposite end of the spectrum with the normal light multiplied seven times brighter.

> **Isaiah 30:26** Moreover **the light of the moon shall be as the light of the sun,** and **the light of the sun shall be sevenfold, as the light of seven days,** *in the day that the LORD bindeth up the breach of his people, and healeth the stroke of their wound.*

This overpowering, brilliant light will shine forth sometime following the piercing darkness and blackening of the heavens. This bright light heralds the coming of the Son of Man from heaven's glory. Imagine when the light of the moon becomes as the sun in its normal strength and the sun shines *"sevenfold, as the light of seven days."*

A good analogy involves how some sports teams, especially in basketball, introduce their star athletes. The arena becomes darkened until a spotlight suddenly appears pointing out the superstar as his name is announced over the loudspeakers. Now multiply this event by the billions to imagine the introduction of the Son of Man in all His glory. The book of Matthew refers to this as *"the sign of the Son of man."*

> **Matthew 24:30** And **then shall appear the sign of the Son of man in heaven**: *and then shall all the tribes of the earth mourn, and they shall see the Son of man coming in the clouds of heaven with power and great glory.*

To the human eye, using human reasoning, these events might seem simultaneous; yet, in reality, the following sequence seems to take place.

- the brightness of the sun will be magnified seven times *(Isaiah 30:26)*;
- the Son of Man appears *(Mark 13:26; Luke 21:27)*;
- all the tribes of the earth mourn *(Matthew 24:30)*;
- a great trumpet will sound *(Matthew 24:31)*;
- Christ sends His angels to gather the elect for protection *(Matthew 24:31)*;
- Christ comes to earth from heaven to execute judgment upon the enemies of Israel *(Revelation 19:11-13, 15-16)*;
- the armies which were in heaven follow Christ to earth *(Revelation 19:14)*; and
- an angel stands in the sun, inviting the fowls of the air to gather for the supper of the great God *(Revelation 19:17-18)*.

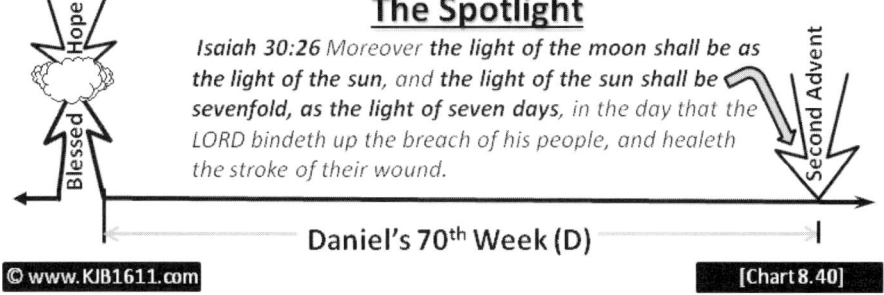

Now, let's consider each of these elements in further detail within their various contexts.

(a) The brightness of the sun is magnified seven times.

> *Isaiah 30:26 Moreover **the light of the moon shall be as the light of the sun**, and **the light of the sun shall be sevenfold, as the light of seven days**, in the day that the LORD bindeth up the breach of his people, and healeth the stroke of their wound.*

(b) The Son of Man appears.

> *Mark 13:26 And **then shall they see the Son of man coming in the clouds** with great power and glory.*

> *Luke 21:27 And **then shall they see the Son of man coming in a cloud** with power and great glory.*

(c) All the tribes of the earth mourn.

(d) A great trumpet sounds.

(e) Christ sends His angels to gather the elect for protection.

> *Matthew 24:30 And **then shall appear the sign of the Son of man in heaven: and then shall all the tribes of the earth mourn**, and they shall see the Son of man coming in the clouds of heaven with power and great glory. 31 And **he shall send his angels with a great sound of a trumpet, and they shall gather together his elect** from the four winds, from one end of heaven to the other.*

(f) Christ leaves heaven and comes to earth to execute judgment upon the enemies of Israel.

(g) The armies which were in heaven follow Christ to earth.

(h) An angel stands in the sun, inviting the fowls of the air to gather for the supper of the great God.

> *Revelation 19:11 And **I saw heaven opened, and behold a white horse; and he that sat upon him** was **called Faithful and True, and in righteousness he doth judge and make war**. 12 His eyes were as a flame of fire, and on his head were many crowns; and he had a name written, that no man knew, but he himself. 13 And he was clothed with a vesture dipped in blood: and his name is called The Word of God. 14 And **the armies which were in heaven followed him** upon white horses, clothed in fine linen, white and clean. 15 And out of his mouth goeth a sharp sword, that with it he should smite the nations: and he shall rule them with a rod of iron: and he treadeth the winepress of the fierceness and wrath of Almighty God. 16 And he hath on his vesture and on his thigh a name written, KING OF KINGS, AND LORD OF LORDS. 17 And **I saw an angel standing in the sun; and he cried with a loud voice, saying to all the fowls that fly in the midst of heaven, Come and gather yourselves together***

unto the supper of the great God; 18 *That ye may eat the flesh of kings, and the flesh of captains, and the flesh of mighty men, and the flesh of horses, and of them that sit on them, and the flesh of all men, both free and bond, both small and great.*

The Angels & the Trumpet

Matthew 24:31 And *he shall send his angels* with *a great sound of a trumpet*, *and they shall gather together his elect from the four winds, from one end of heaven to the other.*

[Chart 8.50]

The scripture, when considered as a whole, ties the sequence of events together! Consider what happens when the light of the sun instantaneously shines as seven days at once. This presumably results in an intense heat upon the earth and its inhabitants. Isaiah prophesied such an event.

> *Isaiah 30:26 Moreover **the light of the moon shall be as the light of the sun**, and **the light of the sun shall be sevenfold, as the light of seven days**, in the day that the LORD bindeth up the breach of his people, and healeth the stroke of their wound.*

Many Bible teachers liken the results of this phenomenon to some man-made calamity like a nuclear bomb. God can use man's devices—but He certainly does not find this necessary! Paul points to the likely cause of this calamity as the Lord's coming in vengeance. The Bible says that Christ will come *"In flaming fire taking vengeance on them that know not God."*

> *2 Thessalonians 1:7 the Lord Jesus shall be revealed from heaven with his might angels, 8 **In flaming fire taking vengeance on them that know not God**, and that obey not the gospel of our Lord Jesus Christ:*

Christ with His Armies

***Revelation 19:11** And **I saw heaven opened**, and behold a white horse; and he that sat upon him was called Faithful and True, and in righteousness he doth judge and make war.*

Time for War

- Christ comes to earth from Heaven to execute judgment upon the enemies of Israel *(Revelation 19:11-13, 15-16)*;
- The armies which were in Heaven follow Christ to earth *(Revelation 19:14)*; and
- An angel stands in the sun, inviting the fowls of the air to gather for the supper of the great God *(Revelation 19:17-18)*.

Daniel's 70th Week (D)

[Chart 8.60]

This brightness of Christ's Second Coming will even cause the horses of God's enemies to be smitten *"with astonishment ... and ... with blindness" (Zechariah 12:4)*.

> ***Zechariah 12:4** In that day, saith the LORD, **I will smite every horse with astonishment, and his rider with madness**: and I will open mine eyes upon the house of Judah, **and will smite every horse of the people with blindness**.*

Notice that the rider will also be smitten with *"madness."* The consuming heat will cause people's flesh, eyes, and tongues to consume away. A nuclear detonation? A natural calamity? Global warming? Maybe so on the last one, but it is not happening as a result of CO_2 emissions caused by man or by beast.

> ***Zechariah 14:12** And this shall be the plague wherewith the LORD will smite all the people that have fought against Jerusalem; **Their flesh shall consume away while they stand upon their feet, and their eyes shall consume away in their holes, and their tongue shall consume away in their mouth**.*

Although many prophetic teachers have said that this description equates to the results of a nuclear holocaust, God certainly does not need some man-made calamity because He controls all. He can simply multiply earth's natural resources to levels beyond human comprehension and certainly beyond man's endurance. Yet, during this time, similar to Israel's time in Egypt, God supernaturally protects the Jews. **We have many examples how easy this task can be performed by the Lord.** For instance, God provided light for the Israelites while covering the Egyptians with darkness *(Exodus 10:21-23)*. In the future, He can certainly "turn up the heat" on His enemies while keeping His people completely protected.

The Lord's Vengeance

Isaiah 30:26 Moreover *the light of the moon shall be as the light of the sun, and the light of the sun shall be sevenfold, as the light of seven days.*

The Revelation

- Lord Jesus and His mighty angels revealed in flaming fire taking vengeance *(2 Thessalonians 1:7-8)*,
- Smites every horse with astonishment and rider with madness *(Zechariah 12:4)*, and
- Their flesh consumed away while they stand upon their feet, and their eyes consumed away in their holes, and their tongue consumed away in their mouth *(Zechariah 14:12).*

Daniel's 70th Week (D)

[Chart 8.70]

During this future event, God will shield His people on earth from the brightness while destroying His enemies. Those enemies not immediately destroyed by the brightness of Christ's coming will be gathered by the armies that have followed the King of kings to earth.

> *Joel 2:1 Blow ye the trumpet in Zion, and sound an alarm in my holy mountain:* **let all the inhabitants of the land tremble: for the day of the LORD cometh***, for it is nigh at hand; 2 A day of* **darkness** *and of* **gloominess***, a day of* **clouds** *and of* **thick darkness***, as the morning spread upon the mountains:* **a great people** *and a strong; there hath not been ever the like, neither shall be any more after it, even to the years of many generations. 3* **A fire devoureth before them; and behind them a flame burneth:** *the land is as the garden of Eden before them, and* **behind them a desolate wilderness***; yea, and nothing shall escape them. 4 The appearance of them is as the appearance of horses; and as horsemen, so shall they run. 5 Like the noise of chariots on the tops of mountains shall they leap, like the*

*noise of a flame **of** fire that devoureth the stubble, as a strong people set in battle array. 6 **Before their face the people shall be much pained: all faces shall gather blackness.** 7 They shall run like mighty men; they shall climb the wall like men of war; and they shall march every one on his ways, and they shall not break their ranks: 8 Neither shall one thrust another; they shall walk every one in his path: and when they fall upon the sword, they shall not be wounded. 9 They shall run to and fro in the city; they shall run upon the wall, they shall climb up upon the houses; they shall enter in at the windows like a thief. 10 The earth shall quake before them; the heavens shall tremble: **the sun and the moon shall be dark, and the stars shall withdraw their shining:** 11 And the LORD shall utter his voice before **his army:** for his camp is very great: for he is strong that executeth his word: **for the day of the LORD is great and very terrible;** and who can abide it?*

While Christ's coming is a fearful time for the enemies of the Lord, it serves as a time of great rejoicing and relief for the believing Jews. The heads that once hung down in shame will be lifted up as the Jews finally witness the arrival of their long awaited physical redemption. God's enemies will scatter through the intense suffering while the Jews will be gathered with the expectation of redemption, peace, and safety.

Luke 21:28 *And **when these things begin to come to pass,** then look up, and **lift up your heads; for your redemption draweth nigh**.*

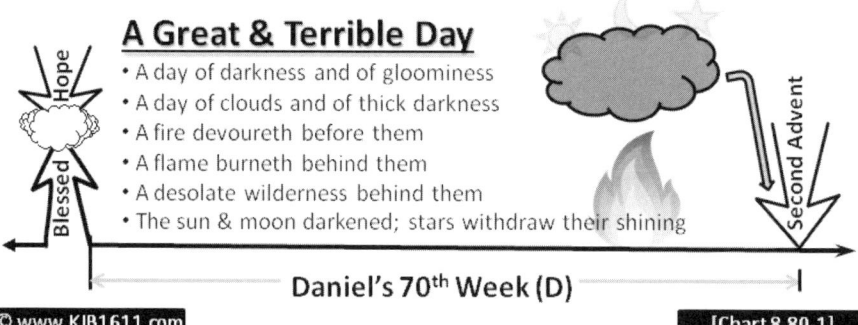

The Day of the Lord Cometh

Joel 2:1 Blow ye the trumpet in Zion, and sound an alarm in my holy mountain: let all the inhabitants of the land tremble: for the day of the LORD cometh, for it is nigh at hand;

A Great & Terrible Day
- A day of darkness and of gloominess
- A day of clouds and of thick darkness
- A fire devoureth before them
- A flame burneth behind them
- A desolate wilderness behind them
- The sun & moon darkened; stars withdraw their shining

Daniel's 70th Week (D)

[Chart 8.80-1]

Joel 2:31 The sun shall be turned into darkness, and the moon into blood, before the great and the terrible day of the LORD come. 32 And it shall come to pass, that whosoever shall call on the name of the LORD shall be delivered: for in mount Zion and in Jerusalem shall be deliverance, as the LORD hath said, and in the remnant whom the LORD shall call.

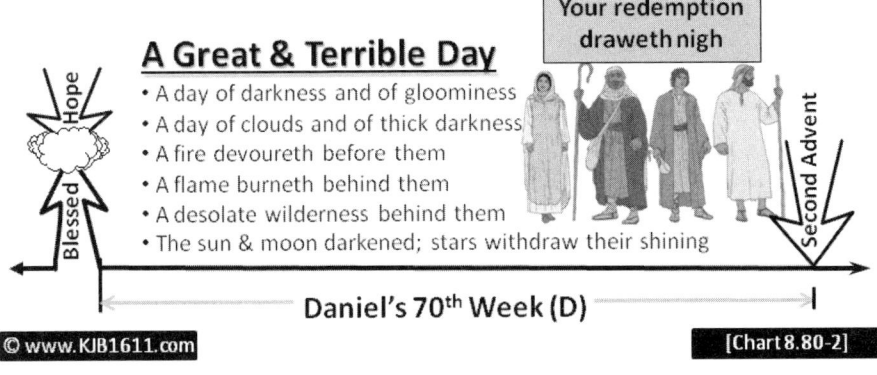

(3) The Sending of Christ's Angels *(Matthew 24:31)*

This next issue reveals the importance of every word of scripture. Those who insist that the Church will enter Daniel's Seventieth Week fail to distinguish certain key elements and differences between two major events. Most confusion can be eliminated by simply noticing the differences between Christ's return for the Church before the beginning of Daniel's Seventieth Week and His return for the Jewish remnant toward the end of that period.

Nowhere in any of Paul's writings where he refers to the Rapture is there any indication of angels being sent to gather God's children. Instead, all believers will be brought up to meet the Lord Jesus in the clouds.

*1 Thessalonians 4:16 For the Lord **himself shall descend from heaven** with a shout, with the voice of the archangel, and with the trump of God: and the dead in Christ shall rise first:*

The Lord meets all believers in the clouds to take the Church home to heaven where we (the believers) remain with Christ until His Second Advent. This is not the scenario presented throughout the Old Testament or the Gospels when describing Christ's return at the close of Jacob's Trouble to establish a kingdom for the Jews. Instead of Christ HIMSELF gathering at the Second Coming, the Bible says that Christ sends His angels to gather the elect (believing Israel) to protect them from the onslaught of judgment proceeding from the Saviour. In fact, the Bible is clear that Christ is leading His armies into battle, not meeting with believers in the clouds at this time *(Revelation 19:11, 14)*. This is likely the reason He must send His angels ahead of Him.

> ***Matthew 24:31** And **he shall send his angels** with a great sound of a trumpet, and **they shall gather together his elect** from the four winds, from one end of heaven to the other.*

Unfortunately, many Bible teachers and students fail to grasp three of the key components of this passage concerning Christ's Second Coming: (1) the identity of the elect, (2) the meaning of the four winds, and (3) the heaven referred to within the context. It has already been demonstrated in this work that the elect of Matthew chapter 24 consist of believing Israel *(Isaiah 45:4)*. Now, the four winds and heaven must be defined in light of the context and other correlating scriptures.

If the angels are going to gather the elect from the four winds, it would make sense that the elect first had to be scattered into the four winds. The Bible repeatedly mentions this scattering of the Jews toward all the winds. Here are four examples:

Notice that the Bible clearly says that God scattered His people into and toward all the winds.

> ***Ezekiel 5:10b** the whole remnant of thee will I **scatter into all the winds**.*

> ***Ezekiel 17:21** And all his fugitives with all his bands shall fall by the sword, and they that remain shall be **scattered toward all winds**: and ye shall know that I the LORD have spoken it.*

The scattering into all winds is defined as the utmost corners of the earth.

*Jeremiah 49:32 And their camels shall be a booty, and the multitude of their cattle a spoil: and **I will scatter into all winds them that are in the utmost corners**; and I will bring their calamity from all sides thereof, saith the LORD.*

The four winds are mentioned in conjunction with the four quarters of heaven.

*Jeremiah 49:36 And upon Elam will I bring **the four winds from the four quarters of heaven, and will scatter them toward all those winds**; and there shall be no nation whither the outcasts of Elam shall not come.*

Those whom God scattered toward the four winds will now be gathered by the angels sent ahead of Christ and His armies. Any diligent Bible student can recognize that these four winds cover the earth and are associated only to the first heaven[2] where the winds blow. John, in the book of Revelation, provides additional confirmation in **Revelation 7:1** when he prophetically wrote of another event further clarifying the

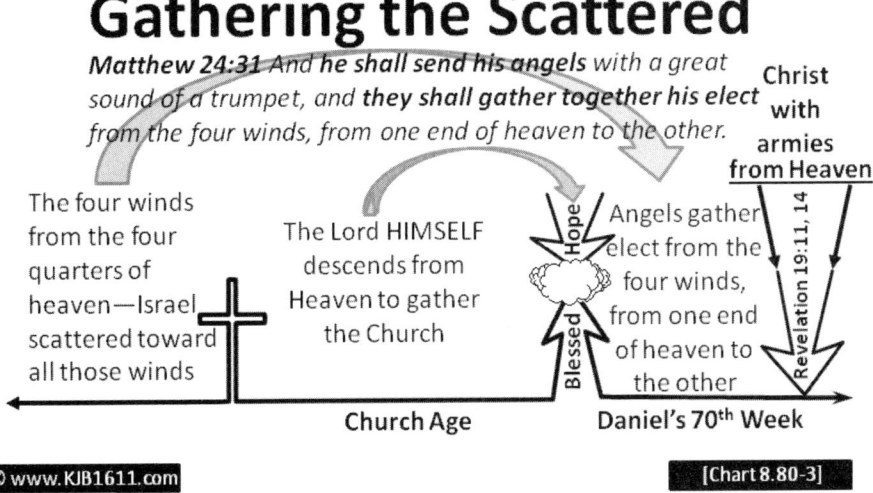

---

[2] The first heaven is the atmospheric heaven where the birds fly, referred to as the *"open firmament of heaven" (Genesis 1:20)*. The second heaven is the starry heaven that we call outer space and is referred to as the *"firmament of the heaven" (Genesis 1:14)*. The third heaven is where God dwells and is referred to as *"heaven" (Genesis 1:1)* or the *"heaven of heavens" (Deuteronomy 10:14)*.

four winds during Daniel's Seventieth Week: *"I saw four angels standing on the **four corners of the earth**, holding the **four winds of the earth**."*

Again, the Lord will gather His elect (Israel) from over the entire earth—*from the four winds, from one end of heaven to the other.* Contextually, neither the second heaven nor the third Heaven (of God's abode) is mentioned as a place of gathering during the Second Coming.

Some Post-tribulationists assume that the mere mention of *heaven* means the third Heaven (God's abode); however, the context remains consistent since the passage refers not to the Heaven of God's abode but to the first heaven where the *winds* blow **(1 Kings 18:45** – see below; also **Psalm 78:26; Daniel 7:2; Daniel 8:8; Daniel 11:4)**.

> *1 Kings 18:45 And it came to pass in the mean while, that **the heaven was black with clouds and wind**, and there was a great rain. And Ahab rode, and went to Jezreel.*

Other passages clearly associate the four winds with the first heaven. For example: *"I bring the four winds from the four quarters of heaven"* **(Jeremiah 49:36)** and *"the four winds of the heaven"* **(Zechariah 2:6)**. In each case, the winds and the heaven refer to the first heaven and never the *"third Heaven"* of God's abode **(2 Corinthians 12:2)** where the Church will have resided for around seven years. Read the passage again with these points in mind.

> ***Matthew 24:31** And **he shall send his angels** with a great sound of a trumpet, and they shall **gather together his elect from the four winds, from one end of heaven to the other.***

Those who had been scattered by God all over the earth will then be gathered by His angels just prior to Christ and His armies arriving to the earth! (Note: The Rapture of the Church at the end of this present age, like many other Church Age truths, was revealed years later through the apostle Paul.) Those persecuted will then be protected and preserved! Those accused and attacked by Satan will be redeemed and secured in Jesus! Jacob's testimony that once was *"all these things are against me"* **(Genesis 42:36)** will now become *"If God be for us, who can be against us?"* **(Romans 8:31)**. The words of David's psalms will ring true as the renewed people of God welcome the victory offered in Christ.

> ***Psalm 124:1** If it had not been the LORD who was on our side, **now may Israel say**; 2 If it had not been **the LORD who was on our side**,*

when men rose up against us: 3 *Then they had swallowed us up quick, when their wrath was kindled against us:* 4 *Then the waters had overwhelmed us, the stream had gone over our soul:* 5 *Then the proud waters had gone over our soul.* 6 **Blessed be the LORD,** *who hath not given us as a prey to their teeth.* 7 *Our soul is escaped as a bird out of the snare of the fowlers: the snare is broken, and* **we are escaped.** 8 **Our help is in the name of the LORD,** *who made heaven and earth.*

Psalm 129:1 *Many a time have they afflicted me from my youth,* **may Israel now say:** 2 *Many a time have they afflicted me from my youth: yet* **they have not prevailed against me.** 3 *The plowers plowed upon my back: they made long their furrows.* 4 *The LORD is righteous: he hath cut asunder the cords of the wicked.* 5 *Let them all be confounded and turned back that hate Zion.* 6 *Let them be as the grass upon the housetops, which withereth afore it groweth up:* 7 *Wherewith the mower filleth not his hand; nor he that bindeth sheaves his bosom.* 8 *Neither do they which go by say,* **The blessing of the LORD be upon you: we bless you in the name of the LORD.**

Conclusion

Matthew, at the time of his writing, neither knew of nor wrote of the New Testament Church's removal from the earth. Paul clearly distinguished between the Church's departure and the gathering of the Second Advent by pointing out that the Lord HIMSELF will come and get His Church but send His angels at the Second Advent while He leads His armies to earth. If this gathering at the Rapture is the same as Matthew chapter 24, why no mention by Paul of the armies following the Lord **(Revelation 19:14)**?

There is no general **catching up** in the days approaching the Second Advent. It is simply not a rapture at all. This is why the Lord sends His angels to *gather* together His elect for supernatural protection upon the earth. This protection takes place toward the end of Daniel's Seventieth Week and almost simultaneously with His return in vengeance on the Day of the Lord.

The Lord will gather His elect (Israel) from all the earth—*from the four winds, from one end of heaven to the other.* This passage is in no way synonymous with the Rapture of First Thessalonians chapter 4. In fact, there is no Rapture or catching away FROM the earth in **Matthew 24:31**.

After the Tribulation?

Before closing this chapter, two more points need additional clarification: when does "the Tribulation" end and what is meant by *great* tribulation? Many Post-tribulation pontificators point to the passage from Matthew that says *"after the tribulation"* and incorrectly assume that this is the point where "the Tribulation" ends and the Rapture takes place. Again, context determines the meaning of any passage or phrase and every word of God's word is vital!

What saith the scripture IN CONTEXT? Read the two verses from Matthew and Mark paying close attention to the bold wording and see if you can detect the key words which clue the reader into the correct context. HINT: *"of those days"* in Matthew and *"that"* in Mark change the entire context and meaning from what is generally taught by those wanting the Church to go through Daniel's Seventieth Week.

__Matthew 24:29 Immediately after the tribulation of those days__ shall the sun be darkened, and the moon shall not give her light, and the stars shall fall from heaven, and the powers of the heavens shall be shaken:

__Mark 13:24__ But in those days, __after that tribulation,__ the sun shall be darkened, and the moon shall not give her light,

Neither passage is intended to indicate that every event before these verses is the so-called Tribulation period and these two verses serve as the terminus of "the Tribulation." Instead, the verses simply state in Matthew that the sun and moon go dark "after the tribulation of THOSE DAYS," referring to the tribulation mentioned in verses 4-28. Mark says the same thing: the sun and the moon go dark "after THAT tribulation," which refers to the suffering mentioned in verses 5-23.

This incorrect application of the term "THE TRIBULATION" is the primary reason that true Bible believers should be very careful in their terminology. It is best always to be sure to use Bible terminology by referring to the so-called Tribulation as Daniel's Seventieth Week. Neither Matthew nor Mark says that this period ends at either of these verses with the sun and moon going dark *(Isaiah 13:10; Ezekiel 32:7; Joel 2:10; Joel 2:31; Joel 3:15; Acts 2:20; Revelation 6:12).*

The Tribulation?

Matthew 24:29 Immediately after the tribulation of those days shall the sun be darkened, and the moon shall not give her light, and the stars shall fall from heaven, and the powers of the heavens shall be shaken:

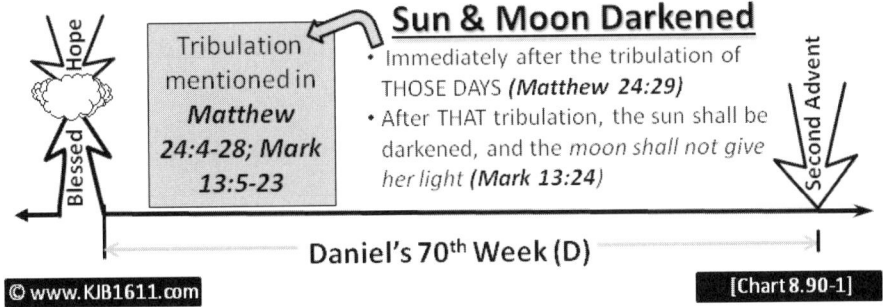

The Great Tribulation?

This misapplication of truth also applies to those who inadvertently change the Bible to refer to the second half of the Daniel's Seventieth Week as THE GREAT TRIBULATION. Nowhere in the Bible is this designation used. The problem arises when some who pervert God's word want to use this designation to justify their dogmas and traditions. Read the three instances in the full verse context and you will see that none of them uses the designation to refer to the second half of the Daniel's Seventieth Week.

*Matthew 24:21 For **then shall be great tribulation**, such as was not since the beginning of the world to this time, no, nor ever shall be.*

*Revelation 2:22 Behold, I will cast her into a bed, and them that commit adultery with her into **great tribulation**, except they repent of their deeds.*

*Revelation 7:14 And I said unto him, Sir, thou knowest. And he said to me, These are they which **came out of great tribulation**, and have washed their robes, and made them white in the blood of the Lamb.*

In each passage, "great" is simply used as an adjective to describe the type of tribulation that people will suffer during Daniel's Seventieth Week. It will be great or intense. It answers the question of how bad the tribulation or suffering will turn out to be. It is described as "*great* tribulation." This again shows why we should use Bible terminology as often as possible and refer to "the Tribulation period" as Daniel's Seventieth Week and not necessarily THE TRIBULATION nor the GREAT TRIBULATION period. These designations only cause confusion since Christians and the Jews have always suffered some level of *tribulation* throughout man's 6,000 year history upon the earth.

> **John 16:33** *These things I have spoken unto you, that in me ye might have peace.* **In the world ye shall have tribulation**: *but be of good cheer; I have overcome the world.*

> **Romans 12:12** *Rejoicing in hope;* **patient in tribulation**; *continuing instant in prayer;*

> **2 Corinthians 1:4** **Who comforteth us in all our tribulation**, *that we may be able to comfort them which are in any trouble, by the comfort wherewith we ourselves are comforted of God.*

Will Christians suffer tribulation? Absolutely! Yet, we will not be here after the Rapture during Daniel's Seventieth Week to experience any part of the escalating tribulation brought upon the world's inhabitants.

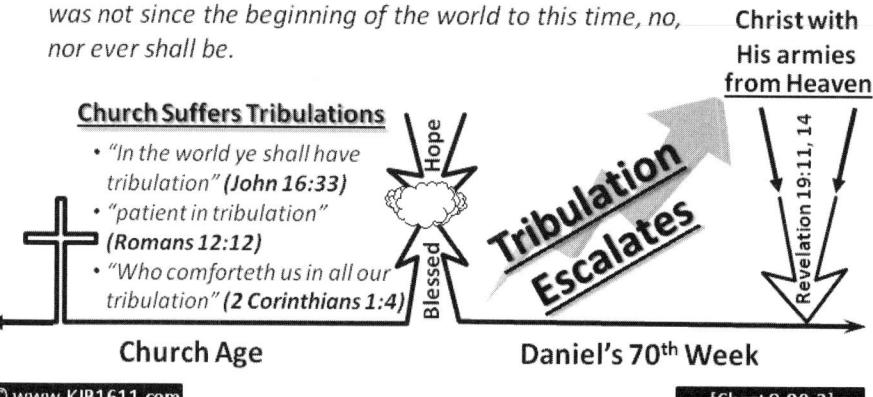

9

The Parable of the Fig Tree

(Matthew 24:32-36)

Immediately following the Lord's teaching on the Second Advent *(Matthew 24:27-31)*, He admonished the apostles to *"Now learn a parable" (Matthew 24:32; Mark 13:28)*. He transitioned into teaching on a parable for good reason. Before exploring the details of the fig tree parable, some background information about parables should prove beneficial.

The word of God incorporates the word *parable* and its plural form *parables* sixty-five times. Each instance involves either a direct or an indirect association to the Jewish people. According to the testimony of scripture found in the Psalms, *parables* are stories presenting *"dark sayings."* Jesus further defined *dark sayings* as *"things which have been kept secret from the foundation of the world."*

> **Psalm 49:4** *I will incline mine ear to a **parable**: I will open my **dark saying** upon the harp.*

> **Psalm 78:2** *I will open my mouth in a **parable**: I will utter **dark sayings** of old:*

> **Matthew 13:35** *That it might be fulfilled which was spoken by the prophet, saying, I will open my mouth in **parables**; I will utter **things which have been kept secret from the foundation of the world**.*

Parables are dark sayings! Even today, when an individual does not know or understand certain details or information, it is said that he remains *in the dark*. There is no doubt that parables present truths cloaked in various layers or depths of meaning. As such, many people remain ignorant as to the true purpose of God incorporating parables within scripture.

When the Lord was asked why He used parables to speak **to the masses**, He confirmed that parables allowed His true disciples to understand and grasp the truth. In turn, the parables hid the deeper truths from those who did not truly love and follow the Saviour. Even today, many people struggle with understanding and correctly interpreting the parables because these dark sayings are not open to them. Notice the distinction given between the two groups ("you" versus "them").

*Matthew 13:10 And the disciples came, and said unto him, **Why speakest thou unto them in parables?** 11 He answered and said unto them, **Because it is given unto you to know the mysteries of the kingdom of heaven, but to them it is not given.** 12 For whosoever hath, to him shall be given, and he shall have more abundance: but whosoever hath not, from him shall be taken away even that he hath. 13 **Therefore speak I to them in parables: because they seeing see not; and hearing they hear not, neither do they understand.***

Christ's parables were intended to keep the mysteries of the kingdom a secret **(Mark 4:11; Luke 8:10)**. In a sense, parables allowed the Lord and His followers to distinguish between His true disciples and those who were unbelieving or those who merely sought to entrap Him in His own words. For this reason, the four Gospels contain nearly three fourths of parables in scripture (forty-seven of the sixty-five usages). The Lord frequently incorporated this style of teaching during His earthly ministry.

The parable under consideration—the parable of the fig tree—was the first of several parables mentioned in the Olivet Discourse (Matthew chapter 24, Mark chapter 13, and Luke chapter 21). Based upon its location, context, and content, this parable was obviously intended to teach on Israel's last days and the Lord's subsequent Second Coming.

The Purpose of the Parable

In many ways, a man's words serve as the window to his heart. The words spoken many times reveal a man's thoughts and feelings along with his purpose for speaking those words. Each of the three Synoptic Gospel passages express the purpose for Jesus speaking the parable of the fig tree. Twice within the parable, the word *"know"* occurs indicating that Christ spoke this parable so that His disciples/apostles might *know* some things. In two of those same passages (Matthew and Mark), the Lord admonished His followers to *"now learn."*

> **Matthew 24:32 Now learn** *a parable of the fig tree; When his branch is yet tender, and putteth forth leaves, ye* **know** *that summer is nigh: 33 So likewise ye, when ye shall see all these things,* **know** *that it is near, even at the doors.*

> **Mark 13:28 Now learn** *a parable of the fig tree; When her branch is yet tender, and putteth forth leaves, ye* **know** *that summer is near: 29 So ye in like manner, when ye shall see these things come to pass,* **know** *that it is nigh, even at the doors.*

> **Luke 21:29** *And he spake to them a parable; Behold the fig tree, and all the trees; 30 When they now shoot forth,* **ye see and know** *of your own selves that summer is now nigh at hand. 31 So likewise ye, when ye see these things come to pass,* **know ye that the kingdom of God is nigh at hand.**

The parables incorporate one of the most fundamental teaching tools: taking a person from what he *knows* in order to teach what he does not know. This teaching method has been used for millennia to help grasp truths otherwise unattainable. This is why Bible parables always take the hearer (or reader) from a truth he presently understands to something less familiar but in need of comprehension. This tool of taking someone from the known to the unknown is a primary characteristic of any good teacher.

In this case, the teacher (Jesus) begins with what the student knows and understands (the development of the fig tree) to lead the student to expand his understanding into the new knowledge (concerning elements associated to the timing of His coming kingdom).

Understandably, the most important truth in this method is the end or intended application. The record of Christ's teachings presents many wonderful examples of Him using this technique to teach His audiences to grasp heavenly truths. The Bible points out that if any man failed to grasp the earthly truths, he certainly had no opportunity to appreciate that which was heavenly or spiritual. One such example is the Lord's dialogue with Nicodemus. This man was someone who was a recognized master of spiritual matters in Israel.

> ***John 3:10** Jesus answered and said unto him, Art thou **a master of Israel**, and knowest not these things? 11 Verily, verily, I say unto thee, We speak that we do know, and testify that we have seen; and ye receive not our witness. 12 If I have told you **earthly things**, and ye believe not, how shall ye believe, if I tell you of **heavenly things?***

Of course, we know that one of the earthly truths presented to the Jewish disciples in our passage incorporated the seasons of the fig tree. This concept would be a very familiar element to the Jews because the fig tree held a prominent place since the time of the garden in Eden. It all began after the fall of man when Adam and Eve stripped a fig tree of some leaves in hopes of covering their nakedness *(Genesis 3:7)*.

The fig tree was also indicative of the apparent blessings found within the land of Canaan. Prior to conquering the land, the spies were sent in to examine the land. In order to demonstrate the land's value, they chose to gather a sampling of figs from a fig tree which would demonstrate God's goodness upon the land of promise *(Numbers 13:23)*. In fact, when describing that land, the Bible said that it was *"A land of ... fig trees" **(Deuteronomy 8:8)***. No doubt the disciples/apostles were keenly aware of the fig tree's historical significance. This is likely why Jesus chose the fig tree to make an application of such prophetic significance.

The Lord pointed the disciples' attention to the expected seasonal changes of the fig tree. He emphasized that watching the changes in the fig tree should indicate to the Jewish people that summer was near. He reminded them that when they saw the fig tree's branches become tender and shoot forth leaves, then they knew that summer was near at hand.

> ***Matthew 24:32** Now learn a parable of the fig tree; **When his branch is yet tender, and putteth forth leaves, ye know that summer is nigh:***

> ***Mark 13:28** Now learn a parable of the fig tree; **When her branch is yet tender, and putteth forth leaves, ye know that summer is near:***

> ***Luke 21:29** And he spake to them a parable; **Behold the fig tree**, and all the trees; 30 **When they now shoot forth, ye see and know of your own selves that summer is now nigh at hand.***

The Lord used the comparison from this earthly application concerning the fig tree to illustrate the return of summer and the deeper spiritual truth of the nearness of His return. In all three Synoptic Gospels, the Lord used words and phrases to emphasize the correlation. Two examples are His use of *"likewise"* and *"in like manner."*

> **Matthew 24:33** *So **likewise ye, when ye shall see all these things**, know that it [the Kingdom of God] **is near, even at the doors.***

> **Mark 13:29** *So ye **in like manner, when ye shall see these things come to pass**, know that it [the Kingdom of God] **is nigh, even at the doors.***

> **Luke 21:31** *So **likewise ye, when ye see these things come to pass, know ye that the kingdom of God is nigh at hand.***

The point of the parable was not to instruct the Jews to look for tender branches and new leaves upon fig trees. Instead, the Jews were instructed to look for *"all these things"* **(Matthew 24:33)**, referring to the events previously mentioned from the earlier part of His Olivet Discourse **(Matthew 24:4-31)**. Christ also mentioned some applicable things at the end of Matthew chapter 23. When the Jews recognize all *"these things"* coming to pass, they will know that the Lord's return is imminent, *"even at the doors."* Christ specifically points out that all *"these things"* indicate that the Kingdom of God is very near!

The Jews are told to continually watch for the occurrence of specific events that will help them to recognize the signs of the times. Yet, the Church received no such admonition. The events unfolding prior to the Rapture of the Church will not fulfill these requirements. As the JEWS see these things coming to pass, they will recognize the imminence of Christ's return for the deliverance of *the elect* **(Matthew 24:22, 24)** and the judgment of the unrepentant **(Revelation 9:20; Revelation 16:9, 11)**. Yet, the Church's only indicators of its *last days* are the spiritually perilous times described repeatedly such as in *2 Timothy 3:1-7*.

Additionally, the Church, according to scripture, has been in its *last days* since the Church's inception. Thus, once the return of Christ (at the Rapture) was first revealed, it has always truly been imminent.

> **Hebrews 1:2** *Hath **in these last days** spoken unto us by his Son, whom he hath appointed heir of all things, by whom also he made the worlds;*

Interestingly, the indicators for the Rapture are completely open-ended rather than a defined point of demarcation. For instance, Christians are told that men shall continue to wax *"worse and worse"* which has no ending point.

> ***2 Timothy 3:13*** *But evil men and seducers shall wax **worse and worse**, deceiving, and being deceived.*

Fig Tree Parable

Matthew 24:33 *So likewise ye, when ye shall see all these things, know that it* **[the Kingdom of God]** *is near, even at the doors.*

Church's Last Days
- Perilous times *(2 Timothy 3:1-7)*
- *"in these last days spoken unto us by his Son"* **(Hebrews 1:2)**
- *"depart[ing] from the faith"* **(1 Timothy 4:1)**
- *"evil men and seducers shall wax worse and worse"* **(2 Timothy 3:13)**

Fig Tree Parable
- Timing of His coming kingdom
- Look for *"all these things"* (Matthew 24:33), referring to the events previously mentioned from the earlier part of His Olivet Discourse *(Matthew 24:4-31)*
- Imminence: deliverance of the elect; judgment of unrepentant

Christ with His armies from Heaven — Revelation 19:11, 14

Hope / Blessed

Church Age — **Daniel's 70th Week**

© www.KJB1611.com [Chart 9.10]

How bad will the apostasy get *(2 Thessalonians 2:3)* involving people *"depart*[ing] *from the faith"* *(1 Timothy 4:1)*? When the Lord thinks it has gotten *"worse"* enough, He will fulfill His promise to the Church by catching us up to meet Him in the clouds! Some people question if things have always been really that bad? Paul clearly and repeatedly described the spiritually precarious situations in the early church. For example:

- Paul disassociated himself from the MANY who were perverting the scripture before it was even completely penned *(2 Corinthians 2:17)*.
- Paul warned that after he left the church in Ephesus, grievous wolves would enter in among the believers trying to destroy their faith *(Acts 20:29)*.

- Additionally, Paul warned those Ephesian elders that deceivers would arise from within their midst to draw away disciples to themselves *(Acts 20:30)*.
- Paul even warned of specific men who were overthrowing the faith of believers by teaching falsehoods and blasphemy *(2 Timothy 2:17-18; 1 Timothy 1:20)*.
- Paul felt compelled to commend the Thessalonian believers because they did not treat God's word as simply the words of men, presumably like many other guilty parties *(1 Thessalonians 2:13)*.

Truly, the Church was in the last days since its inception and has only been getting worse. Paul anticipated the Lord's imminent return. In fact, Paul incorporated the self-inclusive pronoun of "we" repeatedly including himself with those who could be alive at Christ's return for His Church *(1 Thessalonians 4:15, 17)*. That's imminence! This concept is completely contrary to what Jesus taught His disciples during the Olivet Discourse.

The Misinterpretation of Replacement "Theology"

The Jews' hope and their understanding concerning Christ's coming and their association to His earthly kingdom were not merely resulting from the fig tree application. Their hope in Christ's return to deliver them and to establish His 1,000-year reign on earth was based upon the full context of His statements here, as well as, the truths found throughout scripture. That being said, there is an interesting point that deserves special mention.

Obviously, there was never any compelling need for Christ to emphasize the trueness of His words to His disciples. Yet, as always, He carefully chose His every word. In this case, He chose the word *"verily"* to emphasize the particular promises associated with what He was about to reveal.

Matthew 24:34 Verily I say unto you …

Mark 13:30 Verily I say unto you …

Luke 21:32 Verily I say unto you …

Verily means *"in truth; in fact; certainly; with great confidence."* Christ's emphatic remark seems predictive. He knew that His words and solemn promises to Israel would be called into question, even by believers today. In fact, Bible teachers have been increasingly misinterpreting the accurate application of Christ's promises. This particularly applies to the *timing* of the fulfillment of Christ's prophetic utterances. Most of these misinterpreters simply do not distinguish between the three primary people groups—Jews, Gentiles, Church of God **(1 Corinthians 10:32)**.

Furthermore, the teachers through their incorrect application cause Christ's words to become confusing **(1 Corinthian 14:33)**. Some even suggest that *"these things"* took place in AD 70 when Jerusalem was ransacked by the Roman general Vespasian. Yet, the Lord intended His prophetic pronouncements to serve for a time even yet future rather than for man to relegate them to any historical application.[1] One of the primary guides to correct application is found early in the chapter when the disciples asked about the application of His pronouncements. *"Tell us, when shall these things be? and what shall be the sign of thy coming, and **of the end of the world?"** (Matthew 24:3)*.

In order for the words of Christ to have applied to and been fulfilled in the lives of the audience to which He spoke, Christ would have had to return in their lifetimes and establish His millennial, earthly kingdom. That would mean Christ's kingdom has been ongoing for nearly twice as long as He prophesied or the new heaven and earth are now 1,000 years old and God's promises of restoration have simply failed. Additionally, that would mean that we are either living in an extended millennial kingdom period or sometime after the 1,000-year kingdom. Thankfully, this present sin-sick world is not our eternal hope. Our enjoyment of Christ's kingdom and the new heaven and earth remain yet future.

The Jews will in the future endure the difficult times chronicled in Matthew chapter 24 and yet will, in the end, enjoy Christ's victorious deliverance. Those future truths that may seem less significant to Church Age Christians will be the great truths to the Jews living during Daniel's

---

[1] Replacement Theologians fall flat on their faulty foundation by misapplication of Christ's reference to "this generation." They relegate this reference to a single generation and apply it to the generation of people alive when Christ walked the earth rather than prophetically applying these truths as Christ intended. On the opposite spectrum, another error is taught by those who split Daniel's Seventieth Week into two periods interrupted by the Church Age. However, Daniel splits the full Seventy Weeks of years into three sections: sixty-two weeks, seven weeks and one week (of years) and the Seventieth Week into only one section.

Seventieth Week. If they live to see the signs of the times, they too will live to see the coming Christ (barring their martyrdom at the hands of the Antichrist). The Lord so strongly guaranteed the outcome of these truths that He staked His word upon the certainties of their fulfillment. Although heaven and earth will one day be a distant memory, Christ gave His solemn word that His prophecies will all come to pass. As He returns to earth, He will also destroy the wicked and adulterous generation that has plagued God's people and creation for so long.

***Matthew 24:35** Heaven and earth shall pass away, but **my words shall not pass away**.*

***Mark 13:31** Heaven and earth shall pass away: but **my words shall not pass away**.*

***Luke 21:33** Heaven and earth shall pass away: but **my words shall not pass away**.*

Some might argue that portions of these promises were fulfilled historically, but that is not what the Lord guaranteed. He did not say, *"**my word** shall not pass away"* (singular).[2] Christ specifically said, *"**my words** [all inclusive] shall not pass away."* If every prophetic word in the context did not come to pass shortly following Christ's departure, then it is not the time (nor the fulfillment) which the Lord prophesied. His promise concerned the complete and total fulfillment of each of these events. He emphasizes the truth of this fulfillment as more sure than the continued existence of the heaven and earth.

The Privacy of the Hour

There can be no doubt for the Bible believer as to the validity of Christ's promise concerning the events of the End-Times, including His Second Coming and the end of the world. However, by design, there is an element of uncertainty that still remained in Jesus' day as to the "when" of these prophetic fulfillments. Jesus expressed as much when He revealed that God did not want anyone to know the precise timing, at least prior to the events commencing.

***Matthew 24:36** But of that day and hour **knoweth no man**, no, not the angels of heaven, but my Father only.*

---

[2] It is important to note that the overall statements of Christ could be referred to as **the word of God**, or in this case, the general promise. This is not the same as Him referring to His very words (plural).

***Mark 13:32 But of that day and that hour knoweth no man,** no, not the angels which are in heaven, neither the Son, but the Father.*

Unfortunately, far too many well-meaning preachers have used this same passage concerning Israel's last days to explain why no one can know the timing of the Rapture. Although there are certainly some overlapping truths between the Rapture and the Second Coming, these truths concerning not knowing the day and hour were intended to apply uniquely and exclusively to truths being expressed about **Israel's last days**.³ Understanding the context and correct application of this passage is not a license for men to attempt to predict, as many have unwisely done, the day or hour of the Rapture of the Church. If the day and hour of the Jewish End-Times are currently unpredictable, it stands to reason that man has no basis to try to date the day and hour of the Church's departure.

The context reveals that the calamities mentioned in the Olivet Discourse will come to pass upon a people living their lives with no expectation of the impending doom. Although we certainly do *not* know the day or hour of Christ's return for the Church at the Rapture, we should always be living with the expectation of His return today. **In fact, we should *live* every day as though Christ could come today, yet *plan* as though He might *not* return in the foreseeable future.** Keep in mind that the Jewish last days and Christ's Second Advent will prove quite different from the Church's last days.

Although we can understand some principles based upon the time and extent of Daniel's Seventieth Week, we should not even attempt to predict the timing of the day or hour. Not only does *"no man"* presently know the timing, but Christ proclaimed that at the time of His pronouncement neither *"the angels which are in heaven"* nor Christ Himself knew the timing ***(Mark 13:32)***. He stated this knowledge was limited to His *"Father only"* ***(Matthew 24:36)***. What may have been true during Christ's first advent does not necessarily hold true today.

Christ willingly limited His knowledge concerning the Jewish End-Times. However, these self-imposed limitations while on this earth were most likely limited to that span of time and not thereafter. The emphasis

---

³ The reader is again cautioned not to take license with any verse by removing the verse out of its proper context in order to refute the false and dangerous practice of Rapture date-setting.

of scripture revolves around whether or not men are adequately prepared for the inevitability of those events when they do come.

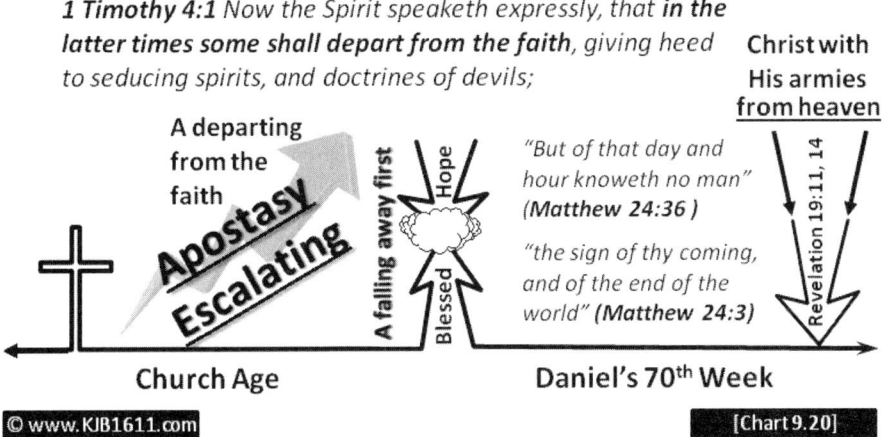

The problem of reconciling all of the facts disturbs any astute student of God's word. The time frame of Daniel's Seventieth Week (at least from the midpoint) is easily pinpointed as to the timing, whether the ending point is defined by the time, times, and half a time *(Daniel 12:7; Revelation 12:14)*; or the given number of months (42 months—*Revelation 11:2, 13:5*); or the given number of days (1260—*Revelation 11:3*). How can anyone alive at that time not be able to pinpoint the day of Christ's return at the Second Advent? The answer might lie in the fact that His return may not take place at the end of Daniel's Seventieth Week.

Perhaps even now the branches of the fig tree are becoming tender waiting to shoot forth their leaves. The Church could depart at any moment and God's attention will again turn to the Jewish people. The promise of these things coming to pass is sure! The only uncertainty that remains is whether or not men will be ready when the pangs, troubles, and tribulations come upon those still here after the Rapture of the Church.

As we shall soon explore, the people will be so distracted by the routines of life and sin of this world that Christ's return will blindside them. For an affirmation of this particular truth, one needs only to consider the complete and total lack of preparedness of those living during the days of Noah and Lot. People were more interested in the pleasures of sin than any possible judgment of God. In the worst of situations, men always seek for some semblance of normalcy. Without hope, men will eat and drink with little regard for the oncoming calamity.

> "These admonitions to valiantly endure tribulations also apply to those who will be persecuted and afflicted PRIOR to the Rapture and the commencement of Daniel's Seventieth Week."

[Excerpt from *"Reviving the Blessed Hope,"* page 39]

10

The Days of Noah and Lot

(Matthew 24:37-42)

It is always important to believe, teach, and follow the right doctrine; but no one has ever—or will ever—master the Bible. Unfortunately, even Christians who try to consistently follow sound doctrine sometimes fail in the simplest teachings.

A prime example of frequent, improper usage from the Olivet Discourse concerns misapplication of the references to the days of Noah and the days of Lot. Since the Rapture of the Church is not in view in the Olivet Discourse, no Bible teacher should apply teachings from Matthew chapter 24 to the Rapture. In order for the Bible student to be *"approved unto God" (2 Timothy 2:15)*, every scriptural application must take into account God's intended context.

The Example from the Past

Ironically, the clearest proof that Matthew chapter 24 has nothing to do with the Rapture of the Church happens to be one of the most referenced events by preachers and teachers as being applicable to the Church's last days. This teaching concerns God's supernatural protection and intervention in Noah's and Lot's days. No scripturally sound and consistent teaching would ever liken those two events to God's interaction with the Church at the Rapture.

The deliverance of Noah and Lot from the heaven-sent catastrophic judgment may offer hope to the unaware members of the audience, but misapplication of the scriptures always creates confusion. This is easy to prove on several fronts. For instance, those mentioned as TAKEN in the context of Matthew chapter 24 are *not* the ones that **escaped** judgment! In fact, they were the ones actually **TAKEN in judgment and death.** The average believer may innocently applaud the concept of such a misapplied context (Noah's and Lot's deliverance) and feel good and excited about the Saviour's soon return, but a closer look at the passage proves the error of such an interpretation.

> ***Matthew 24:37** But **as the days of Noe were, so shall also the coming of the Son of man be**. 38 For as in the days that were before the flood they were eating and drinking, marrying and giving in marriage, until the day that Noe entered into the ark, 39 And knew not until the flood came, and **took them all away**; so shall also the coming of the Son of man be.*

Many believers reading this passage focus upon the behaviour of the wicked preceding Noah's flood. Yet, the reader does not need to get so focused upon the *"eating and drinking, marrying and giving in marriage"* in verse 38 that he fails to consider the details of what took place when the judgment fell. The people of the world in Noah's day (and in Lot's day) were living as though there would be no flood and no judgment. It is also true that the world presently lives oblivious to the fact that the Rapture could take place at any time. Likewise, during Daniel's Seventieth Week, the world will be living as though there will be no Second Advent. The lesson learned: regardless of the calamities falling upon man, he always finds a way to find pleasure in sin.

The unbelieving world has always been careless concerning the things of God and will be *"eating and drinking,"* completely ignorant of their impending doom. They will also be *"marrying and giving in marriage"* but even that takes on new meaning in our depraved societies. However, in order to understand the full gist of the Second Coming of Christ, one must dig further into the events of Noah's day. One must ask himself if the careless and ignorant behaviour of those in Noah's day is really the only reason why the Lord Jesus referenced those days for a testimony to the Jews concerning the future Advent.

Good Bible study is similar to the work of a good detective. Only by asking the right questions can one arrive at the right answers. The first question that might come to mind concerns the careless and ignorant behaviour of those in the past and how that behaviour will be prominent at Christ's return. Yet, far too many stop at this single question rather than asking the even more pertinent questions. For example, when the floods came in Noah's day, who was the recipient of the judgment? Who was providentially protected and preserved? When the floods came, who was TAKEN from the earth? Who was LEFT BEHIND and allowed to remain upon the earth after the flood waters assuaged?

Simply answering these questions leads the Bible student away from any thought that the days of Noah are likened to the coming Rapture. In both cases (the days of Noah and the Second Advent), the wicked are taken in death and the righteous are left upon the earth. The Rapture offers the opposite: the believers are TAKEN to meet the Lord and the lost are left upon the earth. Understanding the conditions of Noah's day helps the Bible student grasp and appreciate the comparison between the flood and the Second Advent.

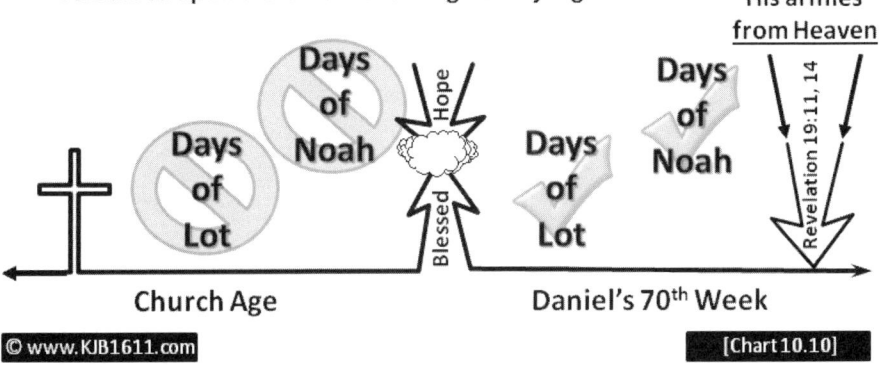

The Bible leaves no doubt concerning the norm in Noah's day—intense wickedness. The description is quite extensive but exploring these few narratives should provide the gist of what was taking place. Beyond the wickedness of the intermarrying between *"the sons of God"* and *"the daughters of men" (**Genesis 6:2**), "the wickedness of man was great in the earth, and ... every imagination of the thoughts of his heart was only evil continually" (**Genesis 6:5**). "The earth also was corrupt before God, and the earth was filled with violence" (**Genesis 6:11**). "It repented the LORD that he had made man" (**Genesis 6:6)* and God determined that man had only *"an hundred and twenty years" (Genesis 6:3)* remaining before He would *"bring a flood of waters upon the earth, to destroy all flesh" (Genesis 6:17)*. This was the condition of the world when you had eight believers on earth and only one preacher *(2 Peter 2:5)*. Now, imagine a world completely void of believers the moment the Rapture takes place!

God the Father knew the flood's date (see *Matthew 24:36*) and instructed Noah to build an ark *"to the saving of his house" (Hebrews 11:7)*. Certainly, the timing of the flood did not take Noah by surprise. In fact, as the day of the flood approached, God invited Noah and his family into the ark *(Genesis 7:1)* with a warning that the rains would begin in just *seven days (Genesis 7:4)*. This one detail fully exposes the true context of the reference of Matthew chapter 24. Matthew refers to those who were taken away as those who *"knew not"* in *Matthew 24:39*. If Noah and his family knew, then who was it that was taken away that *knew not*? It was the lost. This simply cannot be referring to Noah and his family because God gave them the exact timing.

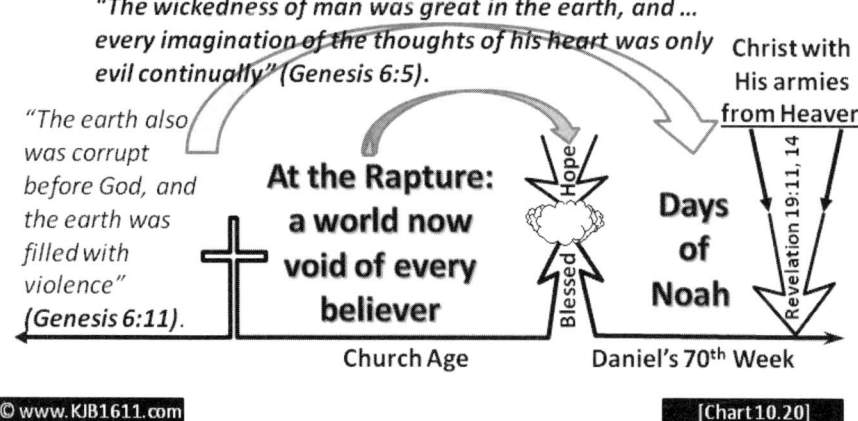

Likewise, it stands to reason that God the Father will do the same for those believers upon the earth before the Second Advent. Things are too precise once the clock starts ticking. Those who know God's word, especially the timing mentioned in Daniel, may not know the hour or exact time, but very definitely could know *the day* of Christ's Second Advent *(Matthew 24:36)*. The Lord will likely reveal the day to those saints living in Daniel's Seventieth Week the same as He did for Noah and for Lot.

Noah and his family were gathered into the ark for protection just prior to the onset of the flood. However, it is important that every Bible student understand the correct application of **Matthew 24:39** as it applies to the unbelieving world. This same parallel will take place at the Second Advent. In Noah's day, it was the **unbelievers** upon whom *"the flood came, and took them all away"* [removed from the earth] and *"so shall also the coming of the Son of man be" (Matthew 24:39)*. Toward the end of Daniel's Seventieth Week, God gathers His elect *(Matthew 24:31)* for protection upon the earth as He pours His wrath upon an unbelieving, unrepentant world *(2 Thessalonians 1:7-8)*.

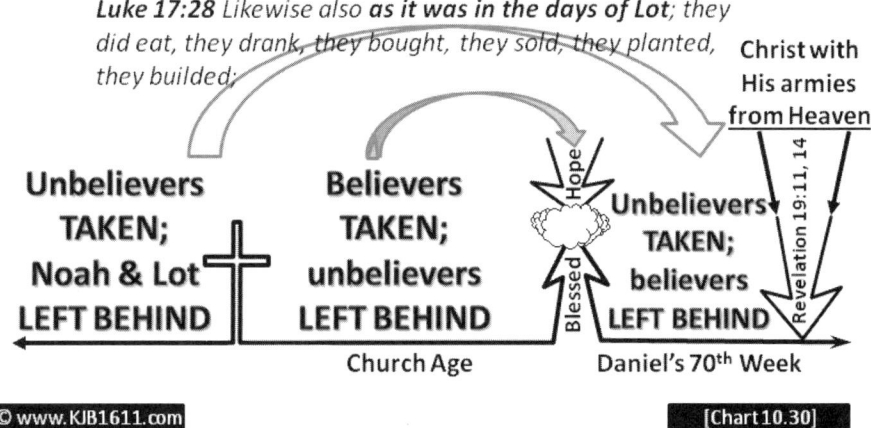

The book of Luke offers a parallel witness to these truths. Lot's protection from the wrath poured upon Sodom serves as a synopsis of the events surrounding the Lord's Second Advent. The day the ANGELS gathered Lot, the destruction poured forth upon the wicked. The wicked were destroyed and removed from the earth, but Lot lived upon the earth after the wrath passed. Just as the angels gathered Lot and protected him from the destruction inflicted upon Sodom, the angels will gather the elect [believing Jews] and protect them from God's impending judgment.

> *Luke 17:28 Likewise also **as it was in the days of Lot**; they did eat, they drank, they **bought**, they **sold**, they planted, they builded; 29 But **the same day that Lot went out of Sodom** it rained fire and brimstone from heaven, and **destroyed them all**. 30 Even thus shall*

> *it be in the day when the Son of man is revealed. 31 In that day, he which shall be upon the housetop, and his stuff in the house, let him not come down to take it away: and he that is in the field, let him likewise not return back. 32 Remember Lot's wife.*

Take note of the statement that the people destroyed in Lot's day were those who *"bought"* and *"sold."* On the surface, the inclusion of this description may seem quite odd. Yet, God's words are never without purpose and plan! This particular wording clearly associates the destruction of Sodom directly to those who are destroyed at the end of Daniel's Seventieth Week. We know this because only those with the Mark of the Beast can buy and sell during Daniel's Seventieth Week **(Revelation 13:17)**. This peculiar wording offers another confirmation how Lot's deliverance is a picture of the supernatural protection of the believers during that fateful time to come and not the Church Age saints delivered by the Rapture.

The admonition to the Jews alive at Christ's Second Advent is that they should *"Remember Lot's wife"* **(Luke 17:32)**. In other words, they should be aware of the inherent dangers of looking back even to their beloved city as the angels seek to gather them for protection from the imminent wrath. For this and other reasons, Lot and Noah do NOT serve as pictures and types of the Church's protection and deliverance. Instead, Lot and Noah picture the protection of those alive just prior to the Lord's Second Advent. Unfortunately, these truths and pictures are consistently misapplied by teachers on both sides of the debate concerning the Pre-tribulation Rapture.

Every Bible student must simply clear his mind of all the fog and allow the Bible to be the absolute authority. This allows all of the various passages to tie beautifully together and make perfect sense. The false, preconceived presumptions about Noah and Lot representing God's protection and removal of the Church make the scriptures appear jumbled and contradictory.

The Examples to Come

Those teachers who fail to remain contextually consistent have produced many of the problems addressed herein. Unfortunately, this includes those teachers with the best of intentions. This is why Bible teachers should never limit themselves to topical Bible studies. Teach and study the whole context of every verse, passage, chapter, and book of the Bible.

For instance, those who fail to study the Bible God's way may use the days of Noah and Lot to warn Christians that they may be LEFT BEHIND at the Rapture. How sad! The context of these passages was never intended to teach anything of the sort.

Those alive at the Lord's Second Advent will be overjoyed that they were the ones LEFT BEHIND, rather than the ones *"taken"* in judgment, death, and destruction. Since Noah and Lot are the chosen examples of God's past protection, these truths will offer future believers much hope. Both Noah and Lot were LEFT BEHIND and came out on the other side of judgment unharmed. The same application applies to those in the field, those grinding at the mill, and those sleeping in the bed. Plainly put, these are not pictures of the Rapture!

> ***Matthew 24:40*** *Then shall two be in the field;* ***the one shall be taken, and the other left****. 41 Two women shall be grinding at the mill;* ***the one shall be taken, and the other left.***

> ***Luke 17:34*** *I tell you, in that night there shall be two men in one bed; the* ***one shall be taken, and the other shall be left****. 35* ***Two women shall be grinding together; the one shall be taken, and the other left****. 36 Two men shall be in the field;* ***the one shall be taken, and the other left.***

Again, understanding the context is crucially important. The passages combined offer three scenarios: (1) Two men in the field, (2) Two women grinding at the mill, and (3) Two men in one bed. Each scenario presents the distinctions in judgment and protection at the Lord's Second Coming. Additionally, the contextual reference to Noah and Lot sheds light on the outcomes.

Again, in both Noah's and Lot's days, those taken *(Matthew 24:39)* were taken in judgment and those LEFT BEHIND were the ones protected and providentially preserved on the earth after the judgment passed. In like manner, the man or woman that is taken in each scenario is taken to judgment *(Matthew 24:39)*. The ones left will be those who benefit from God's grace, protection, and preservation. Those who are left alive upon the earth will be the ones who enter the earthly, millennial kingdom.

While each of these should be self-explanatory, because of modern culture's propensity to pervert that which is otherwise sound and pure, one may require some further exploration. Unfortunately, there are some who have suggested that the two men in the bed are sodomites. With that assumption, at the coming of Christ, one sodomite will be taken to judgment and the other left to enter the kingdom.

This is problematic for multiple reasons! The suggestion that two men in one bed were sodomites is to allow the perversion of modern culture to interpret the scripture rather than allowing the Bible to be the defining authority. The answer is found when the student considers the final days of king David. According to scripture, David *"gat no heat"* **(1 Kings 1:1)** and his servants *"sought ... a young virgin"* to lie in his bosom. They did this so that David *"may get heat"* **(1 Kings 1:2)**. Thankfully, the Bible even clarifies that nothing inappropriate took place between the two when it says that *"the king knew her not"* **(1 Kings 1:4)**.

> *1 Kings 1:1 Now king David was old and stricken in years; and they covered him with clothes, but **he gat no heat**. 2 Wherefore his servants said unto him, Let there be sought for my lord the king a young virgin: and let her stand before the king, and let her cherish him, and **let her lie in thy bosom, that my lord the king may get heat**. 3 So they sought for a fair damsel throughout all the coasts of Israel, and found Abishag a Shunammite, and brought her to the king. 4 And the damsel was very fair, and cherished the king, and ministered to him: **but the king knew her not**.*

One Taken, Other Left

Luke 17:34 *I tell you, in that night there shall be* **two men in one bed;** *the one shall be taken, and the other shall be left.* 35 **Two women shall be grinding together;** *the one shall be taken, and the other left.* 36 **Two men shall be in the field;** *the one shall be taken, and the other left.*

[Chart 10.40]

The days preceding David's death were certainly primitive and the same will likely be true in the days preceding Christ's Second Advent. The two men during Daniel's Seventieth Week are in one bed in order to provide each other heat. In the past, wars were fought with swords on horseback. Historically and prophetically, *"if two lie together, then they have heat"* **(Ecclesiastes 4:11)**. Christians should never force a depraved assumption based upon man's current degenerate state. *"Let God be true, but every man a liar" (**Romans 3:4**)*.

The Exhortation for the Present

In the days of Noah, God gave man a preacher of righteousness **(2 Peter 2:5)** to warn the people of the coming judgment, yet few heeded the warnings. This same scenario will be repeated in the time following the Rapture of the Church. Thus, the Lord Jesus gave a sober warning concerning the personal obligation each Jew will have when Christ's return draws near.

> **Matthew 24:42 Watch** *therefore: for ye know not what hour your Lord doth come.*

> **Mark 13:33 Take ye heed, watch and pray**: *for ye know not when the time is.*

> **Luke 21:34** *And take heed to yourselves, lest at any time your hearts be overcharged with surfeiting, and drunkenness, and cares of this life, and so* **that day come upon you unawares**. *35 For as a snare shall it come on all them that dwell on the face of the whole earth. 36* **Watch** *ye therefore, and* **pray** *always, that ye may be accounted worthy to escape all these things that shall come to pass, and to stand before the Son of man.*

As the people continue to multiply their pleasures and riches, the cares of this world will likewise multiply. The people will become less concerned with their true surroundings and circumstances. Yet, the Lord admonished the Jews that their hearts could *"be overcharged with surfeiting, and drunkenness, and cares of this life"* **(Luke 21:34)**. Those who drop their guard will find that Christ's return will come upon them when they least expect it **(Luke 21:34)**. The reality concerning the unbelieving world is that *"as a snare shall it* [that day] *come on all them that dwell on the face of the whole earth"* **(Luke 21:35)**. It does not have to be that way for the Jews. God has provided a way of escape—faith.

In light of these basic concerns, the Lord called the Jews to a three-pronged response: (1) take heed, (2) watch, and (3) pray. Although these actions work together, they also function independently of each other.

1) The admonition to take heed involves personal responsibility or accountability to oneself. Specifically, the Lord charged, *"**take heed** to yourselves, lest at any time your hearts be overcharged with surfeiting, and drunkenness, and cares of this life, and so that day come upon you unawares"* **(Luke 21:34).**

2) The admonition to *watch* can include the personal call to take heed but extends to being circumspect as to the circumstances of life surrounding all of mankind upon the earth. In other words, these folks should watch the unfolding of prophetic events and the efforts of the faithless Jews, faithless nations, and the Antichrist.

3) Lastly, the Lord admonished the people to *pray*. Heeding and watching is quite useless unless the people seek God's help to thwart the plans of Satan and preserve the believing Jews. The end desire for these Jews is that they will *"escape all these things that shall come to pass"* and be LEFT BEHIND *"to stand before the Son of man"* **(Luke 21:36).**

> "Concerning this future week of years, several passages specifically mention Israel while the Church remains conspicuously absent. The post-tribulationist must force the Church into passages where the Church is NEVER mentioned."

[Excerpt from **"Reviving the Blessed Hope,"** page 46]

11

The Exhortations to Watchfulness

(Matthew 24:43-51)

As the Lord gave His closing statements concerning the days of Noah, He admonished His audience to *"Watch therefore: for ye know not what **hour** your Lord doth come" (**Matthew 24:42**)*. Throughout His Olivet Discourse, the warnings to watch refer to the specific time of day as unknown ("in" a day or the hour, not "on" a certain or particular day). The Lord's words that follow this admonition to watch and pray are followed by two thought-provoking scenarios. These two settings explain how and why those believers should watch. They refer to:

- a **goodman** whose house was *"broken up"* by a thief, and
- a **servant** whose lord departed but was soon to return with lofty expectations

These two scenarios indicate that those who are fully trusting in the Lord with an expectancy of His return will be rewarded for their faithful attentiveness. However, those who get weary in well doing will be judged accordingly. Here are both scenarios (the goodman of the house and the servant) in full.

> *Matthew 24:43 But know this, that if the **goodman** of the house had known in what **watch** the thief would come, he would have watched, and would not have suffered his house to be broken up. 44 Therefore be ye also ready: for in such an **hour** as ye think not the Son of man cometh.*

***Matthew 24:45** Who then is a faithful and **wise servant**, whom his lord hath made ruler over his household, to give them meat in due season? 46 Blessed is that servant, whom his lord when he cometh shall find so doing. 47 Verily I say unto you, That he shall make him ruler over all his goods. 48 But and if that evil servant shall say in his heart, My lord delayeth his coming; 49 And shall begin to smite his fellowservants, and to eat and drink with the drunken; 50 The lord of that servant shall come **in a day** when he looketh not for him, and in **an hour** that he is not aware of, 51 And shall cut him asunder, and appoint him his portion with the hypocrites: there shall be weeping and gnashing of teeth.*

The Watch of the Goodman

In the first parable of the goodman of the house *(see also Luke 12:39-41)*, the Lord Jesus likened man's uncertainty concerning the timing of His return to a goodman's surprise when a thief unexpectedly shows up. In order to more fully comprehend the severity of this parallel, it is important to understand that a *goodman* is a husband *(Proverbs 7:19)* and the ruler of the house *(Matthew 20:11)*.

Regardless of the actions of others, the goodman must remain attentive to the possibility of a thief. All decisions for security belong to the goodman who takes full responsibility for restoration of any loss caused by his unpreparedness. The goodman is not only responsible for the things within the house but also the consequences resulting from the loss of the things contained therein.

Obviously, the goodman would gain a tremendous advantage if he knew (*"what watch"*) a thief intended to show up! Historically, the Jews divided the night into military watches instead of hours. These watches represented the period for which sentinels remained on duty. If the goodman knew which watch, he could be alert and watchful resulting in his not allowing *"his house to be broken up"* **(Matthew 24:43)**.

If the goodman received some intelligence concerning the timing of a thief's arrival, he would have to choose whether or not to believe the information. If he chose to believe the information, he would make the necessary preparations to get ready for the thief's arrival. Although he might not know the exact time the thief would come, he would not be caught completely off guard. Likewise, although the Jews do not know the hour of the Lord's return, they have sufficient information available to them in the word of God to enable them to be prepared for His return.

The purpose of the goodman illustration was not to reveal the exact hour of the Lord's return, but whether or not the Jews would be prepared to meet Him at the precise moment of His return. In fact, the Lord repeatedly drove home this point with comments like *"Therefore be ye also ready" (Matthew 24:44)*. Unfortunately, as we have already discovered, only a remnant of Jews will be left upon the earth and only a portion of them will be ready for the Lord's coming. Yet, the blame for their unpreparedness lies directly with the Jews who refuse to heed the warning. After all, Christ's return is likened to a thief coming in the night.

2 Peter 3:10 But the day of the Lord will come as a thief in the night;

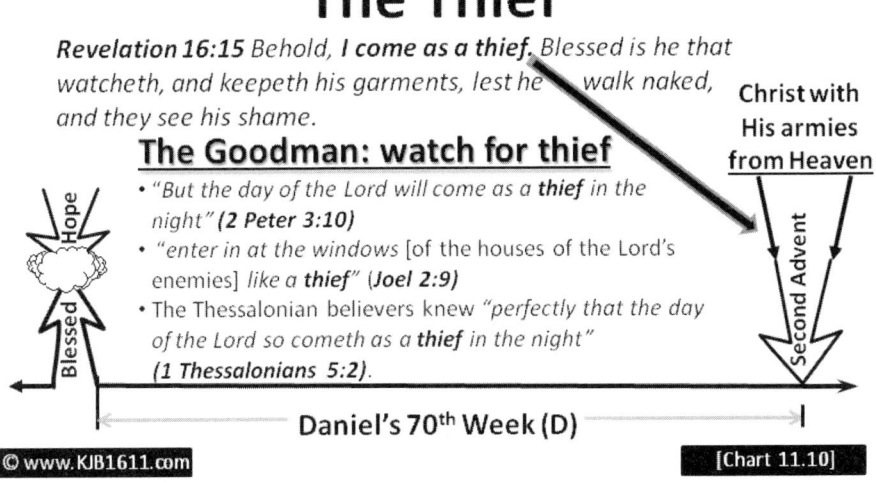

Interestingly, the Bible frequently equates the Lord's return with the actions of a thief. According to ***Joel 2:9***, the Lord's army (which consists of saved saints from Heaven according to ***Revelation 19:14***) will *"enter in at the windows* [of the houses of the Lord's enemies] *like a thief."* The Lord also reminded the Thessalonian believers that they knew *"perfectly that the day of the Lord so cometh as a thief in the night"* **(1 Thessalonians 5:2)**. This is why it very important to distinguish between the Day of the Lord[1] and the Rapture of the Church. In a similar context, Simon Peter

---

[1] For more in-depth Bible teaching on the Day of the Lord, see **Reviving the Blessed Hope of Thessalonians** by the same authors.

warned that *"the day of the Lord will come as a thief in the night"* ***(2 Peter 3:10)***. The Lord Jesus pinpointed the application when He promised, *"Behold, I come as a thief"* and admonished, *"Blessed is he that watcheth, and keepeth his garments, lest he walk naked, and they see his shame"* ***(Revelation 16:15)***.

When the Lord returns at His Second Advent, His return is likened to that of a thief coming upon an unsuspecting and ill-prepared world. This worldwide unpreparedness will be so prevalent in the End-Times that the Lord posed the question during His earthly ministry, *"when the Son of man cometh, shall he find faith on the earth?"* ***(Luke 18:8)***. Additionally, while the majority of the Gentiles will be consumed with their desire to destroy the Jews, many of the Jews will have lost faith and succumbed to the offer of the Antichrist to take the Mark of the Beast.

Those Jews with no faith—who regret having caved in to the pressures and fears of the time—now attempt to justify their actions by turning to their good works. Others will simply betray their fellow kinsmen without remorse, while still others will use their ability to buy and sell to do good works toward their fellow Jews. Each of these groups choose the wrong path by failing to patiently trust in the Lord's deliverance and to faithfully watch and wait for the Messiah's return.

The Servant Chooses His Path (Matthew 24:45-51)

On the heels of the warning for readiness, the Lord raised a relevant question, *"Who then is a faithful and wise servant?"* This question begins His second parable addressing **watchfulness**. The scenario establishes that *"the Son of man is as a man taking a far journey, who left his house, and gave authority to his servants, and to every man his work, and commanded the porter to watch"* ***(Mark 13:34)***. Mark's gospel considers the overall picture while Matthew's gospel hones in on the account of one servant.

> ***Matthew 24:45*** *Who then is a **faithful and wise servant**, whom his lord hath made ruler over his household, to give them meat in due season?*

According to Matthew, before the lord's departure, he elevated a certain servant to rule over his household. *"In due season,"* his fellowservants were to come to this servant to find out their responsibilities for fulfilling the overall obligations of the departed lord. According to

Mark, before departing, the lord *"commanded the porter to watch"* **(Mark 13:34)**. In both accounts, the servants were admonished to be ready and watchful for the lord's return at an unexpected time.

As we follow the story of the promoted servant, we learn of two possible PATHS the servant could take:

He could faithfully and wisely fulfill the obligations set forth by the lord *(Matthew 24:45)*, or

He could assume his lord delayed his return causing the servant to turn to worldly pleasures and mistreating those under his care *(Matthew 24:48-49)*.

In the lord's absence, the wise servant obeys his lord's instructions and righteously manages the household. He knows that the lord could soon return. He is called a *"faithful and wise servant"* who rules well and provides for his lord's household.

> **Matthew 24:45** Who then is a **faithful and wise servant**, whom his lord hath made ruler over his household, to give them meat in due season?

Unfortunately, this same servant could lose sight of his lord's return and choose the wrong path. In doing so, he begins *"to eat and drink with the drunken"* and *"to smite his fellowservants."* The parable refers to him as the *"evil servant."*

> **Matthew 24:48** But and if that **evil servant** shall say in his heart, My lord delayeth his coming; 49 And shall begin to **smite his fellowservants, and to eat and drink with the drunken;**

Regardless of the servant's decision and chosen path concerning faithfulness, his lord will return. The man who chooses to be faithful and wise will be *"blessed,"* but the *"evil servant"* will be so consumed by his worldliness that his lord's return comes at a time *"when he looketh not for him, and in an hour that he is not aware of."* Here is the contrast between the faithful and the wicked:

> **Matthew 24:46 Blessed is that** [faithful] **servant**, whom his lord when he cometh shall find so doing.

> **Matthew 24:50** The lord of **that** [wicked] **servant** shall come in a day when he **looketh not for him, and in an hour that he is not aware of,**

The actions are at opposite ends of the spectrum and the consequences caused by those actions are likewise contrasting. The faithful and wise servant will be rewarded for his watchfulness and service and will be made *"ruler over all his* [the lord's] *goods."*

Matthew 24:47 *Verily I say unto you, That he shall make him [the faithful servant]* **ruler over all his goods.**

God richly blesses the faithful servant. The evil servant, however, will be cut asunder and appointed *"his portion with the hypocrites."* His judgment brings forth *"weeping and gnashing of teeth."* The two outcomes are clear—be promoted to a time of rule (in the kingdom) or be judged in hell with *"weeping and gnashing of teeth."*

Matthew 24:51 *And shall cut him [the wicked servant] asunder, and appoint him* **his portion with the hypocrites**: *there shall be* **weeping and gnashing of teeth.**

Any astute Bible student quickly realizes the problems associated with equating this teaching on judgment to the Christian possessing ETERNAL life. Granted, the unfaithful Christian will see his life's work burn up at the Judgment Seat of Christ *(1 Corinthians 3:15)*, but he can never lose his salvation and be cast into hell. Yet, this misapplication inevitably happens with the false assumption that Matthew chapter 24 addresses the Church and speaks of the Rapture of the Church.

The Servant: Wise or Evil?

Mark 13:34 For the Son of man is as a man taking a far journey, who left his house, and gave authority to his servants, and to every man his work, and commanded the porter to watch.

Wise Servant	**Evil Servant**
(Matthew 24:45-47)	*(Matthew 24:48-51)*
• Faithfully and wisely fulfills the obligations set forth by the lord	• Turns to worldly pleasures and mistreating those under his care
• Blessed is that servant	• Cut asunder, and appointed his portion with the hypocrites:
• Made ruler over all his goods	there shall be weeping and gnashing of teeth

Daniel's 70th Week (D)

[Chart 11.20]

Unfortunately, these misapplications of Matthew chapter 24 have renewed the oft rejected heresy concerning the future lot of unfaithful Christians. Some teach that unfaithful Christians will spend the millennial kingdom in the lake of fire before eventually being delivered for a heavenly rescue. For many people, this sounds similar to the Roman Catholic doctrine of purgatory and that is exactly what it is. Fortunately, the Bible student realizes that the scripture does not contradict itself by implying that Christians can and will atone for their own sins through some type of Christian purgatory.

Instead, the Lord simply directs His warnings toward Jews who fail to trust in the Lord and thereby fail to ready themselves for His Second Coming. They are the faithless ones at His coming *(Luke 18:8)*. In fact, the Lord repeatedly pointed to this faithless group during His ministry:

- They are *"the children of the kingdom"* who will be *"cast out into outer darkness" (Matthew 8:12)*, while *"many ... come from the east and west, and ... sit down with Abraham, and Isaac, and Jacob, in the kingdom of heaven" (Matthew 8:11)*.
- They are the ones *"thrust out"* of the kingdom *(Luke 13:28)*, while others come and *"sit down in the kingdom of God" (Luke 13:29)*.
- They are the ones who will be cut asunder and appointed their portion with the hypocrites and who will experience weeping and gnashing of teeth *(Matthew 24:51)*.

On the heels of these parables, the gospel of Mark includes a final admonition. This admonition opens and closes with the word *"Watch."* In between these bookends recommending watchfulness, Christ admonished that *"the master of the house"* could return *"at even, or at midnight, or at the cockcrowing, or in the morning."* The faithless and unbelieving servants will be shocked when the master suddenly comes and finds them spiritually slumbering. The Lord's admonition is to avoid this pitfall: *"I say unto all, Watch."*

> **Mark 13:35 Watch** *ye therefore: for ye know not when the master of the house cometh, at even, or at midnight, or at the cockcrowing, or in the morning: 36 Lest coming suddenly he find you* **sleeping.** *37 And what I say unto you* **I say unto all, Watch.**

Who Are the Evil Servants?

Matthew 24:51 And shall cut him [the wicked servant] *asunder, and appoint him **his portion with the hypocrites**: there shall be **weeping and gnashing of teeth**.*

- They are *"the children of the kingdom"* who will be *"cast out into outer darkness"* **(Matthew 8:12)**, while *"many ... come from the east and west, and ... sit down with Abraham, and Isaac, and Jacob, in the kingdom of heaven"* **(Matthew 8:11)**.
- They are *"thrust out"* of the kingdom **(Luke 13:28)**, while others come and *"sit down in the kingdom of God"* **(Luke 13:29)**.
- They are cut asunder and appointed their portion with the hypocrites who will experience weeping and gnashing of teeth **(Matthew 24:51)**.

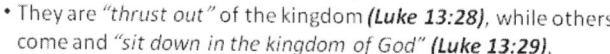

Daniel's 70th Week (D)

[Chart 11.30]

The three main points of emphasis presented in these scenarios are watchfulness, preparedness, and readiness. This particular theme serves as a thread uniting the end of Matthew chapter 24 with the entirety of Matthew chapter 25.

Matthew chapter 24 closes with this admonition to the Jews. They are cautioned to be prepared for Christ's Second Coming. As the study continues, we will see that Matthew chapter 25 opens with two parables promoting this same theme among the Jews. These parables are followed by the pronouncement of a judgment that rewards or condemns the same actions among the Gentile nations.

12

The Parable of the Ten Virgins

(Matthew 25:1-13)

Matthew chapter 25 opens with the word *"Then"* which indicates a continuation of the context of the Olivet Discourse in chapter 24 and specifically the Lord's message concerning *"the sign of thy* [Christ's] *coming, and of the end of the world" (Matthew 24:3)*. Not only does the message of the previous chapter continue into chapter 25, but the nature of the delivery continues as the Lord uses a parable to express His truths.

As we have seen, the Lord offered specific event details throughout the majority of chapter 24 *(Matthew 24:3-31)* concerning His Second Advent, in addition to those comments found at the end of Matthew chapter 23 *(Matthew 23:34-39)*. Interestingly, beginning in **Matthew 24:32,** the Lord expressed the truths using parables, parallels, and different scenarios. This communication method continued throughout the remainder of chapter 24 and into chapter 25.

As we begin the study of Matthew chapter 25, the chapter opens with the parable of the *"ten virgins" (Matthew 25:1-13)* followed by the parable of the *"talents" (Matthew 25:14-30)*. After the two parables, the book of Matthew returns to the chronology of the End-Times in **Matthew 25:31** with the account of the Judgment of the Nations *(Matthew 25:31-46)*. Here is snapshot of the discourse leading up to Matthew chapter 25:

- *Matthew 23:1-33*—The Lord rebukes the hypocrisy of the religious leadership.

- *Matthew 23:34-39*—The Lord begins His discussion concerning His return and the judgment to come.
- *Matthew 24:1-2*—The Lord is interrupted by the comments concerning the Temple to which He replies indicating its prophetic destruction in AD 70.
- *Matthew 24:3-31*—The Lord answers the questions raised at the end of Matthew chapter 23 concerning His return and the judgment to come.
- *Matthew 24:32-36*—The Lord speaks the parable of the fig tree.
- *Matthew 24:37-42*—The Lord parallels His return to the days of Noah (and Lot in Luke chapter 17) and explains that the few will be protected while the vast majority are judged.
- *Matthew 24:43-51*—The Lord exhorts the Jews to be watchful.

The Picture of the Parable

Matthew 25:1 Then shall the kingdom of heaven be likened unto ten virgins,

The first parable of Matthew chapter 25 likens Christ's return to the readiness, or lack of readiness, of *"ten virgins ... to meet the bridegroom."* However, before proceeding, some background study may prove useful. The word *virgin* in scripture appears in various forms sixty-five times. The first usage occurs in Genesis when the Bible says, *"the damsel was very fair to look upon,* **a virgin, neither had any man known her***" (Genesis 24:16)*. In another place, the Bible says, *"for his sister* **a virgin***, that is nigh unto him,* **which hath had no husband***" (Leviticus 21:3)*. This dual emphasis may seem a bit peculiar today, but in Bible times *a virgin* was a woman who was both unmarried and never had relations with a man.

Additional important insights into the Second Advent are gleaned from the book of Leviticus. In fulfillment of the Old Testament Law, the Lord Jesus Christ, as *"the high priest,"* will *"take a wife in her virginity."* Specifically, the high priest takes *"a virgin of his own people to wife."* The parable of the ten virgins parallels the record in the book of Leviticus.

Leviticus 21:10 And he that is the **high priest** *among his brethren ... 13 And he* **shall take a wife in her virginity***. 14 A widow, or a divorced woman, or profane, or an harlot, these shall he not take: but he shall take a virgin* **of his own people to wife.**

The virgins mentioned in the Old Testament books, along with those mentioned during the earthly ministry of the Lord Jesus Christ, were never intended to symbolize the New Testament Church. Yet, in spite of the multitude of evidence against such a teaching, many teachers mistakenly attribute these references to the Church. In fact, the following references express something completely different from what is commonly taught. The virgin, bride, or wife is most definitely Israel. This matches the Law's assessment that our High Priest **(Hebrews 9:11)** will *"take a virgin of his own people to wife" (Leviticus 21:14)*. There is no question as to Israel's husband. He is her Maker, the LORD of hosts; her Redeemer, the Holy One of Israel; and the God of the whole earth!

> *Isaiah 54:5 For **thy Maker is thine husband**; the LORD of hosts is his name; and thy Redeemer the **Holy One of Israel**; The God of the whole earth shall he be called.*

The LORD will rejuvenate Israel and her land and rejoice over them as His virgin bride. The LORD (the bridegroom) will be betrothed to Israel.

> *Isaiah 62:4 Thou shalt no more be termed Forsaken; neither shall thy land any more be termed Desolate: but thou shalt be called Hephzibah, and thy land Beulah: **for the LORD delighteth in thee, and thy land shall be married**. 5 For as a young man marrieth a virgin, so shall thy sons marry thee: and **as the bridegroom rejoiceth over the bride, so shall thy God rejoice over thee**.*

> *Hosea 2:19 And **I will betroth thee unto me for ever; yea, I will betroth thee unto me** in righteousness, and in judgment, and in lovingkindness, and in mercies. 20 **I will even betroth thee unto me in faithfulness: and thou shalt know the LORD.***

> *John 3:29 **He that hath the bride is the bridegroom**: but the friend of the bridegroom, which standeth and heareth him, rejoiceth greatly because of the bridegroom's voice: this my joy therefore is fulfilled.*

Even the apostle John looked ahead to the time *after* the millennial kingdom and *"saw the holy city, new Jerusalem, coming down from God out of heaven,* **prepared as a bride** *adorned for her husband" **(Revelation 21:2)***. When an angel came to John, he said, *"Come hither, **I will shew thee the bride, the Lamb's wife"** (Revelation 21:9)*; the angel showed

John *"that great city, **the holy Jerusalem**, descending out of heaven from God" **(Revelation 21:10)**.*

Biblical historians have acknowledged that the lighting of lamps by virgins to go forth and meet the bridegroom was a practice implemented in the east (which would include the people of Israel). For example, Benjamin Keach (1640-1704), in his *Exposition of the Parables*, wrote concerning the Jewish custom of the marriage feast:

> *No doubt our Lord hereby alludes to the custom of the Jews and other people in those eastern countries, who held their nuptial or marriage feasts in the night, from whence this parable is taken. The custom was this, viz. : – Young men and virgins in the night went forth to meet the bridegroom, as he was coming to the marriage chamber; among the Jews, it was with lamps, ... such who had not lamps lighted and burning, were not admitted into the wedding-chamber.*

Unfortunately, far too many Bible expositors have identified the virgins in Matthew chapter 25 as representing the New Testament Church. This misapplication especially applies to those tainted by the false doctrine of Replacement Theology (a doctrine that teaches that the Church has replaced the nation of Israel and therefore usurps their manifold promises).

Even Benjamin Keach, mentioned above, in his other writings mistakenly associated the virgins with the New Testament Church. However, many of those who believe in this replacement teaching fail to realize the associated problems created by such a teaching. For instance, there are ten virgins mentioned, but only five of the ten virgins were allowed to enter the marriage ceremony.

Those who attempt to apply this parable to the Church at the Rapture have also taught that some Christians will miss the kingdom. They say that these Christians are the five foolish virgins. Unfortunately, this false doctrine has been gaining some popularity of late because of teachers who are now rejecting the Pre-tribulation eschatology. Regardless of one's position on whether or not the New Testament Church eventually became part of the bride of Christ, it is obvious that the references to the bride found in the gospel accounts have absolutely nothing to do with the yet to exist New Testament Church.

Any honest Bible student who rightly divides the word of truth *(2 Timothy 2:15)* would readily see that the parable of the ten virgins depicts events that will occur at the Second Advent and not at the Rapture. The parable involves the preparation (or lack thereof) of the Jews to meet their bridegroom, the Lord Jesus Christ, during Daniel's Seventieth Week. The preparations (or lack of preparations) of the nations will be addressed by the Lord at the Judgment of the Nations following this parable. The judgment for the Church (the Judgment Seat of Christ—see *Romans 14:10*) will already have taken place in Heaven before the parable even comes into focus.

"The marriage of the Lamb" (Revelation 19:7) takes place after the Rapture, after the Judgment Seat of Christ, after the conclusion of Daniel's Seventieth Week, and follows upon the heels of Christ's Second Advent. The marriage of the Lamb will be followed by *"the marriage supper of the Lamb" (Revelation 19:9),* an event that takes place upon the earth and not in Heaven as the Lord establishes His earthly, millennial kingdom. This is why the Lord warned of preparation for a marriage during His earthly ministry *(Matthew 22:1-14; Matthew 25:1-13)*, but any such instructions directed toward Christ's Body are noticeably missing in the Pauline epistles.

It is in this context, that Jesus opened the 25th chapter of Matthew with a parable to warn the Jews of the looming decision to prepare for the coming of the bridegroom, the Lord Jesus Christ *(Matthew 9:15; Matthew 25:1, 5, 6, 10; Mark 2:19-20; Luke 5:34-35; John 3:29)*. Again, it is important to distinguish between the Church's future and that of the nation of Israel. While the apostle Paul seemingly plays a major role in presenting the Church to Christ at the Rapture *(2 Corinthians 11:2; Colossians 1:28)*, the *"friend of the bridegroom"* will likely play the major role in this presentation concerning the nation of Israel. The friend of the bridegroom is none other than John the Baptist *(John 3:29; Judges 14:20)*. He serves as the equivalent to the Western thinking of the best man in a wedding ceremony.

The Preparations of the Virgins

Matthew 25:1 Then shall the kingdom of heaven be likened unto **ten virgins***, which* **took their lamps, and went forth to meet the bridegroom***.*

The particular emphasis and purpose of the parable of the ten virgins is clearly stated. The parable is designed to promote the Jews' preparation for the coming bridegroom, Jesus Christ. In the parable, all ten virgins took lamps with oil in them and went forth to meet the bridegroom. However, only the five *wise* virgins made the necessary preparations for the bridegroom's delayed arrival. When the bridegroom finally arrived after having tarried, it was too late for those who were unprepared.

Matthew 25:2 *And five of them were **wise**, and five were **foolish**. 3 They that were foolish took their lamps, and **took no oil with them**: 4 But the wise **took oil in their vessels** with their lamps. 5 While the **bridegroom tarried**, they all slumbered and **slept**.*

Far too many students focus their attention upon the details of the parables rather than their specific applications. In order to arrive at the intended scriptural interpretation of the parable, we must consider both the heart conditions and resulting actions of the wise and the foolish virgins.

Students must focus upon what takes place at the bridegroom's arrival. All ten virgins took burning lamps, but only five of the ten took additional oil in vessels. This means that the five other virgins who were foolish took only the oil in their lamps. But what does all this mean?

It is correct that the virgins whose oil ran dry and their lamps quit burning were refused entry into the marriage. Yet, it is very important not to miss the greater truth being taught. Those who were not allowed to enter the marriage were kept out because they were *foolish*. This particular thread of foolishness is emphasized throughout scripture. A man's heart condition is the cause of his speech **(Luke 6:45)**. A man's thoughts affect his being and actions **(Proverbs 23:7)**. A man's internal faith causes his external works **(see Hebrews chapter 11)**. In other words, the source of all success or failure is that which is found within the heart and the intent should draw one's focus.

Five virgins took their lamps with extra vessels of oil to keep their lamps burning *(Matthew 25:4)*. The Bible says they did this because they were *wise*. However, the other five virgins took their lighted lamps, but "took no oil with them" *(Matthew 25:3)*. Why? Because they were foolish!

It is important to again focus upon the intent of the subject matter: a parable is used to depict a future real life scenario and event. The parable points to the Lord Jesus Christ returning to find that many of the Jews will not have made the appropriate preparations to enter the millennial kingdom. Why? Because they acted foolishly!

It may be hard to imagine how the Jews could miss the preparations for the coming bridegroom, but remember that the vast majority of Jews missed the Lord's first coming. In fact, they were so ill-prepared that many of them even aided in His crucifixion. Only those with an existing relationship with the Father were prepared for the arrival of the Messiah *(Luke 2:25-35)*. This truth was again emphasized when the Lord Jesus said that those who came to Him, first belonged to the Father.

> *John 17:6 I have manifested thy name unto the men which thou gavest me out of the world: **thine they were, and thou gavest them me;** and they have kept thy word.*

The same type of people who missed the Lord's incarnation will also miss the Lord's Second Advent. After all, according to the parable, *"the bridegroom tarried"* and all the virgins *"slumbered and slept" **(Matthew 25:5)***. In other words, the Lord's return is going to catch men by surprise just as He warned, *"for in such an hour as ye think not the Son of man cometh" **(Matthew 24:44)*** and *"The lord of that servant shall come in a day when he looketh not for him, and in an hour that he is not aware of" **(Matthew 24:50)***. The wise are prepared and the foolish simply repeat the same mistakes of the past.

The Presence of the Bridegroom

> *Matthew 25:6 And at midnight there was a cry made, Behold, the bridegroom cometh; go ye out to meet him.*

The bridegroom will come as promised and prophesied. He will also come at a time in which the vast majority of the population will be unprepared. According to the parable, the cry of the bridegroom's arrival will go forth at midnight—while *"they all slumbered and slept" **(Matthew 25:5)***. Some infer this to be an announcement concerning the specific time of the Lord's arrival. After all, midnight is the time in which the Lord went forth to destroy Egypt thus initiating the Passover and deliverance of Israel *(Exodus 11:4; Exodus 12:29)*. While this is true, it is more likely that the Lord's intended purpose of specifying midnight was to note that He would come when people were careless, sleeping, or disinterested.

The Bridegroom Cometh

Matthew 25:1** Then shall the kingdom of heaven be likened unto **ten** virgins, which **took their lamps, and went forth to meet the bridegroom.

While the bridegroom tarried, they all slumbered and slept.

5 Wise Virgins
- Took oil in their vessels
- Told the foolish to go buy from those who sell
- Allowed to enter the marriage (Kingdom)

5 Foolish Virgins
- Took no oil with them
- They go and buy from those who sell *(Revelation 13:17)*
- Refused entry into the marriage (Kingdom)

Daniel's 70th Week (D)

© www.KJB1611.com   [Chart 12.10]

This midnight cry[1] serves as an invitation to meet the bridegroom *(Matthew 24:31)*. It looks to match the sounding of the trumpet and invitation of the angels to be gathered to safety in the final outpouring of God's wrath at Christ's Second Advent. The wise virgins of the parable represent the *"elect"* or believing Jews who are gathered *"from the four winds"* and brought to safety. Death and destruction reign upon all those who have chosen the world over the Messiah.

The Practice of the Virgins

> ***Matthew 25:7** Then all those virgins arose, and trimmed their lamps. 8 And the foolish said unto the wise, Give us of your oil; for our lamps are gone out. 9 But the wise answered, saying, Not so; lest there be not enough for us and you: but **go ye rather to them that sell, and buy for yourselves.** 10 And while **they went to buy, the bridegroom came;** and they that were ready went in with him to the marriage: and the door was shut. 11 Afterward came also the other virgins, saying, Lord, Lord, open to us. 12 But he **answered and said, Verily I say unto you, I know you not.***

At the defining hour, the five foolish virgins find themselves completely unprepared. In their haste, they look to the wise and ask them for

---

[1] Contrary to some popular Christian music, the midnight cry has nothing to do with the Rapture of the Church. This is just one of many examples of how faulty doctrine has been introduced into churches through music.

their supplies so that they could go into the marriage. The wise virgins admonish the foolish virgins that they cannot go to the marriage on the preparations of the wise.

It is important to take note of the particular wording of the parable in order not to miss the application of the truth found in the book of Revelation. The wise tell the foolish to go *buy* oil from those who *sell*. Yet, during Daniel's Seventieth Week, only those with the Mark can BUY or SELL.

> **Revelation 13:17** *And that **no man might buy or sell, save he that had the mark,** or the name of the beast, or the number of his name.*

This simple truth has been missed by prophecy teachers and its importance cannot be overemphasized here. As the foolish virgins soon learn, the bridegroom has come and their past decisions will now haunt them for all eternity. The door is forever shut—*"while **they went to buy**, the bridegroom came; and they that were ready went in with him to the marriage: and the door was shut" **(Matthew 25:10)**.* When these foolish virgins returned with their purchased oil, they requested entrance, but the Lord responded, *"Verily I say unto you, **I know you not" (Matthew 25:12)**.* This expressed lack of recognition by the LORD is indicative of those who do not know the Lord.

The reader must be careful not to get lost in the details of virgins leaving to buy oil only to return to find the door shut. The purpose of the parable was to promote a readiness among the Jews living during Daniel's Seventieth Week. When the trumpet sounds and the angels gather the elect, those unbelieving Jews will be refused entrance to the Lord's earthly, millennial kingdom. They will hear the ominous words, *"I know you not" **(Matthew 25:12)**.* These words are similar to the Lord's warnings in Matthew chapter 7. The Lord said there would be *"many"* who did things in His name, but would one day hear Him say, *"I never knew you: depart from me, ye that work iniquity."*

> **Matthew 7:21** *Not every one that saith unto me, Lord, Lord, shall enter into the kingdom of heaven; but he that doeth the will of my Father which is in heaven. 22 **Many** will say to me in that day, Lord, Lord, have we not prophesied in thy name? and in thy name have cast out devils? and **in thy name done many wonderful works**? 23 And then will I profess unto them, **I never knew you: depart** from me, ye that work iniquity.*

This event specifically pointing toward the Jews should not be equated to the Judgment of the Nations *(Matthew 25:41)*. The passage toward the end of Matthew chapter 25 chronicles Christ's dealings with the nations, but our subject passage completely focuses upon the nation of Israel. Both Matthew chapter 7 and our present text from chapter 25 testify of Christ's dealings with Jews. Interestingly, some of them claimed to prophesy in the Lord's name, to cast out devils, and to have done many wonderful works *(Matthew 7:22)*. Yet, these people are called workers of iniquity. It will not be their works that save them but their willingness to trust in the LORD for their provisions.

Yet, many will be deceived into taking the Mark in order to buy and sell. They are the foolish virgins of our passage which could indicate a fateful decision they made to sell their soul so that they did not have to depend upon the LORD.[2] The book of Psalms offers further insight into what God thinks about the foolish workers of iniquity.

Psalm 5:5 *The foolish shall not stand in thy sight: thou hatest all workers of iniquity.*

The book of Second Kings *(2 Kings 4:1-7)* offers a real life scenario matching the behaviour of the five wise virgins. This story tells of a woman (like Israel) whose husband had died (like Jesus). She sought the prophet's help and her vessels were supernaturally and secretly filled with oil that enabled her family to pay the creditors and then live off the rest the oil. The five wise virgins picture believing Jews who took their vessels by faith and experienced supernatural provisions through the remainder of Daniel's Seventieth Week.

The Proposition of the Parable

Matthew 25:13 Watch therefore, *for ye know neither the day nor the hour wherein the Son of man cometh.*

---

[2] The book of Daniel offers two examples of what the Jews will face during this fateful time, how they are expected to respond, and how God can and will supernaturally protect them. Shadrach, Meshach, and Abednego refused to bow down to the idol and ended up in the fiery furnace *(Daniel 3:12-18)*. Daniel did not allow the laws to influence his worship of the true God but openly prayed to the God of Heaven *(Daniel 6:10-16)*. Daniel ended up in the den of lions. Likewise, those trusting in God during Daniel's Seventieth Week can be delivered from the fire and from the mouth of the lion.

After finishing the parable, the Lord concluded with the admonition for which the parable was delivered—*"Watch therefore."* This parable reiterates that the Jews during Daniel's Seventieth Week will need to turn to the Lord and trust His messengers prior to Christ's Second Advent. Once the trumpet sounds and the angels gather the elect, there will be no opportunity for repentance from a damnably foolish decision. Those *"foolish"* virgins for which Christ died will immediately be on the same side of God's wrath as the nations that fought against Israel during this turbulent time. If that were not ominous enough, the Lord's return promises to come as an element of surprise. The Jews *"know neither the day nor the hour wherein the Son of man cometh."*

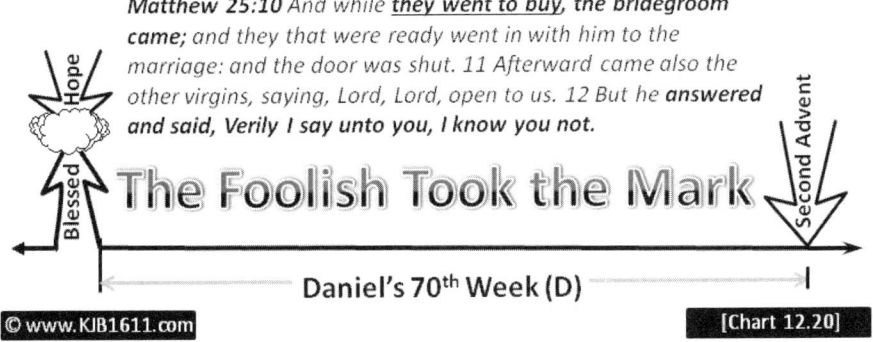

The *"foolish"* virgins (unbelieving Jews) will be *"the children of the kingdom"* who *"shall be cast out into outer darkness" (Matthew 8:12)*. They are *"the way side" (Matthew 13:4, 19)*, the *"stony places" (Matthew 13:5, 20-21)*, and the *"thorns" (Matthew 13:7, 22)* of which the Lord warned concerning His word not taking root. They are *"the tares"* that grow up with the wheat *(Matthew 13:24-30)*. While the wheat will be gathered into the barn, the angels will gather the tares for burning *(Matthew 13:36-43)*. While the wise virgins enter into the safety of protection and then into the millennial kingdom, the *"foolish"* virgins will have the door shut only to hear the condemnation, "Depart!"

Who Are the Foolish Virgins?

While the wise virgins enter into the safety of protection and then into the millennial kingdom, the "foolish" virgins will have the door shut only to hear the condemnation, "Depart!"

- They are *"the children of the kingdom"* who *"shall be cast out into outer darkness" (Matthew 8:12)*.
- They are *"the way side" (Matthew 13:4, 19)*, the *"stony places" (Matthew 13:5, 20-21)*, and the *"thorns" (Matthew 13:7, 22)* of which the Lord warned concerning His word not taking root.
- They are *"the tares"* that grow up with the wheat *(Matthew 13:24-30)*. While the wheat will be gathered into the barn, the angels will gather the tares for burning *(Matthew 13:36-43)*.

© www.KJB1611.com   [Chart 12.30]

The purpose of the parable of the ten virgins helps to visually distinguish between those who place their faith in God's supernatural provision and protection versus those who place their trust in their good works and the world system. The foolish virgins are simply those who have sold their souls to buy from those who sell.

"Lot and Noah are NOT pictures for the Church, but of those alive at the inception of the Day of the Lord. Unfortunately, these truths and pictures are consistently misapplied by teachers on both sides of the Pretribulation Rapture debate."

[Excerpt from *"Reviving the Blessed Hope,"* page 53]

13

The Parable of the Talents

(Matthew 25:14-30)

The Parable of the Talents follows the Parable of the Ten Virgins. It is important to remember that *parable* or *parables* are found sixty-five times in scripture with each use directly or indirectly associated with the Jewish people. Generally speaking, a *parable* is a story presenting *"dark sayings" **(Psalm 49:4; Psalm 78:2)**.* In one instance, Jesus defined *"dark sayings"* as *"things which have been kept secret from the foundation of the world" **(Matthew 13:35)**.*

When the Lord was asked about His use of parables, Christ confirmed that parables allowed His true followers to understand and grasp the truth. Yet, the same truths revealed by the parables remained hidden from those who did not truly love and follow the Saviour ***(Matthew 13:10-13)***.

Additionally, one's understanding or lack of understanding of the parables could have been used to distinguish between the Lord's true disciples and those who merely sought to entrap the Lord with His own words. Not surprisingly, forty-seven of the sixty-five parables are found in the gospels that record the Lord's earthly ministry. Based upon the location and context of this Parable of the Talents, the Lord obviously intended for the parable to teach concerning man's readiness for the His Second Coming.

The emphasis of this parable focuses upon the Lord's return and subsequent establishment of His earthly kingdom, not upon the time of Jacob's Trouble. Again, it is important to understand biblical terminology. *Kingdom* simply means the domain of a king, thus, the kingdom of heaven points to all things pertaining to the establishment of Christ's heavenly kingdom upon the earth. This applies to both the preparation for and realization of that kingdom. The Lord repeatedly pointed His followers' attention to this earthly kingdom. A great case in point is found in the prayer of Matthew chapter 6 and especially the words of **Matthew 6:10** where Christ instructs His followers to pray: *"Thy kingdom come. Thy will be done in earth, as it is in heaven."*

The Picture of the Parable

> ***Matthew 25:14 For the kingdom of heaven is as a man travelling into a far country, who called his own servants, and delivered unto them his goods.*** *15 And unto one he gave five talents, to another two, and to another one; to every man according to his several ability; and straightway took his journey.*

In this parable, like the others, the Lord presented a hypothetical, temporal, *earthly* scenario in hopes of driving home some eternal *spiritual* truths. This method of communicating truths was frequently and effectively incorporated by the Lord. He utilized these earthly truths and developed these scenarios to enlighten mankind and to enable men to grasp the crucial, deeper spiritual truths. In this illustration, the earthly scenario involves a man preparing to travel into a far country only to return again.

Prior to his departure for the *"far country,"* the man *"called his own servants, and delivered unto them his goods."* Among those goods were eight talents (a talent is a measurement of goods or money based upon its value in weight). Three servants were called and the lord distributed his goods *"to every man according to his several ability."* As always, the wording here is very important—the distribution was based on one's God-proven ability. The Lord never gives anyone more than he can handle. Once the goods were divided and distributed amongst the lord's three servants, he *"took his journey."*

While the text of this parable does not specifically reveal the identity of the man, the location of the far country, or the identity of the three servants, at least two of these areas seem to be clearly identified later in the chapter. Based upon the opening line of the passage depicting the

Judgment of the Nations, it appears that the man travelling is *"the Son of man"* and that the far country is Heaven.

> **Matthew 25:31** *When **the Son of man** shall come in his glory, and all the holy angels with him, then shall he sit upon the throne of his glory:*

These truths might seem quite obvious to us who live in the Church Age, yet they likely astounded the hearers present prior to the cross! They were anticipating the immediate establishment of the Lord's earthly kingdom. These parables pointed to the fact that the Lord Jesus was going away rather than immediately establishing His kingdom.

The Lord was emphasizing to His disciples that He was going to take His journey into a far country PRIOR to His kingdom being established. These truths would soon turn out to be the harsh reality with which the disciples would become all too familiar.

Jesus repeatedly taught these truths to His disciples: *"Ye have heard how I said unto you, **I go away**, and come again unto you"* **(John 14:28)**, and *"It is expedient for you that **I go away**: for if I go not away, the Comforter will not come unto you"* **(John 16:7)**. Yet, when the armed men came to arrest Jesus, Simon Peter pulled his sword from its sheath. He was determined to fight for his King and for the earthly establishment of the kingdom **(John 18:10)**.

When the disciples' focus and words are examined, these references as to the timing of the kingdom are repeated. For instance, just before the Lord's ascension, the Jewish disciples asked, *"Lord, wilt thou **at this time** restore again the kingdom to Israel"* **(Acts 1:6)**. To which the Lord responded, *"It is not for you to know the times or the seasons, which the Father hath put in his own power"* **(Acts 1:7)**. He further added that they would *"receive power, after that the Holy Ghost"* was come upon them **(Acts 1:8)**. The kingdom was not now! Yet, God would not leave them powerless.

It is important to couple these truths with Paul's historical account when he wrote, *"But unto every one of us is **given grace according to the measure of the gift of Christ**. Wherefore he saith, When he ascended up on high, he led captivity captive, and gave gifts unto men"* **(Ephesians 4:7-8)**. In other words, before the Lord Jesus departed for a far country, He called His servants together and distributed to them His goods. We see from the Bible that these goods included **grace, the Holy Ghost, spiritual gifts, spiritual leaders, etc.**

This Parable of the Talents in the book of Matthew does not give the reason for the lord's journey into a far country. Yet, a similar parable from Luke's gospel gives the necessary insights: *"A certain nobleman went into a far country **to receive for himself a kingdom**, and to return"* **(Luke 19:12)**. The parable further confirms, *"And it came to pass, that **when he was returned, having received the kingdom**, then he commanded these servants to be called unto him, to whom he had given the money, that he might know how much every man had gained by trading"* **(Luke 19:15)**. The story of the lord or nobleman obviously points to the Lord Jesus Christ. He left this earth and journeyed to a far country TO RECEIVE A KINGDOM.

The Lord Jesus Christ cannot return for **the servants mentioned in these parables** until He receives His kingdom. With these truths, we can now piece together the timing of these events. Revelation chapter 11 records the earliest point that the receipt of the kingdom will take place. The Bible says, *"And the seventh angel sounded; and there were great voices in heaven, saying, **The kingdoms of this world are become the kingdoms of our Lord,** and of his Christ; and he shall reign for ever and ever"* **(Revelation 11:15)**.

There is no ambiguity concerning this scenario and sequence of events. Yet, there are those who think that the Lord was talking TO and talking ABOUT the New Testament Church in these parables, which He certainly was not! True Bible believers know and teach that the Lord was talking to the Jews about the future establishment of His earthly kingdom. Of primary importance is that every reader acknowledges that the Lord could *not* fulfill His kingdom promise until sometime after **Revelation 11:15**.

Unfortunately, a growing number of people are teaching that the parables depicting the kingdom of heaven were intended for the Church's preparation and the Lord's return. Yet at the same time, they teach that the Rapture of the Church will take place either in Revelation chapter 6 or chapter 7. This type of convoluted scenario is simply unrealistic and impossible! The King must first receive His kingdom, THEN He can return to establish it upon the earth!

The Practice of the Servants

> *Matthew 25:16 Then he that had received the **five talents** went and traded with the same, and made them other five talents. 17 And likewise he that had received **two**, he also gained other two. 18 But he that had received **one** went and digged in the earth, and hid his lord's money.*

In this earthly scenario, the lord's servants were left to the devices of their own free will. Once the lord embarked upon his journey to the far country, each servant had to decide what he was going to do with the lord's goods. We read that the servant who received five talents actively traded and his investment doubled! Likewise, the servant who received two talents took those two talents and with great wisdom also doubled his goods! However, the third servant, already lacking his lord's confidence, took his single talent and hid it in the earth.

Most people miss the underlying spiritual truths intended by the parables by solely focusing upon the details expressed in the parables. Parables are not meant to convey truths in the same manner as those passages which were intended to be interpreted literally. After all, they present underlying and hidden spiritual truths.

After Christ's ascension, He gave His gifts to men for use during what would become the Church Age. The recipients of those gifts included three types of people: those who already knew the Lord, others who would later come to trust in the Lord, and yet others who chose never to trust the Lord for salvation.

In the previous Parable of the Ten Virgins, we read that the Lord delayed His return *(Matthew 25:5)*. Historically, we know that the New Testament Church is parenthetically placed into this period of "delay." For this reason, the focus shifts away from Israel and directly upon the "one body" of Jew and Gentile together. Yet, this transfer is only temporary—it lasts throughout the Church Age but ends at the Rapture when God turns His focus again upon Israel.

After the Rapture of the Church, these parable truths are then propelled forward in time as Daniel's prophetic clock begins again. Daniel's Seventieth Week reinstitutes God's dealings with the Jews. The Jews living at that time will be in possession of many other of the Lord's gifts (goods) which include the word of God, the Holy Ghost *(Mark 13:11)*, the grace of God, prophets, and His witnesses. What will God's chosen people do with such great treasures?

According to Christ's testimony in this parable, some of these Jews will squander their God-given opportunities. History repeats itself! As did their fathers, some of the Jews will *"resist the Holy Ghost"* *(Acts 7:51)*. As did their fathers, some will do *"despite unto the Spirit of grace"*

(Hebrews 10:29). Additionally, some will persecute the prophets *(Acts 7:52)*. Thankfully, others will do right! Instead of rebelling against the truth, these believers will welcome the working of the Holy Ghost, receive God's grace, and heed the message of God's messengers. There are only two groups: those who reject the Lord and those who trust in Him. Those rejecting the Lord will be judged and subsequently removed from the earth in death. Those who trust the Lord will be ushered into the Lord's earthly, millennial kingdom.

The Presence of the Lord

***Matthew 25:19 After a long time** the lord of those servants cometh, and **reckoneth** with them.*

There is no imminence in this teaching as the parable indicates that the lord's return would come *"After a long time."* Additionally, none of what has been mentioned up to this point matters if the lord of the servants was not returning for a time of reckoning! Yet, he will return to reckon with both the faithful and the unfaithful. The *faithful* servants will be rewarded with greater authority in the kingdom while the *unfaithful* servants are severely punished.

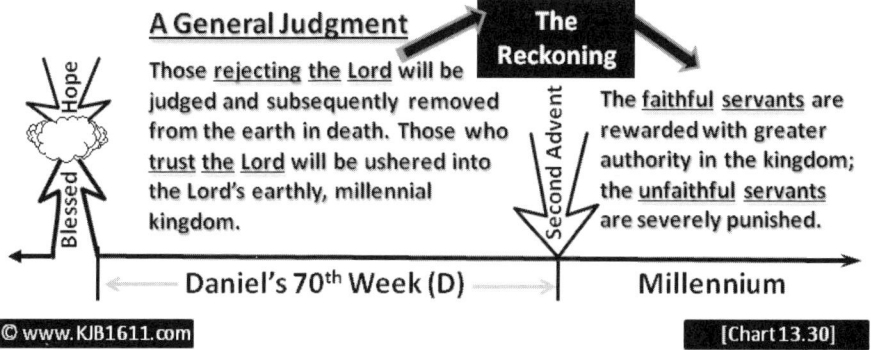

This teaching of a general judgment (one judgment including the faithful and the unfaithful) and after *"a long time"* should prick the interest of those familiar with the primary judgments in the Bible. Paul's epistles show that these concepts are contrary to the prospects of the New

Testament Church. Every astute Bible student knows that the *New Testament saints* will stand before Christ at the Judgment Seat of Christ long before the *lost* stand in judgment at the Great White Throne Judgment.

Furthermore, the apostle Paul's epistles do not teach that Christ's return for the Church would take place *"after a long time."* Instead, quite the contrary! Paul anticipated being alive and remaining when Christ returned for the Church *(1 Thessalonians 4:15, 17)*. While he was yet alive, Paul believed that he could be part of that group that would not die *(1 Corinthians 15:51)*. This teaching of imminence means that no further events prior to Christ's return for the Church would need to take place.

The Punishment or Praise of the Lord

On that day of reckoning, the two faithful servants were called upon first to give an accounting concerning their use of the talents. These faithful servants joyfully recounted how they each took their talents and doubled them. This news greatly pleased the lord so he promoted them to a higher level of authority within the lord's domain.

> *Matthew 25:20 And so he that had received five talents came and brought other **five** talents, saying, Lord, thou deliveredst unto me five talents: behold, I have gained beside them five talents more. 21 His lord said unto him, **Well done, thou good and faithful servant:** thou hast been faithful over a few things, I will make thee ruler over many things: **enter thou into the joy of thy lord**. 22 He also that had received **two** talents came and said, Lord, thou deliveredst unto me two talents: behold, I have gained two other talents beside them. 23 His lord said unto him, **Well done, good and faithful servant;** thou hast been faithful over a few things, I will make thee ruler over many things: **enter thou into the joy of thy lord.***

It is important to remember that God usually provides sufficient information in the context to determine the meaning of any particular passage. This parable is no exception to that rule. The key statement *"enter thou into the joy of thy lord"* occurs twice. Unfortunately, far too many Bible teachers assume that this statement addresses those who are about to enter into Heaven. Yet, this parable does not even have the entering of Heaven in view, nor does any part of Matthew chapters 24 and 25. In fact, those who *"endure unto the end"* *(Matthew 24:13)* of Daniel's

Seventieth Week are *not* leaving this earth. Instead, those who endure are delivered into the *"joy of the lord"* and hear the pronouncement to enter just prior to entering into Christ's earthly, millennial kingdom.

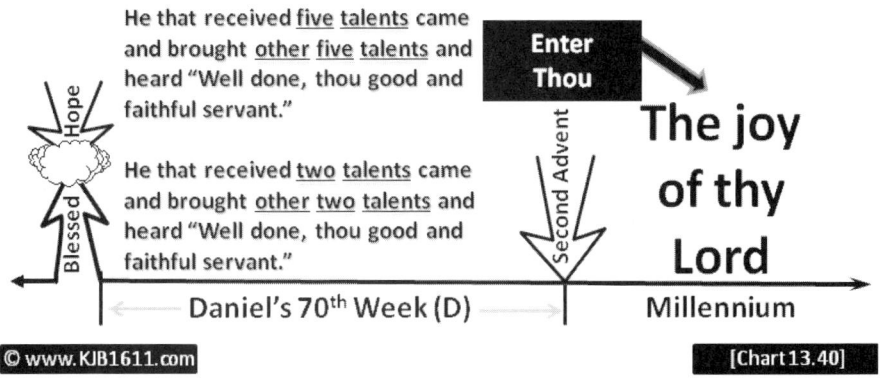

The misapplication of this parable is on par with those who apply some type of rapture to the two people in the field and the two women at the mill *(see Mathew 24:40-41)*. Again, Heaven is not in view and neither is any type of rapture. In fact, those *taken* in each of those scenarios are not raptured anywhere. Those taken are taken in death and condemnation. Additionally, the faithful are the ones **not** taken but preserved UPON THE EARTH. This fact parallels the days of Noah and Lot who remained upon the earth following God's judgment.

Those in this parable who are instructed to enter the *joy of the lord* represent the faithful who are ushered into Christ's earthly kingdom. As depicted in the parable of the talents, these rewarded Jews will enter the kingdom with varying levels of authority.

Unfortunately, there was a third servant mentioned who was given the single talent. As this final servant was called upon to give an account for his actions during the lord's absence, there can be no doubt that he experienced a wide spectrum of emotions. He was fearful because he thought the lord to be *"an hard man"* but optimistic in that he had at least preserved his lord's talent.

*Matthew 25:24 Then he which had received the **one talent** came and said, Lord, I knew thee that thou art an **hard man,** reaping where thou hast not sown, and gathering where thou hast not strawed: 25 And **I was afraid,** and went and hid thy talent in the earth: lo, there thou hast that is thine.*

Any optimism quickly disintegrates as this servant hears his lord's fateful pronouncement, *"Thou wicked and slothful servant."* We find out that this servant not only lost what was given to him prior to the lord's departure, but he was also *"cast … into outer darkness"* where there will be *"be weeping and gnashing of teeth."*

*Matthew 25:26 His lord answered and said unto him, **Thou wicked and slothful servant,** thou knewest that I reap where I sowed not, and gather where I have not strawed: 27 Thou oughtest therefore to have put my money to the exchangers, and then at my coming I should have received mine own with usury. 28 **Take therefore the talent from him,** and give it unto him which hath ten talents. 29 For unto every one that hath shall be given, and he shall have abundance: but from him that hath not shall be taken away even that which he hath. 30 And **cast ye the unprofitable servant into outer darkness: there shall be weeping and gnashing of teeth.***

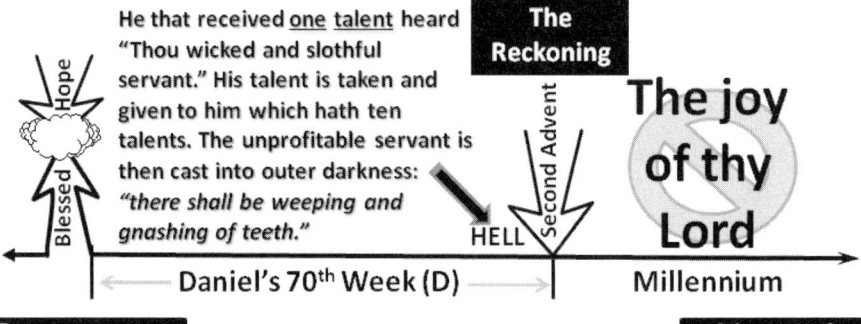

Those who teach that this parable addresses the New Testament Church have a disturbing problem: how to handle this third servant who is obviously condemned to hell. Those looking for ways out of their doctrinal blunders have devised many types of unsavory resolutions. In fact, the confused brethren never cease to come up with new and improved hypotheses. Some of these propositions even resemble some sort of Baptist/Protestant version of the Roman Catholic purgatory. One doctrinal mishap often leads to another.

The faulty, doctrinal assumption that these three servants represent Christians causes another damaging, doctrinal quandary by suggesting that unfaithful Christians spend the millennium in the lake of fire until purged of their sins. It seems not to matter that this teaching goes contrary to everything taught in the Bible and especially Paul's epistles. The answer is quite simple.

The unfaithful servant does not represent an unfaithful Christian, but rather represents unbelievers during Daniel's Seventieth Week. In fact, when the Lord returns to establish His kingdom, there will be many unbelievers who hear the fateful words heard by the third servant, *"Thou wicked and slothful servant."* In turn, they will be told to *"Depart!"* Their faithlessness determined their eternal destiny.

> "The Rapture involves the Lord taking the Church to His Heavenly abode, while the Second Advent serves as the introduction of Christ's earthly Kingdom. At this return, the Lord Jesus does not actually set foot upon the earth—a detail distinguishing the Rapture from the Second Advent."

[Excerpt from **"Reviving the Blessed Hope,"** page 54-55]

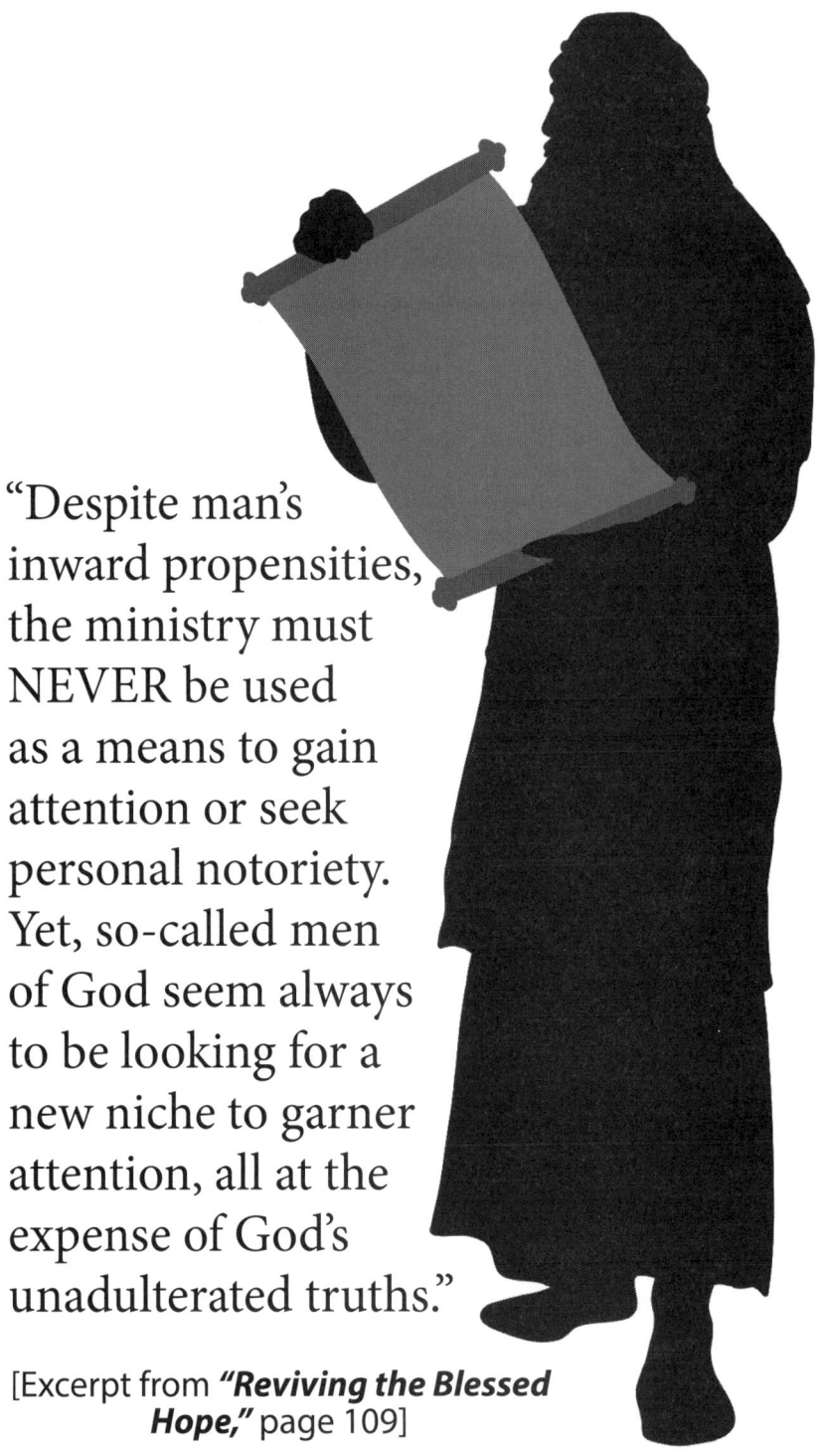

"Despite man's inward propensities, the ministry must NEVER be used as a means to gain attention or seek personal notoriety. Yet, so-called men of God seem always to be looking for a new niche to garner attention, all at the expense of God's unadulterated truths."

[Excerpt from *"Reviving the Blessed Hope,"* page 109]

14

The Judgment of the Nations

(Matthew 25:31-46)

At Christ's First Advent, He came as *the Lamb of God (John 1:29, 36)*, meek and lowly. Yet, Christ will return at His Second Advent in all His glory with power and majesty and judgment. When reading passages like the next one under consideration, it is important to take all scriptural correlations into consideration. This passage simply says that Christ comes with His holy angels, then sits upon His throne; yet judgment ensues between His return and the throne.

> *Matthew 25:31 When the Son of man shall come in his glory, and all the holy angels with him, then shall he sit upon the throne of his glory:*

This account picks up the context established prior to the introduction of the parables. The context is unmistakable: *"When the Son of man shall come in his glory."* After all, in **Matthew 24:30**, Jesus said, *"they shall see the Son of man coming in the clouds of heaven with power and great glory."* Of course, this is the Second Coming—the coming that emphasizes Christ's power, glory, and majesty.

At this coming, Christ returns to establish His earthly, millennial kingdom. However, before doing so, the Lord will execute judgment upon an unbelieving world. In fact, unbelievers will be refused entrance into the kingdom while believing nations hear the joyful words, *"Come, ye blessed of my Father, inherit the kingdom prepared for you from the foundation of the world"* **(Matthew 25:34)**. These nations do not enter the kingdom as a result of some Calvinistic override of their will; rather, they enter because of their faith in the word and their obedience to the will of God. In other words, these nations are *not* here because the kingdom was prepared for them in the sense that they played no part in being here. Instead, the kingdom was prepared for them and we know this because they are here.

Although there are many facets to the Lord's Second Advent, the focus of this particular section is upon the Judgment of the Nations. This scenario corresponds to the prophetic truths found in Psalm chapter 9. King David did not fully grasp the truths captured by his pen, yet they eloquently set the stage for the Judgment of the Nations.

In that psalm, David spoke of a time *"When mine enemies are turned back, they shall fall and perish at thy presence"* **(Psalm 9:3)**. He acknowledged that the Lord *"satest in the throne judging right"* **(Psalm 9:4)**. He saw that the Lord *"rebuked the heathen ... destroyed the wicked ... put out their name for ever and ever"* **(Psalm 9:5)**. David wrote that God *"prepared his throne for judgment"* **(Psalm 9:7)** and that God would *"judge the world in righteousness"* and *"minister judgment to the people in uprightness"* **(Psalm 9:8)**. In closing, David understood that *"The wicked shall be turned into hell, and all* **the nations** *that forget God"* **(Psalm 9:17)**. In fact, the fruition of the judgment is an answer to David's prayer found in the concluding remarks of the psalm:

> **Psalm 9:19 Arise***, O LORD; let not man prevail:* **let the heathen be judged in thy sight***.* 20 **Put them in fear***, O LORD:* **that the nations may know themselves to be but men***. Selah.*

The Particulars of the Judgment

As stated, the Judgment of the Nations will take place at the Lord's Second Advent. However, there are three particulars set forth in our passage that serve as indicators to the timing of the event: (1) the Son of man shall come in His glory, (2) all the holy angels will be with Him, and (3) He shall sit upon the throne of His glory.

> **Matthew 25:31** *When the Son of man shall* **come in his glory***, and all the* **holy angels with him***, then shall he* **sit upon the throne** *of his glory:*

Those who do not espouse the Pre-tribulation Rapture could argue that the first particular (the Son of man coming in His glory) could take place at the Rapture or the Second Advent. Yet, the other two aspects directly point to the Second Advent. However, it is just as important to recognize that the world will see Christ descend in all His glory, not at the Rapture, but at the Second Advent.

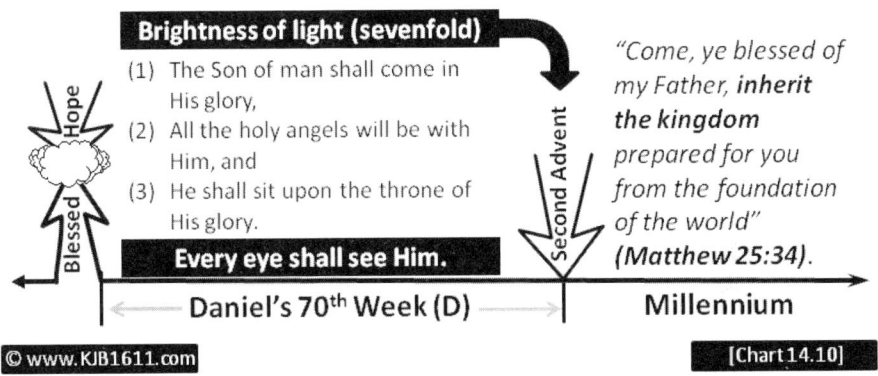

What did Christ mean when He said that *"the Son of man shall come in his glory"*? In the scripture, there is a strong association between glory and LIGHT.

- Isaiah wrote, *"Arise, shine; for thy **light** is come, and the **glory** of the LORD is risen upon thee" (Isaiah 60:1)*.
- Isaiah also wrote, *"the LORD shall be unto thee an everlasting **light**, and thy God thy **glory**" (Isaiah 60:19)*.
- Ezekiel plainly declared the association of light to glory when he said, *"As the appearance of the bow that is in the cloud in the day of rain, so was the appearance of the **brightness** … This was the appearance of the likeness of the **glory** of the LORD" (Ezekiel 1:28)*.
- Ezekiel also emphatically stated, *"the court was full of the **brightness of the LORD'S glory**" (Ezekiel 10:4)*.
- Simeon declared that Christ was *"A **light** to lighten the Gentiles, and the **glory** of thy* [God, the Father] *people Israel" (Luke 2:32)*.
- Paul said of Christ that He was *"the **brightness of his*** [God, the Father] ***glory**" (Hebrews 1:3)*.

John prophesied of the New Jerusalem that *"the **glory** of God did **lighten** it, and the Lamb is the **light** thereof" (Revelation 21:23).* Each of these associations shows that Christ's return in glory will be accompanied by the brightness of light. The Lord provides ample witness to those searching for truth. Christ's Second Advent is undeniably accompanied by the brightness of His glory. Isaiah said of that time, *"the light of the moon shall be as the light of the sun, and the light of the sun shall be sevenfold, as the light of seven days, in the day that the LORD bindeth up the breach of his people, and healeth the stroke of their wound" (Isaiah 30:26).*

When Christ comes in His glory, *"every eye shall see him" (Revelation 1:7).* How will the entire world see Him? This happens because His glory manifests itself by the brightness. Paul alluded to the specific details of this time when he said, *"And then shall that Wicked be revealed, whom the Lord shall consume with the spirit of his mouth, and shall destroy with **the brightness of his coming**" (2 Thessalonians 2:8).* These elements concerning Christ's Second Coming may indicate why the Lord gathers His Church to meet Him in the clouds. Not only do the clouds serve as Christ's chariot *(Psalm 104:3)*, but they also serve as a veil for Him from the world. Unlike the Second Advent, the clouds serve as a veil at the Rapture.

> **Psalm 18:11 He made darkness his secret place**; *his pavilion round about him were dark waters and **thick clouds of the skies.***

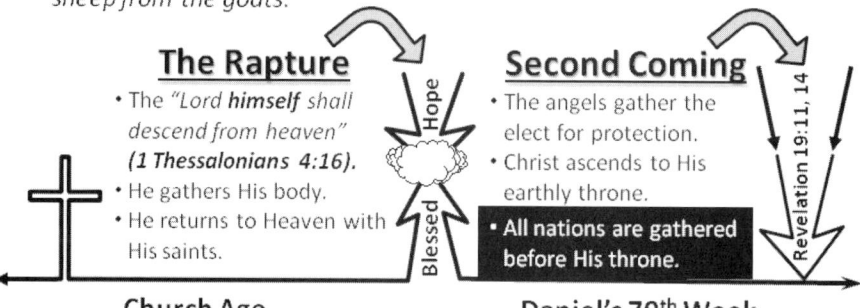

Believers who reduce the final judgments to one do harm to a good number of doctrinal truths. As the following chart indicates, there are significant differences between the three End-Time judgments: (1) the Judgment Seat of Christ, (2) the Great White Throne Judgment, and (3) the Judgment of the Nations. The Judgment Seat of Christ (a judgment in Heaven involving only the saved) should not be confused with the Great White Throne Judgment (a judgment where the unsaved will be raised from the dead to receive their final sentence as they are all condemned to the lake of fire). Yet, the particular judgment in our subject text is a national judgment involving national consequences.

Judgment	Key Passage(s)	Location	Timing	People	Focus	Result
The Judgment Seat of Christ	1 Corinthians 3:11-15; 2 Corinthians 5:1-11	Heaven	Follows the Church's Rapture; during Daniel's Seventieth Week	Saved people	The believer's body of work	Reward or loss of reward
The Judgment of the Nations	Matthew 25:31-46	Earth	At the conclusion of Daniel's Seventieth Week; prior to Christ's millennial kingdom	Nations	Treatment of the Jews during Daniel's Seventieth Week	Entrance into the earthly, millennial kingdom or sentencing to hell
The Great White Throne Judgment	Revelation 20:11-15	Heaven and earth have fled	Follows the millennial kingdom and Satan's final attempt to defeat the saints	The lost	The works of those who knew not God	Sentencing to the lake of fire for all eternity

The Practice of the Judgment

As the nations appear before the Lord, He divides them into two distinct categories: sheep and goats. We shall see later what these two categories represent, but for now it is important that we simply note that the Lord divides the people—*"as a shepherd"* divides the flock.

The Western mind-set and culture may find it odd that shepherds often kept sheep and goats together as both were *"of the flock"* (see **Leviticus 3:6, 7, 12**). It is equally important to recognize that shepherding entails much more than simply being a herder of the sheep. For instance, sheep and goats frequently display a striking resemblance to each other. Only those familiar with shepherding could easily distinguish between the two. The shepherd knows that the most distinguishable characteristic between the animals involves their behavior: sheep tend to follow and goats tend to go their own way.

> **Matthew 25:32** *And before him shall be **gathered all nations**: and he shall **separate them one from another**, as a shepherd divideth his sheep from the goats: 33 And he shall set the **sheep on his right hand, but the goats on the left**.*

When the Lord divides the nations, He places the sheep nations on His right hand and the goat nations on His left. Some teachers have incorrectly interpreted this dividing as applying to the Christians and non-Christians and that is simply not the case. Additionally, this national separating is in no way designed to distinguish between Israel and the nations, but only between sheep and goat nations. The sheep nations are those who followed the word of God and treated Israel appropriately during Daniel's Seventieth Week. The goat nations are those who went their own way and turned against God's chosen people. Once the Lord rests His case in judgment, there will be no doubt where these nations stood in this regard.

The Pillars of the Judgment

Once the division is completed, the Shepherd's work is done and the nations are staring into the face of *"the King."* The Bible says, *"Then shall the King say."* As the Shepherd, Christ will separate using His knowledge of the differences between the sheep and the goats. Now as King, He executes His rightful authority to judge.

As is often the case, the judgment begins with those deemed righteous. Yet, curiously, the judgment seems to be somewhat surprising to its recipients. The judgment opens with the pronouncement of award— *"Come, ye blessed of my Father, inherit the kingdom prepared for you from the foundation of the world."*

> **Matthew 25:34** *Then shall the King say unto them on his right hand, **Come, ye blessed** of my Father, **inherit the kingdom** prepared for you from the foundation of the world:*

Once again, when the hyper-Calvinists read verses like these, they always make a mess in interpretation. The reality is that the kingdom was prepared from the foundation of the world for whoever would inherit it. This does not mean that these inheritors lacked any free will; after all, the Lord identified them as sheep that chose to follow His way. Additionally, the beneficiaries of this inheritance do not enter into Heaven but into an earthly kingdom.

As the sheep (the righteous nations) hear of their inheritance, they also receive word as to the outward cause for their reward. The Lord provided six examples of their rewarded faithfulness: (1) *"ye gave me meat,"* (2) *"ye gave me drink,"* (3) although a stranger, *"ye took me in,"* (4) *"ye clothed me,"* (5) *"ye visited me"* when I was sick, and (6) *"ye came unto me"* when I was in prison.

> *Matthew 25:35 For I was an **hungred**, and ye gave me meat: I was **thirsty**, and ye gave me drink: I was a **stranger**, and ye took me in: 36 **Naked**, and ye clothed me: I was **sick**, and ye visited me: I was in **prison**, and ye came unto me.*

Interestingly, these nations demonstrate a spiritual ignorance pertaining to the Lord's recollection of their deeds. As the Lord pronounces their reward, three times the people ask the Lord *"when"* these things took place.

> *Matthew 25:37 Then shall the righteous answer him, saying, Lord, **when** saw we thee an hungred, and fed thee? or thirsty, and gave thee drink? 38 **When** saw we thee a stranger, and took thee in? or naked, and clothed thee? 39 Or **when** saw we thee sick, or in prison, and came unto thee?*

The Lord's answer to this question reveals the entire foundation of this judgment. He says, *"Inasmuch as ye have done it unto one of the least of these my brethren, **ye have done it unto me."*** In other words, the Lord Jesus (a Jew according to the flesh) said that when these nations blessed His brethren (the Jews), it was as though they had done it to the Lord.

> *Matthew 25:40 And the King shall answer and say unto them, Verily I say unto you, Inasmuch as ye have done it unto one of the least of these **my brethren**, ye have done it unto me.*

This truth concerning Israel is transdispensational! Thousands of years ago, the Lord told Abraham, *"I will bless them that bless thee, and curse him that curseth thee"* **(Genesis 12:3)**. That Bible truth will be the required object of faith to pass the test of the Judgment of the Nations.

Those who follow the Lord in obedience are the sheep who *"inherit the kingdom."* Those who do not abide by this admonition are the goats that will experience the ultimate *"curse."* This application applies throughout time, yet the Judgment of the Nations in the context only applies to the national treatment to Israel during Daniel's Seventieth Week.

Unfortunately, many modern Bible teachers espousing a Post-tribulation Rapture also tend to adopt an anti-Semitic position. Many of these same people have never trusted in the Lord for salvation nor find the eternal security of the believer plausible. Consider what this means. This leads them to believe that there is no need to be saved today because their trust is focused upon seeing the signs of the so-called Tribulation period prior to it coming to pass. When Daniel's Seventieth Week commences, they will consider the Jews as their enemies and refuse to come to their aid. Thus the false teachings will cause a host of people to end up on the wrong side of the Judgment of the Nations resulting in eternal condemnation.

One has to wonder what the other nations will think as they hear the pronouncement of the reward for the righteous nations. Any optimism will be dashed as their hopes quickly fade into despair. Again, the Lord starts the judgment with their sentence—*"Depart from me, ye cursed, into everlasting fire, prepared for the devil and his angels."*

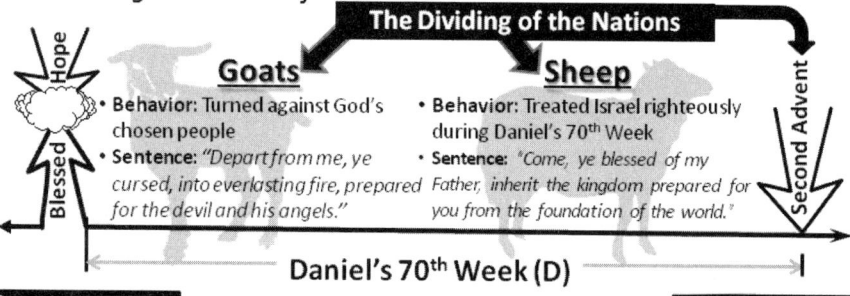

*Matthew 25:41 Then shall he say also unto them on the left hand, Depart from me, ye cursed, **into everlasting fire, prepared for the devil and his angels:***

The Bible clearly distinguishes between God's purpose for the kingdom and His purpose for creating hell. The kingdom was prepared for man whereas hell was *"prepared for the devil and his angels."* In other words, these nations end up in hell against God's plan and His perfect will.

The Lord expressed six scenarios whereby these nations could have ministered to Him by doing good to God's chosen people. Yet, the Bible says that the goat nations failed by giving the Lord no meat, giving Him no drink, not taking Him in, and not clothing Him or visiting Him when He was sick or imprisoned.

*Matthew 25:42 For I was an **hungred**, and ye gave me no meat: I was **thirsty**, and ye gave me no drink: 43 I was a **stranger**, and ye took me not in: **naked**, and ye clothed me not: **sick**, and in **prison**, and ye visited me not.*

The context shows that this judgment reflects their actions during the one week of years known as Daniel's Seventieth Week. When these nations refuse to faithfully aid the Jews in obedience to the word of God, they seal their condemnation. The condemned too will ask *when* they were given the opportunity to do good to the Lord.

*Matthew 25:44 Then shall they also answer him, saying, Lord, **when** saw we thee an hungred, or athirst, or a stranger, or naked, or sick, or in prison, and did not minister unto thee? 45 Then shall he answer them, saying, Verily I say unto you, Inasmuch as ye did it not to one of the least of these, ye did it not to me. 46 And **these shall go away into everlasting punishment**: but the righteous into life eternal.*

Before proceeding, it is necessary to again clear some confusion. Some falsely teach that these nations are, in fact, unfaithful Christians who spend the millennium in the lake of fire only to be raised to be with the Lord at the conclusion of Christ's 1,000-year reign. It is hard to imagine how these Bible teachers could make this bizarre presumption when the truth is so blatantly obvious. The Bible says that those judged *"shall go away into EVERLASTING PUNISHMENT"* which indicates that there will be no reprieve at the end of the millennium. Simply stated—this judgment is not for unfaithful Christians, but unbelieving nations.

This judgment is not a temporary measure as a means for purging one's sin. For those who refuse to believe the word of God and refuse to demonstrate that faith by assisting the Jews, this is their eternal lot. The confusing part for the recipients of God's praise and reward was not that they had helped the Jews, but that by helping the Jews, they had in fact been ministering to the Lord.

The reality is that Daniel's Seventieth Week will cause the Jews to be hungry, thirsty, naked, sick, and imprisoned. Those nations in direct opposition to *the New World Order* will adopt a pro-Jewish policy. At the Judgment of the Nations, they will ultimately find their reward to be well worth any temporary hardships experienced. The story does not end here. These faithful nations enter the promised kingdom in natural bodies and will produce offspring. Sadly, it will be from those offspring that Satan will *"gather ... together to battle: the number of whom is as the sand of the sea"* **(Revelation 20:8)**.

Christians living today should *not* take our absence from Daniel's Seventieth Week as an excuse to spiritually let down our guard. Instead, our doctrinal understanding and spiritual blessedness should move us to live holy lives **(2 Peter 3:11-14)**. A crucially important aspect is for us to remain faithfully adamant witnesses for the Lord Jesus Christ.

Each Christian has an obligation toward all those who do not know Christ as Saviour. The apostle Paul admonished every believer to *"Awake to righteousness, and sin not; for some have not the knowledge of God: I speak this to your shame"* **(1 Corinthians 15:34)**. The Christian's loss of rewards at the Judgment Seat of Christ may come as a shock to those who unworthily stand before a holy, righteous Judge **(1 Corinthians 3:13-15)**.

Appendix

Who Is This Israel in the Land?

The Bible cautions against those claiming that the Jews living in the land are illegitimate simply because they are diametrically opposed to the ways of the Creator. Has the Jewish restoration simply been a fluke or an anomaly as some claim? The question deserves an answer but only by considering the scripture and not any concocted biases. It is true that the vast majority of Israel's inhabitants continue in unbelief and even debauchery. However, the critic simply fails to recognize the reality of Israel in the land along with God's prophesied purpose and plan. Israel's existence in the land is not the fulfillment of Moses' prophecy in **Deuteronomy 30:1-4** which states that Israel will return to their land only after repentance.

The Bible clearly tells why Israel as a nation was restored to their land and it has absolutely nothing to do with their deserving some sort of restoration. Their restoration and rebirth has everything to do with God's name and His glory. Many passages offer the Last Days scenario, but it is best to focus on two chapters in Ezekiel, starting with Ezekiel 36, honing in on verses 17-33. Verse 25 serves as the pivotal verse for understanding the timing.

- **Verse 17**—The house of Israel defiled their own land.
- **Verse 18**—God poured out His fury upon them for the blood shed and the idols in the land.
- **Verse 19**—God scattered them among the heathen.
- **Verse 20**—In the heathen lands, they profaned God's holy name by claiming to remain the people of the Lord while in open rebellion to Him.
- **Verse 21**—God took pity on the children of Israel for His holy name's sake while the children of Israel profaned His holy name.

- **Verse 24**—God gathered them from among the heathen to bring them back into their land.
- **Verses 22-23**—God gathered them not for their sakes, but for His holy name's sake.
- **Verse 25**—THEN (timing) after the gathering into the land, He will cleanse them of their filthiness.
- **Verse 26**—by putting in them a new heart and a new spirit (His spirit—verse 27)
- **Verse 28**—Only then will they be God's people and God will be their God again.
- **Verse 32**—God reminds them that it was not for their sakes that He will do all this.
- **Verse 33**—Key words (*"In that day"* which refers to the Day of the Lord)—He will have cleansed the children of Israel from their iniquities.

Today, Israel is an accepted national entity born from the migrations of millions of Jewish settlers from every corner of the globe. Israel's existence as an autonomous nation is not a mere fluke of fate simply resulting from Satan's hatred for them and his desire to altogether destroy them. Israel is back in the land, not because of a repentant heart, but because of God's displeasure with their continued sinfulness among the nations.

Their regathering and protection (apart from some unseen supernatural intercessions) has not been a matter of repentance but a secular political ambition. Even today in Israel, the Jewish inhabitants have not shown themselves outwardly dependent upon God but their dependence is upon political and military might. They were literally ripped out of the nations in fury only to find themselves in a spiritual wilderness of the land of Israel.

Scripture Index

Genesis 1:1 143
Genesis 1:14 143
Genesis 1:20 143
Genesis 3:7 152
Genesis 3:15 40
Genesis 4:8 35
Genesis 6:2-6 163-164
Genesis 6:5 81
Genesis 6:11 163
Genesis 6:17 164
Genesis 7:1-4 164
Genesis 12:3 . . . . 74, 209
Genesis 18:25 103
Genesis 24:16 180
Genesis 42:36 144

Exodus 4:1-30 50
Exodus 10:21-23 139
Exodus 11:4 185
Exodus 12:29 185
Exodus 20:4 110

Leviticus 3:6-7 207
Leviticus 3:12 207
Leviticus 21:3 180
Leviticus 21:10-14 180-181

Numbers 13:23 152
Numbers 30:3 76

Deuteronomy 1:35 38
Deuteronomy 8:8 152
Deuteronomy 10:14 143
Deuteronomy 13:13 39
Deuteronomy 19:15 . . . . 18, 111
Deuteronomy 30:1-4 213

Joshua 10:12-13 121
Judges 14:20 183

1 Samuel 2:12 39

1 Kings 1:1-4 168
1 Kings 11:5-7 110
1 Kings 18:45 144

2 Kings 4:1-7 188
2 Kings 22:8 80
2 Kings 22:13 . . . . 80, 110

1 Chronicles 16:13 120
1 Chronicles 25:8 20

2 Chronicles 20:12 32
2 Chronicles 24:20-21 35

Psalm 5:5 188
Psalm 9:3-20 204
Psalm 12:7 38
Psalm 18:11 206
Psalm 22:22 23
Psalm 49:4 . . . . 149, 191
Psalm 78:2 . . . . 149, 191
Psalm 78:26 144
Psalm 95:10 38
Psalm 104:3 206
Psalm 105:6 120
Psalm 118:22 21
Psalm 122:6 114
Psalm 124:1-8 144-145
Psalm 127:3 113
Psalm 129:1-8 145
Psalm 135:4 120

Proverbs 7:19 172
Proverbs 23:7 184
Proverbs 29:25 102
Proverbs 30:11-14 40

Ecclesiastes 1:9 71
Ecclesiastes 3:15 71
Ecclesiastes 4:11 169

Isaiah 2:2 119	Daniel 12:11 . . . . 105, 109, 110, 111
Isaiah 8:14 21	
Isaiah 10:5-15 116	Hosea 2:19-20 181
Isaiah 10:20-21 . . . . 116, 122	
Isaiah 11:12 18	Joel 2:1-11 139-140
Isaiah 13:10 . . . . 121, 132, 146	Joel 2:9 173
Isaiah 13:12 81	Joel 2:10 . . . . 132, 146
Isaiah 19:2 61	Joel 2:31-32 . . . . 133, 141, 146
Isaiah 28:16 21	Joel 3:15 . . . . 121, 133, 146
Isaiah 30:26 . . . . 134, 135, 137, 206	
Isaiah 41:8 120	Amos 5:18 55
Isaiah 44:1 120	
Isaiah 45:4 . . . . 59, 120, 142	Nahum 1:15 . . . . 16, 89
Isaiah 52:7 . . . . 16, 89	
Isaiah 54:5 181	Zechariah 2:6 144
Isaiah 60:1 205	Zechariah 9:14 125
Isaiah 60:19 205	Zechariah 12:4 138
Isaiah 61:1 . . . . 16, 90	Zechariah 12:10 51
Isaiah 62:4-5 181	Zechariah 14:2-4 . . . . 46, 61, 123-127
Isaiah 66:1 44	Zechariah 14:9 47
	Zechariah 14:12 . . . . 127, 138
Jeremiah 5:31 80	Zechariah 14:16-20 119
Jeremiah 6:13-14 80	
Jeremiah 8:10 80	Malachi 2:12 20
Jeremiah 30:7 107	
Jeremiah 32:7-8 31	Matthew 1:1 . . . . 38, 39
Jeremiah 49:32 143	Matthew 1:23 49
Jeremiah 49:36 . . . . 143, 144	Matthew 3:7 39
	Matthew 4:17-23 94
Ezekiel 1:5 18	Matthew 4:23 . . . . 86, 88, 89, 90
Ezekiel 1:10 18	Matthew 5:1-48 94
Ezekiel 1:28 205	Matthew 6:10 192
Ezekiel 5:10 142	Matthew 7:21-23 187-188
Ezekiel 10:4 205	Matthew 8:11 177
Ezekiel 17:21 142	Matthew 8:12 . . . . 177, 189
Ezekiel 32:7 146	Matthew 9:15 183
Ezekiel 36:17-33 213-214	Matthew 9:35 . . . . 86, 94, 95
	Matthew 10:1-42 95
Daniel 2:34-25 21	Matthew 10:5 98
Daniel 3:12-16 188	Matthew 10:6 . . . . 19, 98
Daniel 7:2 144	Matthew 10:24 20
Daniel 8:8 144	Matthew 10:28 127
Daniel 9:24 . . . . 27, 35, 107	Matthew 11:5 95
Daniel 9:24-27 55	Matthew 12:34-45 38-39
Daniel 9:27 . . . . 60, 103, 105, 106,	Matthew 13:1-52 94
. . . . 107, 111	Matthew 13:4-7 189
Daniel 11:4 144	Matthew 13:10-13 . . . . 150, 191
Daniel 11:31 105, 108, 109, 110, 111, 112	Matthew 13:15 26
Daniel 12:1 107	Matthew 13:19-43 189
Daniel 12:7 . . . . 120, 159	Matthew 13:35 . . . . 149, 191

Scripture Index

Matthew 13:39. 52
Matthew 13:49. 52
Matthew 15:8. 17
Matthew 15:24. 72
Matthew 16:4. 39
Matthew 16:18. 21
Matthew 16:21-22. . . . . 22, 95
Matthew 16:23. 22
Matthew 17:17. 39
Matthew 18:3. 26
Matthew 18:15-20. 21
Matthew 18:17. 23
Matthew 18:23-35. 94
Matthew 20:1-16. 94
Matthew 20:11. 172
Matthew 20:19. 117
Matthew 21:42. 22
Matthew 22:1-14. 183
Matthew 22:2-14. 94
Matthew 23:1-33. 179
Matthew 23:2. 16
Matthew 23:8. 21
Matthew 23:33. 39
Matthew 23:34-39. . . . . . 33-37, 179-180
Matthew 24:1. . . . . 43, 180
Matthew 24:2. . . . . 43, 44, 50, 180
Matthew 24:3. . . . . 25, 33, 43, 45, 46, 48,
. . . . . 50, 52, 54, 65, 72, 101, 156, 179
Matthew 24:3-31. . . . . 179, 180
Matthew 24:4-6. . . . . 55, 58, 60
Matthew 24:4-31. 153
Matthew 24:6. 65
Matthew 24:7. . . . . 55, 61, 64, 73, 118
Matthew 24:8. . . . . 55, 56, 65, 73
Matthew 24:9. . . . . . 69, 70, 72, 73, 74, 79
Matthew 24:10-12. . . . . 69, 78-81
Matthew 24:13. . . . . 52, 69, 82, 198
Matthew 24:14. . . . . . . 86, 87, 92, 93, 97,
. . . . 100, 101, 104
Matthew 24:14-20. . . . 103-105, 109-113
Matthew 24:21. . . . 56, 74, 103, 115, 117,
. . . . 147
Matthew 24:22. . . . . 83, 84, 86, 115, 119,
120, 153
Matthew 24:23. . . . . 60, 115, 121, 123
Matthew 24:24. . . . 59, 60, 115, 121, 122,
. . . . 124, 153
Matthew 24:25. . . . . 115, 121, 125
Matthew 24:26. . .115, 121, 124, 125, 200
Matthew 24:27. . . . . . . 115, 125, 149, 200

Matthew 24:28. . . . . 115, 149, 200
Matthew 24:29. . . . . . 121, 129, 130, 131,
. . . . 146, 149, 200
Matthew 24:30. . . . 50, 51, 129, 134, 135,
. . . . 136, 149, 200, 203
Matthew 24:31. . . 59, 129, 135, 136, 141,
. . . . 142, 144, 145, 149, 165, 186, 206
Matthew 24:32. . . 36, 149, 151, 152, 179,
. . . . 180
Matthew 24:33. . . . . 50, 149, 153, 180
Matthew 24:34. . . 35, 36, 37, 38, 50, 149,
. . . . 155, 180
Matthew 24:35. . . . . 149, 157, 180
Matthew 24:36. . .149, 157, 158, 164, 180
Matthew 24:37. . . . . 66, 161, 162
Matthew 24:37-42. 180
Matthew 24:38. . . . . 66, 161, 162
Matthew 24:39. . .161, 162, 164, 165, 167
Matthew 24:40. . . . . 161, 167
Matthew 24:41. . . . . 161, 167
Matthew 24:42. . . . . 161, 169, 171
Matthew 24:43. . . . . 171, 172
Matthew 24:43-51. 180
Matthew 24:44-51. . . . . 171-178, 185
Matthew 25:1-13. 179-183
Matthew 25:1-30. 94
Matthew 25:2-4. 184
Matthew 25:5-13. . . . . 183,-186, 196
Matthew 25:14. 192
Matthew 25:14-30. . . . . 179, 191
Matthew 25:15. 192
Matthew 25:16-23. 195-198
Matthew 25:24-25. 200
Matthew 25:31. . . . 74, 179, 193, 203-206
Matthew 25:31-46. . . . . . 74, 86, 179, 203
Matthew 25:32. . . . . 206, 208
Matthew 25:34. . . . . 203, 208
Matthew 25:35-40. . . . . 119, 209
Matthew 25:41. 188
Matthew 25:41-46. 211
Matthew 26:26-29. 21
Matthew 27:25. 75
Matthew 28:9. 24
Matthew 28:16-20. 21
Matthew 28:19. 99

Mark 1:1. 15
Mark 1:14-15. 94
Mark 2:19-20. 183
Mark 4:11. 150

Mark 4:12	26
Mark 8:12	38
Mark 9:31-32	95
Mark 12:10	22
Mark 13:1-3	33, 43-45
Mark 13:4	33, 48, 50
Mark 13:5-7	33, 58,-65
Mark 13:8	33, 56, 61, 64, 65, 73
Mark 13:9	33, 70, 73, 74
Mark 13:10	33, 100
Mark 13:11	33, 77, 196
Mark 13:12	33, 78
Mark 13:13	33
Mark 13:14	33, 105, 109, 110, 111, 112
Mark 13:15-18	33, 112
Mark 13:19	33, 117
Mark 13:20	33, 84, 119, 120
Mark 13:21	33, 60, 122, 123
Mark 13:22	33, 59, 60, 122, 124
Mark 13:23	33, 122, 123, 125
Mark 13:24	33, 121, 131, 146
Mark 13:25	33, 131
Mark 13:26	33, 135, 136
Mark 13:27	33
Mark 13:28	33, 149, 151, 152
Mark 13:29	33, 151, 153
Mark 13:30-32	33, 155-158
Mark 13:33	33, 169
Mark 13:34	33, 174, 175
Mark 13:35-37	33, 177
Mark 15:37	24
Mark 16:14-15	96, 99
Mark 16:20	50, 124
Luke 1:1-3	19
Luke 1:5-25	15
Luke 1:79	16
Luke 2:25-35	185
Luke 2:32	205
Luke 4:17	90
Luke 4:18	16, 90
Luke 4:36	17
Luke 5:34-35	183
Luke 6:45	184
Luke 8:10	150
Luke 9:1	86
Luke 9:2	94
Luke 9:6	86
Luke 9:45	95
Luke 10:1	20
Luke 11:50	38
Luke 11:51	38, 39
Luke 12:39-41	172
Luke 13:28-29	177
Luke 16:8	39
Luke 16:16	94
Luke 17:24-27	66, 125
Luke 17:28	66, 125, 165
Luke 17:29	125
Luke 17:32	166
Luke 17:34-36	126, 127, 167
Luke 18:8	125, 174, 177
Luke 18:31	86
Luke 18:32	86, 117
Luke 18:33	86
Luke 18:34	86, 95
Luke 19:12-15	194
Luke 20:17-18	22
Luke 21:5	43, 44
Luke 21:5-36	33
Luke 21:6	44
Luke 21:7	48, 50
Luke 21:8	58, 60
Luke 21:9	61, 65
Luke 21:10	61, 73
Luke 21:11	64
Luke 21:12	70, 73, 74, 79
Luke 21:14-15	77
Luke 21:16	79
Luke 21:18	84
Luke 21:20	106
Luke 21:21-24	112-117
Luke 21:25	130, 131
Luke 21:26	78, 131
Luke 21:27	135, 136
Luke 21:28	140
Luke 21:29-31	151, 152-153
Luke 21:32	40, 155
Luke 21:33	157
Luke 21:34-36	169, 170
Luke 22:32	26
Luke 23:34	75
Luke 24:11-12	86
Luke 24:47	99
Luke 24:49-53	15
John 1:1-3	15
John 1:11	19, 72
John 1:29	203
John 3:10-12	152

Scripture Index

John 3:29 . . . . 181, 183	Acts 26:26 18
John 4:23 vi	Acts 28:27 26
John 8:19 17	Acts 28:28 63
John 8:32 32	
John 8:37-44 40	Romans 1:23 110
John 8:44 . . . . 39, 56	Romans 3:4 . . . . 40, 169
John 10:11 21	Romans 5:13 103
John 11:48 16	Romans 8:23 . . . . 23, 85
John 12:40 26	Romans 8:31 144
John 14:28 193	Romans 10:15 . . . . 16, 89
John 15:22-24 103	Romans 10:19 63
John 16:7 193	Romans 11:7 122
John 16:13 32	Romans 11:11-25 63
John 16:33 148	Romans 11:17 25
John 17:6 185	Romans 11:25 49
John 17:17 32	Romans 11:26 122
John 18:10 193	Romans 12:12 148
John 19:30 . . . . 25, 56	Romans 13:11 85
John 20:1 25	Romans 14:10 183
John 20:8 96	
John 20:9-22 24-25	1 Corinthians 1:22 . . . . . .48,50, 124-131
JJohn 20:25 96	1 Corinthians 2:2 93
John 20:26 25	1 Corinthians 2:13 33
John 20:31 19	1 Corinthians 3:11 22
	1 Corinthians 3:13-15 . . . . 176, 212
Acts 1:6. . . . . 46, 54, 100, 193	1 Corinthians 10:32 156
Acts 1:7-8. 193	1 Corinthians 14:33 36
Acts 1:9. . . . . 15, 45	1 Corinthians 15:1-4 . . . . 15, 86
Acts 1:12 . . . . 45, 114	1 Corinthians 15:34 212
Acts 1:22 96	1 Corinthians 15:51 198
Acts 2:20 146	
Acts 2:40 38	2 Corinthians 1:4 148
Acts 2:47 . . . . 23, 25	2 Corinthians 1:10 88
Acts 4:11 22	2 Corinthians 2:17 154
Acts 4:12 82	2 Corinthians 4:4 65
Acts 4:13 93	2 Corinthians 11:2 183
Acts 7:38 . . . . 20, 23	2 Corinthians 12:2 144
Acts 7:51-52. 196-197	
Acts 7:55 77	Galatians 1:7-8 91
Acts 8:3. 79	Galatians 2:15 117
Acts 10:12 18	Galatians 3:8 . . . . 91, 92
Acts 13:46 63	Galatians 3:28 . . . . 27, 74
Acts 17:11 98	
Acts 17:29 110	Ephesians 1:7. 22
Acts 18:5-6. 63	Ephesians 1:13. 67
Acts 20:24 90	Ephesians 1:14. 23
Acts 20:28 . . . . 22, 24, 43	Ephesians 2:2. 39
Acts 20:29 . . . . 67, 154	Ephesians 2:20. 22
Acts 20:30 155	Ephesians 3:6. 25
Acts 26:10-11. 79	Ephesians 4:7-8 193

Ephesians 5:6 39

Colossians 1:5-6 101
Colossians 1:14 22
Colossians 1:23 101
Colossians 1:28 183
Colossians 3:6 39
Colossians 3:11 74

1 Thessalonians 2:13 155
1 Thessalonians 4:15-17 .... 63, 155, 198
1 Thessalonians 5:2 173
1 Thessalonians 5:3 80
2 Thessalonians 1:7-8 .... 137, 165
2 Thessalonians 2:3 .... 111, 154
2 Thessalonians 2:4 .... 56, 106, 108-111
2 Thessalonians 2:7 77
2 Thessalonians 2:8 206
2 Thessalonians 2:9 124

1 Timothy 1:20 155
1 Timothy 4:1 .... 62, 154
1 Timothy 6:20 132

2 Timothy 2:15 .... 54, 86, 93, 101, 161, ... 183
2 Timothy 2:17-18 155
2 Timothy 3:1 .... 30, 63, 67
2 Timothy 3:1-7 153
2 Timothy 3:2-4 63
2 Timothy 3:13 154
2 Timothy 4:18 85

Titus 1:2 101

Hebrews 1:2 .... 63, 153
Hebrews 1:3 205
Hebrews 2:3 103
Hebrews 2:12 23
Hebrews 4:2 91
Hebrews 9:11 181
Hebrews 9:12-16 23
Hebrews 9:16-17 20
Hebrews 10:29 197
Hebrews 11:7 164
Hebrews 13:8 98

James 1:27 69
James 2:18 124

1 Peter 2:9 39
2 Peter 1:16 18
2 Peter 1:20 41
2 Peter 1:21 17
2 Peter 2:5 .... 164, 169
2 Peter 3:8 132
2 Peter 3:10 .... 53, 132, 173, 174
2 Peter 3:11-14 .... 53, 212
2 Peter 3:11-12 53

1 John 2:18 59
1 John 3:10-12 40
1 John 3:20 101
1 John 4:8 69
1 John 4:16 69

Revelation 1:7 .... 51, 206
Revelation 2:9 72
Revelation 2:22 147
Revelation 3:9 72
Revelation 6:12 .... 133, 146
Revelation 6:16 134
Revelation 7:1 .... 18, 143
Revelation 7:14 147
Revelation 8:12 121
Revelation 9:20 153
Revelation 11:2-3 .... 120, 159
Revelation 11:3-13 106
Revelation 11:15 .... 52, 194, 195
Revelation 12:6 120
Revelation 12:7-9 107
Revelation 12:14 ...... 104, 120, 159
Revelation 12:17 74
Revelation 13:5 159
Revelation 13:17 .... 117, 166, 187
Revelation 14:6 91
Revelation 16:9-11 153
Revelation 16:15 174
Revelation 19:7-9 183
Revelation 19:11-18 47, 56, 67, 135, 136, 142-145, 173
Revelation 20:3 52
Revelation 20:4-6 47
Revelation 20:8 .... 18, 212
Revelation 20:11 53
Revelation 21:1 53
Revelation 21:2 181
Revelation 21:9 181
Revelation 21:10 182
Revelation 21:23 206

Word Index

Symbols

1260 days 159
144,000 100
1948 37
42 months 159

A

abomination 105, 106, 108
Abomination of Desolation 56, 103, 108
abominations 111
abortions 81
Abraham 92
AD 70 37, 44, 156
Adam and Eve 92, 152
adoption 84, 85
all the world 101
Allah 57
America's greatness 74
Amos 55
angels 59, 142-145, 165, 166, 187, 189
anti-Semitic position 210
Antichrist 59
anxiety 78
apostasy 154
apostles 100
appendix 75
ark 164
armies 144, 145
armies of heaven 67
Arminian 82
army 173
assisted suicides 81
authority 199
autonomous nation 214

B

Word Baptists 74
beginning of the end 104
Benjamin Keach 182
Bereans 98
best man 183
bible versions 70
Bible-believing 74, 76
Blessed Hope 29
blood 24, 26, 43
blood moon 133
body of Christ 74
bride of Christ 182
bridegroom 182-187
brilliant light 134, 206
buy and sell 166, 174, 187-190

C

Calvinist 83, 203, 208
carcasses 126
cataclysmic events 130-132
Christian purgatory 177
Christians suffer tribulation 148
Church Age 27, 196
clouds 142, 154, 206
clue 146
commotions 66
communist 79
computer 87
confusion 78
consuming heat 138
context 28, 37, 54, 59, 87, 101, 142, 146, 158, 161, 162, 167, 198, 211
corners of the earth 142
cosmic and earthly disturbances 129
covenant 60, 107-108, 113-114
cross 86
cursed 75
custom of the marriage feast 182

D

Daniel's Seventieth Week 28, 29, 51, 55, 111, 146, 148
dark sayings 150
Darwinian philosophies 69
David's prayer 204
Day of God 53
day of Pentecost 23, 24
Day of the Lord 53, 56, 70, 80, 127, 132, 133, 134, 145, 173
day or hour 158
deception 58, 60, 65
detective 162
disease 66

diversion 49, 54
diversity of meaning 87
divine judgment 132
doctrine 161

E

eagles 126
earthquakes 64, 66
elect 59, 142, 144, 145, 165, 187, 189
end of the world 48
End-Time judgments 158, 207
endure 81-84, 86, 199
English language 93
eschatology 102
eternal security 210
evil servant 176

F

faithful and wise servant 176
false Christs 127
false covenant of peace 106
far country 193, 194
field 167
fig tree 149-152, 159
fig tree parable 149
final generation 36
First Thessalonians chapter 5 70
five virgins 182-188
five talents 196
flash of lightning 126
flee 112, 127
flood 164, 165
foolish virgins 184, 187, 187, 190
foolish workers of iniquity. 188
forty-two months 108
four winds 142, 143, 144
freewill 83, 209
friend of the bridegroom 183

G

genealogy 39
general inclusiveness 99
general judgment 197
generation 35, 37, 38, 39, 40, 157
Gentiles 98, 99
geronticide 81
gifts 196
glad tidings 89, 91, 92, 93, 94
Global warming 138

glory 206
goat nations 208
God never changes 98
God's wrath 103
Gomorrah 104
goodman 171-173
gospel 15, 89, 90, 91, 94, 95, 97, 100, 101
gospel of the grace of God 100, 101, 102
gospel of the kingdom 86, 94, 95, 96, 97, 99, 100, 101, 102, 104
gospel preached to Abraham 92
grammatical rules 93
GREAT TRIBULATION period 148
Great White Throne 53, 198, 207
Greek 109
grinding at the mill 167

H

Hebrew 109
hell 211
HIMSELF 145
hinge 103
history 70, 71
Holocaust's devastation 74
Holy Ghost 26, 76, 77
holy lives 212

I

idols 110
image 110
imminence 30, 153-155, 197, 198
infants 113
Isaiah 81
Israel 181, 213-214

J

Jacob's Trouble 132, 142
jealousy 63
Jeremiah 31, 32, 79
Jewish remnant 141
Jewish restoration 213
Jews, Gentiles, Church of God 156
John the Baptist 183
Josiah 80
Judaea 113
Judgment of the Nations 74, 86, 183, 188, 193, 204, 207, 209, 210, 212
Judgment Seat of Christ 176, 198, 207, 212

K

King of kings 139
kingdom 46, 93, 96, 99, 100, 192, 193, 199, 203, 208, 211, 212
Kingdom of God 153
kingdom of heaven 94, 96, 98, 192, 195
kingdom prepared for them 204

L

lamps 182, 184
last days 63, 155, 158
LEFT BEHIND 163, 167, 170
lineage 40
Lot 21, 104, 126, 127, 160, 161, 164, 165, 166, 167, 199
love 67, 69, 81

M

Mahdi 57
Man of Sin 56, 106, 108, 110, 114
Mark of the Beast 86, 166, 174, 187-188
marriage of the Lamb 183, 187
Matthew chapter 23 33, 34, 39
Matthew chapter 25 180, 182, 188
mercy seat 23, 24, 26
Michael 107
midnight cry 186
midpoint 159
millennial kingdom 167, 185, 197, 199
millennium in the lake of fire 201
Mohammed 57
Mount of Olives 45, 46
mysteries of the kingdom 150

N

national distinctions 74
national judgment 207
nations 203, 208
New Testament Church 20, 21, 24, 25, 27, 29, 43, 72, 195, 200
New Testament Church is parenthetically 196
Nicodemus 152
Noah 21, 126, 127, 160, 161, 163, 164, 166, 167, 169, 171, 199
nobleman 194
nuclear 132, 137-138

O

oil 188
Olivet Discourse 25, 27, 28, 29, 33, 48
one body 196
one-world system 71
open-ended 154
orthodox 57

P

parable 149-151, 172-200
paranoia 69, 78
parenthetical 63-64
parenthetical diversion 47
peace 60, 80, 108, 140
persecution 72
pestilences 64, 66
Peter and John 93
physical deliverance 84
physical disturbance 66
physical salvation 81
Physical survival 86
pinpoint 159
pleasures of sin 160
Post-tribulationists 74
preacher of righteousness 169
precursors 105, 129, 130
predict 155, 158
preparedness 178
Preterist 71, 75
pro-Jewish policy 212
prognostication 66
pronoun 70, 72
protector of Israel 107
purgatory 177, 201

Q

questions 162

R

Rapture 47, 52, 56, 144, 158, 161, 166
readiness 174, 178, 180, 187, 191
rebirth 213
redemption 84, 140
regathering 214
religious dogma 91
remnant 81, 173
repentance 126
replacement theology 75, 182

restrain 77, 107
resurrection 25, 86
Reviving the Blessed Hope 13
rightly divide 86, 101, 183
rumors of wars 66

S

Sabbath day restrictions 113-114
sacrifices 107, 108
safety 80
salvation 84
salvation chart 67
Samaritans 98
Satan cast from heaven 106
saved 67, 84
scattered 142
scoffers 131
Second Coming 47, 203
secular political ambition 214
senicide 81
sensationalism 13, 67
servant 174, 175, 199, 200
sheep 207, 209, 210
sheep nations 208
Shepherd 208, 208
shepherds 207
shortened 84
shortened the days 86
signs 48-51, 59, 64, 94, 131, 210
smart device 87
social media 67
Sodom 104, 165, 166
Son of Man 134
spiritually perilous times 153
sports teams 134
spotlight 134
Stephen 77
study 93
sun and the moon go dark 146
synagogues 71, 72, 73
Synoptic Gospels 19, 33, 43

T

take heed 170
taken 126, 161, 163, 164, 199
talents 192, 196
tares 189
Temple 44, 45, 50, 106, 106
temple of God 110

temple's destruction 45
ten virgins 180, 182, 183, 184, 190
testator 23, 24
THE GREAT TRIBULATION 147
THE TRIBULATION 146, 148
Theophanies 129
these things 48
thief 172, 173, 174
throne of His glory 204
time, times, and half a time 159
tradition 91
transdispensational 209
transition 63, 100
travel into a far country 192
tribulation 31, 103, 146, 159
twelve disciples 98
two witnesses 100, 106, 111

U

unbelieving nations 212
unbelieving world 203
unfaithful Christian 176-177
United Nations 61

V

vengeance 137
Vespasian 156
vessels 188
virgin bride 181
virgins 181, 182, 184, 187, 187
Vishnu 57
vow 75

W

war against Satan 107
watch 170, 171
watch and pray 171
watches 172
watchfulness 177, 178
waxed cold 81
willful ignorance 93
winter 113
wise virgins 189
world system 72
wrath 86, 104, 165, 186

Z

Zechariah 46